# The Inter-American Development Bank and Political Influence

# R. Peter DeWitt, Jr.

The Praeger Special Studies program—utilizing the most modern and efficient book production techniques and a selective worldwide distribution network—makes available to the academic, government, and business communities significant, timely research in U.S. and international economic, social, and political development.

# The Inter-American Development Bank and Political Influence

## With Special Reference to Costa Rica

PRAEGER SPECIAL STUDIES IN INTERNATIONAL ECONOMICS AND DEVELOPMENT

**Praeger Publishers** New York London

Library of Congress Cataloging in Publication Data

DeWitt, R Peter, 1943-
The Inter-American Development Bank and political influence, with special reference to Costa Rica.

(Praeger special studies in international economics and development)
Bibliography: p.
Includes index.
1. Inter-American Development Bank. Economic assistance in Costa Rica. 3. Loans, Foreign—Latin America. 4. United States—Foreign relations—Latin America. 5. Latin America—Foreign relations—United States. I. Title: The Inter-American Development Bank and political influence ...
HG3881.D44 332.1'53 77-2929
ISBN 0-275-24460-1

PRAEGER PUBLISHERS
200 Park Avenue, New York, N.Y. 10017, U.S.A.

Published in the United States of America in 1977
by Praeger Publishers, Inc.



789 038 987654321





Printed in the United States of America

For Sherri

# PREFACE

This inquiry began as an analysis of the impact of foreign assistance through the Inter-American Development Bank on Costa Rican development. Costa Rica provided a case study illustration of the role of international lending throughout Latin America and the Third World. From the outset it became apparent that a focus purely within the national boundaries of Costa Rica would not be sufficient to elucidate the impact of the Bank's projects on social, political, and economic structure. The impact of foreign aid within Costa Rica could only be understood by considering the global dimensions of the problem. Specifically, the internal and external factors impinging on Costa Rican development had to be defined and studied.

The initial months of the study, conducted in Washington, D.C., made increasingly clear the very considerable indirect leverage of the United States on the Bank through the U.S. Congress and in the executive branch through such agencies as the U.S. Treasury, General Accounting Office, U.S. State Department, and other government bodies. Extensive interviewing during a summer in Washington, D.C., made more apparent the pattern of U.S. influence in the Bank and the now obvious linkage between U.S. leverage and the U.S. connection with actual institutional control over major aspects of the Bank's funding of programs in Latin America. The aspects of U.S. formal and informal control are discussed fully in the initial chapters of this study.

From this fundamental analysis of the Bank it was obvious that the following salient questions must be asked: What is the impact of U.S. national interest on the Inter-American Development Bank? What are the linkages between U.S. influence and the Bank's impact on Costa Rican development?

An analysis of the parameters of U.S. national interest, however, could only shed a partial light on the problems of Costa Rican development. It was necessary, therefore, to expand the theoretical framework to include not only questions of national interest but additionally to link these questions with internal and external factors of Costa Rican development. Contemporary theories of underdevelopment or dependency offered the analytic framework found most useful here in analyzing the global factors of Costa Rican development that go beyond the conceptual boundaries of the nation-state. The dependency theoretical framework does address the questions with which this study is concerned and proves exceedingly useful when linked with the concept of national interest.

Dependency theory, which has been adopted by Marxists, neo-Marxists and non-Marxists alike, has been defined theoretically by such scholars as Bodenheimer (Jonas), Cardoso, Frank, and Dos Santos.[1] The usefulness of dependency to any study in international political economy represents an immense advance, conceptually, over conventional development theories, which advocate development and modernization by diffusion.[2] This is not to say that dependency theory does not have some defects such as the tendency of dependency theorists to be grand theorists who often fail to provide concrete, researchable indicators of dependence. To overcome this fault, traditional economic indicators of development are used to measure the impact of dependency in this study of the Inter-American Bank's role in Costa Rican development.

By employing the dependency conceptual framework and exploring the impact of U.S. national interest in the Bank and on Bank projects in Costa Rica, this study analyzes the following set of interrelated propositions: (1) What is the impact of U.S. national interest on the Bank? (2) What is the impact of the Bank on Costa Rican development? (3) What are the linkages between U.S. influence in the Inter-American Development Bank and the Bank's impact on Costa Rican development? I believe that the discussion here sheds light on these questions and that the example of the Inter-American Development Bank in Costa Rica can be generalized to the issue of international lending throughout Latin America.

This study originated as a dissertation in the Department of Political Science at the State University of New York at Binghamton. Many individuals and organizations were helpful in providing assistance.

I would like to thank the Organization of American States for the research fellowship for field work in Costa Rica. The Department of Political Science at the State University of New York at Binghamton was most generous in providing a National Defense Education Act Fellowship, which allowed the opportunity for a summer of research in Washington, D.C., on the Inter-American Development Bank. A Dissertation Year Fellowship awarded by the Department of Political Science at the State University of New York at Binghamton was used for compiling the Costa Rican research and writing the study.

I owe a great deal to many individuals. James Petras, Edwin Rutkowski, Arthur Smith, and George Westacott read the study and provided helpful suggestions. Many individuals in Costa Rica provided information and criticism, much of it helpful in understanding the Costa Rican polity and economy. In Washington, D.C., many individuals at the Inter-American Development Bank gave generously of their time and contributed to a deeper understanding of the Bank and its operations in Latin America. Interviewees are unnamed in the footnotes of this study to protect the confidential nature of the discussion but are nevertheless due my thanks. Many other people played an important part in this project and are owed my thanks. My wife, Sherri, proofread the manuscript and provided helpful suggestions. She was a constant source of inspiration during the research and writing, and to her this book is dedicated. Patricia Dolaway and Shirley Stacconi typed the manuscript. I also owe a substantial debt to other scholars in both North and South America whose manuscripts and abstracts were of great assistance.

I hope that this study will prove useful to future scholars of international political economy. The shortcomings of this work are, of course, my own.

NOTES

1. For a discussion of dependency, see for example Susanne Bodenheimer, "Dependency and Imperialism: The Roots of Latin American Underdevelopment" and Theotino Dos Santos, "The Structure of Dependence," in Readings in U.S. Imperialism, ed. K. T. Fann and Donald C. Hodges (Boston: Porter Sargent Publishers, 1971); Andre Gunder Frank, "The Development of Underdevelopment," in his Latin America: Underdevelopment or Revolution (New York: Monthly Review Press, 1969); and Fernando Henrique Cardoso, "Dependency and Underdevelopment in Latin America," New Left Review 74 (July-August, 1972): 83-95.

2. For a discussion that contrasts the diffusion model of development with the theory of dependency, see the introduction to Ronald H. Chilcote and Joel C. Edelstein, eds., Latin America: The Struggle with Dependency and Beyond (New York: John Wiley and Sons, 1974).

## CONTENTS

LIST OF TABLES

| Table | | Page |
|---|---|---|
| 6.9 | Projected Balance of Payments Including Aluminum Project, 1975-90 | 114 |
| 6.10 | Community Concerns | 116 |
| 6.11 | IDB Lending for Export Financing, 1961-74 | 119 |
| 7.1 | Credit Allocated by the Central Bank | 127 |
| 7.2 | Costa Rican Trade Balance with CACM Countries, 1965-71 | 129 |
| 7.3 | Importance of Coffee in Relation to All Exports, 1930-39 | 132 |
| 7.4 | Value of Principal Costa Rican Exports, 1962 and 1966-72 | 134 |
| 7.5 | Wage Comparison of Costa Rican Work Force for Key Sectors | 137 |
| 7.6 | Costa Rican Voting Behavior, 1953-66 | 142 |
| 7.7 | Votes for President and Vice President, 1974 Election, by Province | 144 |
| 7.8 | Structure of Public Direct Investment, 1965-72 | 146 |
| 7.9 | Public Sector Investment, 1975 | 146 |
| 8.1 | Military Training in Latin America | 154 |
| 8.2 | U.S. and Multilateral Assistance, by Sector: Summary for 1961-70 | 156 |
| 8.3 | Sector Distribution of ADELA Projects, April 30, 1970 | 158 |
| 8.4 | Investment in Central America by the World Bank Group | 160 |
| 8.5 | Investment in Central America by the U.S. Export-Import Bank | 162 |
| 8.6 | U.S. Percentage of Direct Foreign Investment in Central America in 1969 | 163 |

## LIST OF FIGURES

## LIST OF ACRONYMS

| | |
|---|---|
| CABEI | Central American Bank for Economic Integration |
| CACM | Central American Common Market |
| CODESA | Costa Rican Development Corporation |
| CONDECA | Central American Defense Council |
| Eximbank | U.S. Export-Import Bank |
| IBRD | International Bank for Reconstruction and Development |
| ICE | Instituto Costarricense de Electricidad |
| IDB | Inter-American Development Bank |
| LAFTA | Latin American Free Trade Association |
| NAC | National Advisory Council on International Monetary and Financial Policies |
| OAS | Organization of American States |
| OFIPLAN | Oficina de Planificación |
| PLN | Partido Liberación Nacional |
| USAID | United States Agency for International Development |

# The Inter-American Development Bank and Political Influence

PART

# I

# THE INTER-AMERICAN DEVELOPMENT BANK

CHAPTER

# 1

# HISTORY AND STRUCTURE OF THE INTER-AMERICAN DEVELOPMENT BANK

The agreement establishing the Inter-American Development Bank was concluded in April 1959 by a committee of the Organization of American States. The Inter-American Development Bank (IDB) was the first regional development bank to be established and became fully operational in December 1960.

A long course of events finally led to implementation of the IDB. The seminal idea for creating a regional development bank for Latin America is usually traced to the First Inter-American Conference of 1889-90, held in Washington, D.C., at which a resolution was adopted calling for the establishment of an "inter-national American bank."[1] The resolution, however, served to crystallize the opposition of various U.S. organizations to an inter-American bank.

For some 70 years afterward, the idea for an inter-American bank continued to be stifled by successive U.S. administrations that feared such a bank would compete with existing private banking institutions. Partial U.S. hegemony over Latin America had persisted since the 1823 assertion of the Monroe Doctrine (which prohibited European states from further colonization or direct intervention in the Western Hemisphere). This situation continued throughout the beginning of the twentieth century, bolstered by the Roosevelt Corollary of 1904, in which President Theodore Roosevelt proclaimed the readiness of the U.S. government to act as an international police force in Latin America and intervene on behalf of U.S. interests. U.S. rejection of the resolution calling for an inter-American bank at the Inter-American Conference of 1889-90 was, in sum, an expression of U.S. paternalism in "knowing what was best" for Latin America. Roosevelt expressed this paternalism in a message before the Congress:

> If a nation shows that it knows how to act with reasonable efficiency and decency in social and political matters; if it keeps order and pays its obligations, it need fear no interference from the United States. Chronic wrongdoing, or an impotence which results in a general loosening of the ties of civilized society, may in America, as elsewhere, ultimately require intervention by some civilized nation, and in the Western Hemisphere the adherence of the United States to the Monroe Doctrine may force the United States, however reluctantly, in flagrant cases of such wrongdoing or impotence, to the exercise of an international police power . . . . It is a mere truism to say that every nation, whether in America or anywhere else, which desires to maintain its freedom, its independence, must ultimately realize that the right of such independence cannot be separated from the responsibility of making good use of it.[2]

By the 1930s, the mood of U.S. imperialism had changed relatively with the advent of President Franklin D. Roosevelt's "good neighbor policy" and the move toward retrenchment as a result of the Great Depression. However, U.S. opposition to the establishment of a financial institution that would compete with private U.S. banks continued to block the possibility of an inter-American financial institution. By 1940 the United States had signed a convention calling for the establishment of an inter-American bank and Roosevelt gave it his full support, but the measure failed in the Congress for the same reasons as before.

With the outbreak of World War II the issue of the inter-American bank was buried by the more pressing matters of the conduct of war. At the July 1944 Bretton Woods Conference, which planned postwar international economic policy, there was general agreement that the creation of an inter-American bank would parallel the function of such international institutions as the World Bank (International Bank for Reconstruction and Development) and the Export-Import Bank, which were created at the conference.[3]

The turning point for the establishment of a hemispheric bank came in 1958, precipitated by the conjuncture of a number of events. The hostility Vice President Richard Nixon encountered in Caracas and Lima during his visit to Latin America in 1958, showed that contrary to U.S. State Department opinion, hostility did exist toward U.S. policies in Latin America.[4] The success of the rebels under Fidel Castro in Cuba, which led to the overthrow of the regime of Fulgencio Batista and Castro's rise to prime minister in February 1959, forced the United States to reconsider its policies toward Latin

America and the idea of an inter-American bank. In August 1958 the U.S. representative to the Inter-American Economic and Social Council of the Organization of American States announced that the United States would support a hemispheric bank.

This was a radical departure from the official U.S. position on the bank during the earlier twentieth century and must be seen as the adaptation of U.S. foreign policy interests to the discontent in Latin America toward existing American policies. In 1958 the United States was made forcibly aware of Latin American resentment by the treatment of Nixon on his "good will" tour. By January 1959 the Inter-American Economic and Social Council of the Organization of American States had convened a Specialized Committee for Negotiating and Drafting the Instrument of Organization of an Inter-American Financial Institution to begin working on the bank. On April 8, 1959, the agreement for the establishment of the Inter-American Development Bank was signed and the IDB was inaugurated as the development bank for Latin America.[5]

The creation of the Inter-American Development Bank was not a unique manifestation of the shift in U.S. foreign policy. Shortly afterward came a number of other attempts at U.S.-Latin American cooperation through such institutions as the Alliance for Progress (1961) and the nearly simultaneous creation of the Latin American Free Trade Association (LAFTA) and the Central American Common Market (CACM) in 1960.

The change in the focus of U.S. foreign policy destined the IDB to become one of the most dynamic of all hemispheric agencies with a subscribed capital of $1 billion, of which approximately 55 percent was to be authorized by the Latin American nations. President Dwight Eisenhower summarized the official reasons for the creation of the IDB as follows:

> (1) The special relationship, historical, political, and economic between the United States and the Latin American republics;
> (2) The pressing economic and social problems in the areas resulting from a rapid increase of population and a widespread desire for improved living conditions; and
> (3) The desirability of an institution which will specialize in the needs of Latin America, which will give the Latin American members a major responsibility in determining priorities and authorizing loans.[6]

These same conditions, however, existed throughout most of the twentieth century. It took such events as the failure of the Nixon visit and the success of Castro in Cuba to make apparent the necessity for a shift in U.S. Latin American policy.

The lessening of U.S. opposition to the idea of a hemispheric bank was welcomed by many Latin American governments for several reasons. First, they perceived the IDB, along with the Latin American Free Trade Association and the Central American Common Market, as a vehicle for expanding regional economic integration and trade. The Latin Americans also favored the idea of a multilateral bank, which they felt would allow them greater participation in international lending programs directed toward Latin America. But perhaps one of the strongest forces supporting the IDB was Latin American dissatisfaction with the policies and procedures of the World Bank, which imposed rigid project preparations and monetary restrictions on borrower countries. This outlook on the part of the Latin American governments, coupled with the shift in the U.S. attitude on a regional development bank, assisted in ushering the IDB into existence in 1959.[7]

## THE BANK'S STRUCTURE

When it was established in 1959, the Bank's membership consisted of 19 Latin American countries and the United States. Only members of the Organization of American States were originally eligible for membership. Cuba failed to join, although it had participated in the drafting of the original charter, due to its movement away from the inter-American system. Six other states have since joined: Trinidad and Tobago (1967), Barbados (1969), Jamaica (1969), Canada (1972), Bahamas (1974), and Guyana (1974). In addition, a number of nonregional countries are eligible for membership for the purpose of increasing the Bank's capital resources. The nonregional countries that are potential members include all the nations belonging to the International Monetary Fund and Switzerland.[8] In recent years with the increased demand for development loans due to worldwide inflation, European countries with their surplus of Eurodollars have been courted by the Bank for membership.

Structurally, the supreme authority for the IDB, as with the World Bank, is vested in the Board of Governors. Each member country is represented by a governor, although each governor's voting power is proportional to the size of the capital subscription of the country he represents. The Board of Governors generally meets once a year. The daily business of the Bank, however, is delegated, except on certain specific matters, to the Board of Executive Directors. As with the Board of Governors, representation and voting power within the Board of Executive Directors are weighted according to the size of each country's subscription. In the original agreement establishing the Bank, one executive director is appointed to represent the member country having the largest number of shares in the Bank. The remaining executive directors are elected by the governors of the other member countries. The agreement sets the number of directors at no fewer than six.[9] Currently the Board of Executive Directors consists of nine members, with the United States holding one directorship by virtue of its predominance as a shareholder. The formula for the voting power of a member country is 135 regular votes plus one for each $10,000 subscribed. As of February 1974 the United States controlled 199,839 votes or 40.29 percent of the total member country votes.[10]

The United States, with its 40 percent plus of the total votes on the Board of Executive Directors, maintains a virtual veto over the soft or concessionary loans allocated from the Bank's Fund for Special Operations. The articles of agreement specify that all decisions concerning the Fund for Special Operations shall be approved by two-thirds of the total voting power of the member countries.[11] Table 1.1 illustrates IDB voting power as of 1974.

The Bank's ordinary capital funds, which are lent at the current commercial rate, do not need a vote of at least two-thirds of the total membership for approval. Ordinary capital funds are allocated by a simple majority vote, with no one country retaining a veto. It is apparent from Table 1.1 that the United States, with the support of one other executive director, could block the approval of any ordinary capital loan with a negative or abstaining vote. This seldom occurs, however, as confrontation at the board meeting is usually avoided by resolving differences prior to the actual voting. Decisions at the board meetings are reached in an informal consensus atmosphere, with voting the exception to the rule. Decision making occurs at IDB board meetings through informal communications between members as their objections and reservations on loans under consideration are discussed. Should the dissatisfaction of a member country toward a particular loan not be resolved, that country may instruct its director to speak against the proposed loan.[12] If opposition appears too strong after informal negotiations, rather than risk defeat in a board vote, the loan request has most often been withdrawn.[13] Therefore, voting power among the IDB member countries is structurally defined by the necessity for a two-thirds favorable vote on concessionary loans, a majority vote on ordinary capital loans, and by the number of votes per capital subscription of each member.

The Bank's daily operations are conducted by the president and professional staff. The president is elected by the Board of Governors for five years and is eligible for successive terms. The first president was Felipe Herrera of Chile, who served in 1960-71. Since 1971 Antonio Ortiz Mena, the former finance minister of Mexico, has been president. The executive vice president, the chief administrator of

TABLE 1.1

Voting Power in the IDB, February 14, 1974

| Country of Executive Director and Alternate (A) | Appointed or Elected By | Number of Votes | Percentage of Votes |
|---|---|---|---|
| Brazil | Brazil | 58,985.0 | 11.89 |
| Ecuador (A) | Ecuador | 3,176.6 | 0.64 |
| Total | | 62,161.6 | 12.53 |
| Argentina | Argentina | 58,985.0 | 11.89 |
| Chile (A) | Chile | 16,295.0 | 3.29 |
| Total | | 75,280.0 | 15.18 |
| Canada | Canada | | |
| Canada (A) | | 24,403.0 | 4.92 |
| Nicaragua | Costa Rica | 2,414.2 | 0.49 |
| Costa Rica (A) | El Salvador | 2,414.2 | 0.49 |
| | Guatemala | 3,176.6 | 0.64 |
| | Haiti | 2,414.2 | 0.49 |
| | Honduras | 2,414.2 | 0.49 |
| | Nicaragua | 2,414.2 | 0.49 |
| Total | | 15,247.6 | 3.09 |
| Colombia | Colombia | 16,281.0 | 3.28 |
| Peru (A) | Peru | 7,744.6 | 1.56 |
| Total | | 24,025.6 | 4.84 |
| Uruguay | Bolivia | 4,693.4 | 0.95 |
| Paraguay (A) | Paraguay | 2,414.2 | 0.49 |
| | Uruguay | 6,223.8 | 1.25 |
| Total | | 13,331.4 | 2.69 |
| Venezuela | Barbados | 839.0 | 0.17 |
| Trinidad and Tobago (A) | Trinidad and Tobago | 2,414.2 | 0.49 |
| | Venezuela | 31,665.0 | 6.38 |
| Total | | 34,918.2 | 7.04 |
| United States | United States | 199,839.0 | 40.29 |
| United States (A) | | | |
| | Dominican Republic | 3,176.6 | 0.64 |
| Mexico | Jamaica | 3,176.6 | 0.64 |
| Panama (A) | Panama | 2,414.2 | 0.49 |
| | Mexico | 37,965.0 | 7.65 |
| Total | | 46,732.4 | 9.42 |

Source: Inter-American Development Bank, Annual Report, 1973 (Washington, D.C.: 1974), p. 111.

the Bank, has by convention always been a U.S. citizen. The remainder of the management is comprised of professional staff from all of the member nations, with U.S. citizens making up 18 percent of the total staff and 42 percent of the top management.[14]

## Capital Resources

As of February 1974 the Bank's assets equaled $10.74 billion (counting the U.S. dollar value of foreign currency), which may be broken down into the following categories: ordinary capital resources (hard loans); the Fund for Special Operations (soft loans); and the Social Progress Trust Fund (soft loans), the latter established by the United States and presently administered by the Bank as part of the Fund for Special Operations. Additionally, there are a number of special funds administered by the Bank; these will be outlined in the discussion to follow. The Social Progress Trust Fund represents about $525 million and, as with all concessionary money, the fund is subject to a two-thirds vote of approval by the total membership. Table 1.2 illustrates the resources of the Bank since its operational inception in 1960.

Capital subscriptions by member countries vary according to their size and domestic wealth. Table 1.3 shows the subscription by each member country.

It is apparent from Tables 1.1 and 1.3 that the nations with the most influence in terms of voting power in the Bank are: the United States, Argentina, Brazil, and Mexico. The negative vote of either Argentina, Brazil, or Mexico, combined with that of the United States, would be sufficient to stifle any proposed loan, allowing these nations considerable political influence in the Bank. Venezuela, with a smaller percentage of the total votes, exercises less influence. Recently, however, Venezuela has been playing a more dominant role. At the meeting of the Board of Governors in Santiago, Chile, in April 1974, Venezuela proposed to create a trust fund similar to that of the U.S. Social Progress Trust Fund. The Venezuelan trust fund, made possible largely from its trade surplus accrued through oil revenues, would contribute $500 million to development in Latin America. The Venezuelan fund would be a major departure from the U.S. Social Progress Trust Fund in that Venezuela would not exercise a veto power. President Carlos Andrés Pérez in his inaugural address to the people of Venezuela stated that the trust fund would operate "without humiliating vetoes, with no conditions that it be used to promote the economic activities of interest to the multinational corporations, which in their influence are often able to paralyze the lines of credit to Latin America."[15]

TABLE 1.2

The Bank's Profile in Figures, 1960–73
(thousands of dollars)

| | Subscriptions (end of year) | | | | |
|---|---|---|---|---|---|
| | Ordinary Capital Resources | Fund for Special Operations | Social Progress Trust Fund | Other Funds | Total |
| 1960 | 813,200 | 146,300 | — | — | 959,500 |
| 1961 | 813,200 | 146,300 | 394,000 | — | 1,353,500 |
| 1962 | 813,200 | 146,300 | 394,000 | — | 1,353,500 |
| 1963 | 813,200 | 146,300 | 394,000 | — | 1,353,500 |
| 1964 | 1,285,000 | 218,900 | 525,000 | 9,300 | 2,038,200 |
| 1965 | 1,769,800 | 1,119,500 | 525,000 | 25,200 | 3,439,500 |
| 1966 | 1,769,800 | 1,119,500 | 525,000 | 44,400 | 3,458,700 |
| 1967 | 1,778,800 | 2,321,400 | 525,000 | 60,200 | 4,685,400 |
| 1968 | 2,259,600 | 2,321,400 | 525,000 | 69,500 | 5,175,500 |
| 1969 | 2,282,300 | 2,328,000 | 525,000 | 69,800 | 5,205,100 |
| 1970 | 2,763,000 | 2,328,000 | 525,000 | 81,000 | 5,697,000 |
| 1971 | 3,465,900 | 2,328,000 | 525,000 | 105,800 | 6,424,700 |
| 1972 | 4,373,000 | 3,987,600 | 525,000 | 113,700 | 8,999,300 |
| 1973 | 5,710,300 | 4,383,600 | 525,000 | 125,000 | 10,763,900 |

Source: Inter-American Development Bank, Annual Report, 1973 (Washington, D.C.: 1974), pp. 22–23.

TABLE 1.3

Member Country Subscriptions to the Capital Stock of IDB, 1972-73
(in thousands of dollars)

| Member | Shares | Percent of Total Shares | Total Subscribed Capital | Paid-in Portion of Subscribed Capital: U.S. Dollars | Paid-in Portion of Subscribed Capital: Member Currencies | Callable Portion of Subscribed Capital | Due from Members: Paid-in Capital Subscriptions | Due from Members: Non-negotiable Non-Interest-Bearing Demand Obligations |
|---|---|---|---|---|---|---|---|---|
| Argentina | 58,850.0 | 12.43 | 709,933 | 62,211 | 62,211 | 585,511 | | 48,567 |
| Barbados | 704.0 | .15 | 8,493 | 1,249 | 1,249 | 5,995 | | 1,116 |
| Bolivia | 4,558.4 | .97 | 54,990 | 3,995 | 3,995 | 47,000 | | 4,265 |
| Brazil | 58,850.0 | 12.43 | 709,933 | 62,211 | 62,211 | 585,511 | | |
| Canada | 24,268.0 | 5.13 | 292,755 | — | 48,254 | 244,501 | 16,085 | 14,476 |
| Chile | 16,160.0 | 3.42 | 194,945 | 17,082 | 17,082 | 160,781 | | 14,635 |
| Colombia | 16,146.0 | 3.41 | 194,776 | 17,070 | 17,070 | 160,636 | | 6,944 |
| Costa Rica | 2,279.2 | .48 | 27,496 | 1,998 | 1,998 | 23,500 | | 611 |
| Dominican Republic | 3,041.6 | .64 | 36,692 | 2,663 | 2,664 | 31,365 | | |
| Ecuador | 3,041.6 | .64 | 36,692 | 2,663 | 2,664 | 31,365 | | |
| El Salvador | 2,279.2 | .48 | 27,496 | 1,998 | 1,998 | 23,500 | | 1,267 |
| Guatemala | 3,041.6 | .64 | 36,692 | 2,663 | 2,664 | 31,365 | | |
| Haiti | 2,279.2 | .48 | 27,495 | 1,998 | 1,998 | 23,499 | | 1,358 |
| Honduras | 2,279.2 | .48 | 27,495 | 1,998 | 1,998 | 23,499 | | |
| Jamaica | 3,041.6 | .64 | 36,692 | 2,664 | 2,663 | 31,365 | | 2,610 |
| Mexico | 37,830.0 | 7.99 | 456,359 | 39,990 | 39,990 | 376,379 | | |
| Nicaragua | 2,279.2 | .48 | 27,495 | 1,998 | 1,997 | 23,500 | | |
| Panama | 2,279.2 | .48 | 27,495 | 1,997 | 1,998 | 23,500 | | 1,267 |
| Paraguay | 2,279.2 | .48 | 27,495 | 1,997 | 1,998 | 23,500 | | 1,355 |
| Peru | 7,609.6 | 1.61 | 91,798 | 6,668 | 6,669 | 78,461 | | 2,644 |
| Trinidad and Tobago | 2,279.2 | .48 | 27,495 | 1,998 | 1,997 | 23,500 | | 1,798 |
| United States | 180,366.0 | 38.11 | 2,175,833 | 331,745 | — | 1,844,088 | | 150,530 |
| Uruguay | 6,088.8 | 1.29 | 73,451 | 5,337 | 5,336 | 62,778 | | 1,628 |
| Venezuela | 31,530.0 | 6.66 | 380,360 | 33,331 | 33,332 | 313,697 | | 26,174 |
| Total 1973 | 473,360.8 | 100.00 | 5,710,356 | 607,525 | 324,035 | 4,778,796 | 16,085 | 281,245 |
| Total 1972 | 402,779.0 | 100.00 | 4,373,022 | 480,049 | 252,050 | 3,640,923 | 29,402 | 214,840 |

Source: Inter-American Development Bank, Annual Report, 1973 (Washington, D.C.: 1974), p. 83.

TABLE 1.4

Financial Arrangements with Nonmember Countries and Other Resources
(in thousands of dollars)

| | | Detail by Arrangements | | | |
|---|---|---|---|---|---|
| | Amount | Bond Issues and Loans | Funds Under Administration | Participations and Others | Parallel and Independent Financing |
| Austria | 33,617 | 33,617 | — | — | — |
| Belgium | 18,396 | 17,500 | — | 896 | — |
| Finland | 11,100 | 1,100 | — | 10,000 | — |
| France | 43,478 | 43,478 | — | — | — |
| Germany | 295,971 | 283,582 | 12,284 | 105 | — |
| Israel | 5,000 | 5,000 | — | — | — |
| Italy | 74,041 | 73,171 | — | 870 | — |
| Japan | 136,746 | 118,571 | — | 18,175 | — |
| Netherlands | 67,705 | 23,239 | — | 100 | 44,366 |
| Norway | 6,000 | 4,000 | 2,000 | — | — |
| South Africa | 2,500 | 2,500 | — | — | — |
| Spain | 38,913 | 31,413 | — | 7,500 | — |
| Sweden | 22,778 | 17,778 | 5,000 | — | — |
| Switzerland | 145,024 | 135,385 | 9,231 | 408 | — |
| United Kingdom | 43,949 | 24,193 | 18,481 | 1,275 | — |
| Vatican | 1,007 | — | 1,007 | — | — |
| ICEM* | 1,250 | — | 1,250 | — | — |
| U.N. Agencies | 8,197 | — | — | 8,197 | — |
| Total | 955,672 | 814,527 | 49,253 | 47,526 | 44,366 |

*Intergovernmental Committee for European Migration.

Source: Inter-American Development Bank, Annual Report, 1973 (Washington, D.C., 1974), p. 104.

Venezuela has in addition been urging other Latin American member countries to play a more dynamic role in the Bank by setting up similar trust funds. One proposed method for the establishment of additional funds is to float bond issues backed by the Venezuelan trust fund, particularly in the capital markets of OPEC (Organization of Petroleum Exporting Countries) nations.[16]

The Bank also administers several other funds on behalf of some developed nonmember countries and agencies. Besides the U.S. Social Progress Trust Fund, the Bank administers $955,672,000 for nonmembers as of February 1974. These resources provide additional capital for concessional loan purposes. Table 1.4 outlines these nonmember contributors and the amount of their subscriptions to the IDB.

Overall IDB lending in 1961-72 falls mainly into two sectors: 40 percent from ordinary capital (hard loans) and 49 percent from the soft loan resources of the Fund for Special Operations. The remaining 11 percent came from the special funds administered by the Bank. Since 1972, due to the increased demand pressure on the Bank's resources, the level of the Fund for Special Operations has dropped to 42.5 percent of the Bank's total loan commitment while the resources lent from ordinary capital have increased to 55 percent. The soft loan resources available from other sources also have dropped from 11 percent to 2.5 percent. This reduction of approximately 15 percent in the level of the Bank's concessional spending places a serious burden on the IDB's ability to meet the demand for low interest rate loans most needed by the least developed nations.[17]

During the period ending fiscal year 1973, the IDB disbursed $884 million in loans in the following categories: ordinary capital resources, $453 million; Fund for Special Operations, $427 million; other funds, $4 million. Table 1.5 lists the member countries that were recipients of loans for the period 1971-73.[18]

Table 1.6 outlines the sectors in which loans were made in 1961-73. It demonstrates that a very large percentage of the Bank's loans provide for infrastructure. Infrastructure made up 39 percent of loan costs in 1973, with 24 percent for electric power and 15 percent for loans in transportation and communications. Only a small percentage of loans was granted to social infrastructure projects. Social infrastructure received 17 percent of the total loans granted, while only 10 percent of that total was applied to education. Urban development with 2 percent and sanitation projects with 5 percent likewise had low priority. Programs of dramatic potential social impact such as agrarian reform have received no consideration in the Bank's funding scheme.

The IDB resorts to several means to raise the necessary capital for loan projects. Ordinary capital for conventional (hard) loans is obtained partly from paid-in subscriptions from member nations and

TABLE 1.5

IDB Loans, 1971-73
(in thousands of dollars)

| Country | 1971 | | 1972 | | 1973 | |
|---|---|---|---|---|---|---|
| | Number of Loans | Total | Number of Loans | Total | Number of Loans | Total |
| Argentina | 4 | 73,688 | 3 | 162,661 | 1 | 12,454 |
| Barbados | 1 | 1,000 | 1 | 2,800 | — | — |
| Bolivia | 2 | 21,579 | 6 | 42,082 | 1 | 46,528 |
| Brazil | 9 | 148,929 | 8 | 213,156 | 8 | 274,115 |
| Chile | 2 | 11,600 | — | — | — | — |
| Colombia | 4 | 80,275 | 3 | 49,900 | 8 | 105,900 |
| Costa Rica | 1 | 3,500 | 2 | 8,300 | 1 | 16,000 |
| Dominican Republic | 1 | 3,400 | 3 | 33,700 | 3 | 39,000 |
| Ecuador | 4 | 30,300 | 3 | 39,700 | 4 | 55,700 |
| El Salvador | 1 | 10,000 | 2 | 39,600 | 1 | 8,000 |
| Guatemala | 2 | 9,200 | — | — | 3 | 36,800 |
| Haiti | 2 | 1,800 | 1 | 10,000 | 1 | 22,200 |
| Honduras | 4 | 21,400 | 1 | 9,200 | 1 | 1,200 |
| Jamaica | 3 | 9,060 | — | — | 5 | 30,800 |
| Mexico | 3 | 57,699 | 5 | 115,689 | 4 | 113,467 |
| Nicaragua | 1 | 3,500 | 1 | 12,500 | 3 | 29,200 |
| Panama | 2 | 17,400 | 3 | 15,700 | 2 | 18,000 |
| Paraguay | 4 | 44,782 | — | — | — | — |
| Peru | 3 | 24,052 | 3 | 785 | 4 | 19,280 |
| Trinidad and Tobago | 2 | 7,600 | 2 | 13,100 | 1 | 2,400 |
| Uruguay | — | — | 1 | 10,000 | 2 | 3,100 |
| Venezuela | 4 | 71,001 | 1 | 18,900 | 3 | 43,100 |
| Regional | — | — | 3 | 9,400 | 1 | 6,800 |
| Total | 59 | 651,765 | 52 | 807,173 | 57 | 884,044 |

Source: Inter-American Development Bank, Annual Report, 1973 (Washington, D.C.: 1974).

TABLE 1.6

Distribution of Loans by Sector, 1961-73
(in millions of dollars)

| Sector | 1973 | Percent | 1961-73 | Percent |
|---|---|---|---|---|
| Directly productive | | | | |
| Agriculture | 187 | 21 | 1,464 | 23 |
| Industry and mining | 165 | 19 | 978 | 15 |
| Economic infrastructure | | | | |
| Electric power | 216 | 24 | 1,172 | 19 |
| Transportation and communications | 135 | 15 | 1,099 | 17 |
| Social infrastructure | | | | |
| Sanitation | 48 | 5 | 644 | 10 |
| Urban development | 14 | 2 | 416 | 7 |
| Education | 91 | 10 | 287 | 5 |
| Other | | | | |
| Preinvestment | 14 | 2 | 109 | 2 |
| Export financing | 10 | 1 | 98 | 1 |
| Tourism | 4 | 1 | 42 | 1 |
| Total | 884 | 100 | 6,309 | 100 |

Source: Inter-American Development Bank, Annual Report, 1973 (Washington, D.C.: 1974), p. 25.

partly from the sale of bonds on the international markets. Bond sales are backed by the callable funds pledged by member countries. In the initial years of the Bank's operations, bonds were floated in the U.S. capital market. Recently, in order to reduce its dependence on the United States and partially in response to the U.S. balance of trade deficit, the IDB has drawn from such diverse capital markets as Europe, Japan, and Latin America. The United States has, however, contributed to approximately 40 percent of the total callable capital and 57 percent of all capital resources.

Unlike the ordinary capital, the concessional loans of the Fund for Special Operations are not derived from the international market The low interest rates paid on concessional loans would not make them very attractive in international capital markets. Therefore, these funds are drawn directly from member countries' subscriptions. Currently the subscription of U.S. supplies roughly two-thirds of the concessional contributions and thereby has given the United States considerable influence over the allocation of these funds.

The special accounts of the Bank such as the Social Progress Trust Fund and the funds of the nonmember nations are derived from donations, which are largely for concessional loan purposes.

While the resources of the Bank remain diverse, it is perhaps interesting to comment on the substantial contribution of the United States. Based on an evaluation by the U.S. General Accounting Office in 1972, the United States has contributed about 94 percent of the hard currencies available to the IDB.[19] Recently U.S. contributions have been decreasing. Resources from nonmember countries amounting to $1,368 million, and the financial support of some Latin American nations such as Venezuela with its pledge of the $500 million trust fund, have been cutting into the percentage of U.S. contributions to the Bank's hard currency resources.[20]

## Operating Policies and Procedures

Since the Bank first became operational in 1960 it has shifted its emphasis in sectoral lending and lending policies. In earlier years the Bank placed a fairly heavy emphasis on social development projects. In 1962 some 26.6 percent of its lending was directed to water supply and sewage systems, 27.8 percent to housing projects, and 3.7 percent to education, while only 34.8 percent was being allocated to agriculture and industry, 22.1 percent in agriculture, and 11.7 percent in industry.

By 1965 the pattern of sectoral funding had shifted away from social projects. Water and sewer programs as well as housing were dramatically deemphasized with water and sewage programs down from 26.6 percent to 19 percent, housing down from 27.8 percent in 1962 to 15 percent, and education down from 3.7 percent to 2 percent of the total lending in 1965. At the same time, allocations in industry and mining had more than doubled from 11.7 percent in 1962 to 26 percent, as did transportation and communications from 4.1 percent in 1962 to 9 percent in 1965. By 1965 a shift in lending policies favoring the support of the production sector and infrastructure for that sector was apparent.[21]

In 1968 the Bank's sectoral lending priorities again shifted, with social projects further deemphasized and infrastructure becoming the dominant sector with 48.5 percent of the total lending allocations. In the social project sector, housing was decreased from 15 percent in 1965 to 6 percent in 1968; water and sewage programs decreased from 29 percent to 6.2 percent; and education projects remained about the same at 2.0 and 2.6 percent, respectively, in 1965 and 1968. Industry and mining also decreased from 1965 to 1968 from a high of 23 percent to 13.6 percent, and agriculture dropped in lending allocation from 21 percent to 17.5 percent. However, during this period the Bank made a definite push in infrastructure allocations as transportation and communications projects rose from 9 percent in 1965 to 29.6 percent in 1968, and electric power loans increased from 8 percent in 1965 to 29.6 percent in 1968, and electric power loans increased from 8 percent in 1965 to 18.9 percent by 1968.[22]

In recent years this pattern of lending has remained fairly constant. By 1973 housing and sanitation had become a very low priority, 2 percent and 5 percent, respectively, while education projects were on the increase from 2.6 percent in 1968 to 10 percent in 1973. Overall, however, social projects, with only 17 percent of the total lending allocation, were far outweighted by production and infrastructure projects, which comprised almost 80 percent of the Bank's lending allocations in 1973. Industry and mining increased from 13.6 percent in 1968 to 19 percent in 1973. Agriculture also rose, from 17.5 in 1968 to 21 percent in 1973. Transportation and communications declined from 29.6 percent in 1968 to 15 percent in 1973, yet electric power increased from 18.9 percent in 1968 to 24 percent in 1973. This gave productionist projects 40 percent and infrastructure 39 percent, or a combined total of 79 percent of the 1973 lending allocation.[23] Table 1.7 depicts the movement from 1962 to 1973 away from social projects toward an emphasis of production and infrastructure in the IDB.

The movement away from social projects toward infrastructure and production may be explained by a number of factors. One factor was that in 1965 the function of the U.S. Social Progress Trust Fund was superseded by the Fund for Special Operations. During the initial years of the Bank's operation, the Social Progress Trust Fund had been largely responsible for funding social projects. After 1965, with its expanded responsibility, the Fund for Special Operations instituted more restrictive guidelines, which dampened the interest of Latin American governments in social projects. Fund for Special Operation loans, unlike Social Progress Trust Fund loans, were more restrictive because they no longer financed the local cost with dollars due to the tied purchase aspect of the U.S. contribution. (Tied aid must be spent in the lending country, that is, it is tied to purchases from the lending country.) Latin American governments, therefore, were more attracted after 1965 to projects with a higher import component such as infrastructure, mining, or industrial development than to social projects, which require a large local contribution. The policy transferring the function of the Social Progress Trust Fund to the Fund for Special Operations had a major impact on the IDB's pattern of funding in emphasizing production and infrastructure and deemphasizing social projects.[24]

TABLE 1.7

Sectoral Distribution of IDB Loans, 1962, 1965, 1968, 1973, and 1961-73

| Sector Percentage | 1962 | 1965 | 1968 | 1973 | 1961-73 | 1961-73 (total costs in millions of dollars) |
|---|---|---|---|---|---|---|
| Social projects | | | | | | |
| Housing | 27.8 | 15.0 | 6.0 | 2.0 | 7.0 | 416 |
| Water supply and sewerage | 26.6 | 19.0 | 6.2 | 5.0 | 10.0 | 644 |
| Education | 3.7 | 2.0 | 2.6 | 10.0 | 5.0 | 287 |
| Production and infrastructure | | | | | | |
| Industry and mining | 11.7 | 23.0 | 13.6 | 19.0 | 15.0 | 978 |
| Agriculture | 22.0 | 21.0 | 17.5 | 21.0 | 23.0 | 1,464 |
| Transportation and communications | 5.4 | 9.0 | 29.6 | 15.0 | 17.0 | 1,099 |
| Electric power | 1.2 | 8.0 | 18.9 | 24.0 | 19.0 | 1,172 |

Source: John White, Regional Development Banks, op. cit., p. 5; Inter-American Development Bank, Annual Report, 1973 (Washington, D.C.: 1974), p. 25.

TABLE 1.8

IDB Guidelines for Fund for Special Operations Loans

| Stage of National Development | Maximum Grace Period | Maximum Maturity | Interest[a] |
|---|---|---|---|
| Most developed | 5 years | 25 years | 3% Social<br>4% Economic |
| Intermediate[b] | 7 years | 30 years | 2% |
| Insufficient markets[c] | 8 years | 35 years | 2% |
| Least developed | 10 years | 40 years | 1% for grace period;<br>2% thereafter |

[a]All FSO loans are concessional.

[b]Chile, Colombia, and Peru

[c]Barbados, Costa Rica, Jamaica, Panama, Trinidad and Tobago, and Uruguay

Source: Inter-American Development Bank, Memorandum, June 4, 1974, from Henry J. Costanzo, executive vice president, "New Policy Guidelines of the Fund for Special Operations," p. 1.

Another factor that seems to have played a major role in this policy alteration was the change in U.S. thinking toward the role of the Alliance for Progress in Latin America. In 1960, in the wake of Castro's rise to power in Cuba, the United States had discarded, at least officially, its traditional policy that Latin American economic development should be achieved with private enterprise alone. At the Inter-American Economic Conference held in Bogota in 1960, the United States presented a draft agreement advocating the establishment of a program of social development and private investment. The Act of Bogota, which established the basis for the Alliance for Progress, set forth a program of social development, one of the main instruments of which was to be the Social Progress Trust Fund to be administered by the newly created Inter-American Development Bank. By 1965, however, many serious problems impeded the Alliance for Progress and, with Cuba well contained, the alliance lost some of its fervor for social development.[25] This explains to some degree the alteration in the IDB's sectoral funding policy from 1960 to the present as outlined in Table 1.7.

Another area of funding policy is the distribution of concessional loans to the least developed Latin American nations. It seems only logical that the Bank would distribute most of its low interest loans to the countries least able to afford high interest rates. However, this has not always been the case. In 1961-71 the Fund for Special Operations, the soft loan window of the Bank, distributed 46.8 percent or $1,126 million of its loans to the most developed countries (Argentina, Brazil, Mexico, and Venezuela), while only 24.7 percent or $594 million was distributed to the least developed nations (Bolivia, Dominican Republic, Ecuador, El Salvador, Guatemala, Haiti, Honduras, Nicaragua, Paraguay, and the Central American Regional Organization).[26] In 1972, however, the IDB adopted new policy guidelines for the Fund for Special Operations granting preferential treatment for economically less developed countries and countries of an insufficient market capacity (see Table 1.8). Current data on the Fund for Special Operations do not indicate whether or not these guidelines have been implemented (IDB's annual reports for 1973 and 1974 do not reflect this policy change).

The ordinary capital of the IDB, however, is lent at commercial rates, and there is no special advantage for the least developed nations of Latin America. Ordinary capital funds seem to be fairly equally distributed, although there have been charges that these funds are disbursed on a "fair share" basis, that is, that loans are distributed in proportion to the countries' contributions. A rank order correlation of 0.59, however, demonstrates that the relationship between the level of subscription and loan allocations in 1969-72 is a spurious one and does not support the above contention.[27]

The resources of the member and nonmember trust funds are another source of development capital. There are, however, important restrictions on the use of these funds beyond the limitations of the rates of interest and repayment terms. The Norwegian Fund, the Vatican Fund, and the Swedish Fund provide sources of untied capital. However, the trust funds of several other nations administered by the IDB are usually tied to purchases in the donor country. This restricts the use of some trust fund monies in financing local costs. The Canadian Trust Fund has an 80 percent tied content, the United Kingdom's fund has a 100 percent tied content to the purchase of goods in Britain (although a second smaller trust fund of 2 million pounds sterling was established in 1971 without the tied aspect),[28] and the Netherlands Trust Fund also has a 100 percent tied content.[29]

These aid restrictions, which demand a purchase tied to the goods of the donor nation, curtail the development of projects that have a limited export component. This limitation has usually favored productionist projects in industry or infrastructure and has restricted the development of social projects that demand a sizeable local contribution.

This analysis of the Inter-American Development Bank, its historical development, structure, and some of the salient guidelines that govern its operations, provides a background to an understanding of the Bank's activities in Costa Rica. The United States on a power distribution basis has played a central role since the Bank's founding. The United States was instrumental in bringing the Bank into being and with control of 40 percent plus of all Bank votes has been a major force in shaping Inter-American Development Bank policy.

The shift in emphasis discussed above from projects of a strong social orientation to infrastructure and production projects was supported by the United States within the Bank as it was in other U.S. government projects, such as the Alliance for Progress after 1965. The multilateral or multinational nature of the Bank should be understood in terms of the role of its dominant members. Only within that context can the impact of the Inter-American Development Bank's role in a country like Costa Rica be fully evaluated. The discussion to follow will establish the theoretical parameters for such an evaluation and will provide empirical indicators of the Bank's role in Latin American development.

## NOTES

1. Sidney Dell, The Inter-American Development Bank (New York: Praeger, 1972), p. 3.

2. Federico Gil, Latin American-United States Relations (New York: Harcourt, Brace, Jovanovich, 1971).

3. U.S. House Committee on Foreign Relations, "The United States and the Multilateral Development Banks," 93rd Congress, 2nd Session (March 1974), p. 19.

4. John White, Regional Development Banks: The Asian, African and Inter-American Development Bank (New York: Praeger, 1972), p. 146.

5. Inter-American Development Bank, Third Annual Report, 1962 (Washington, D.C.: 1963), p. 4.

6. "The United States and the Multilateral Development Banks," p. 20.

7. Ibid., pp. 18-19.

8. IDB, "Agreement Establishing the Inter-American Development Bank entered into effect December 30, 1959, with modification made by the Board of Governors, June 30, 1972," p. 1.

9. Ibid., p. 11.

10. IDB, Annual Report, 1973 (Washington, D.C.: 1974), p. 111.

11. IDB, "Agreement," p. 7.

12. White, Regional Development Banks, pp. 154-55.

13. Dell, The Inter-American Development Bank, p. 41.

14. "The United States and the Multilateral Development Banks," p. 215.

15. Inter-American Development Bank, Meeting of the Board of Governors, XV (Washington, D.C.: 1975), p. 6.

16. Ibid., pp. 9-10.

17. "The United States and the Multilateral Development Banks," p. 21.

18. IDB, Annual Report, 1973 (Washington, D.C.: 1974), pp. V, 37.

19. "The United States and the Multilateral Development Banks," pp. 23-25.

20. IDB, Annual Report, 1973 (Washington, D.C.: 1974), p. 104.

21. IDB, Annual Report, 1965 (Washington, D.C.: 1966), p. 5.

22. Statistics from IDB, Annual Report, 1965 (Washington, D.C.: 1966), p. 5; and John White, Regional Development Banks (New York: Praeger, 1972), p. 172.

23. Statistics taken from White, Regional Development Banks, p. 172, and IDB, Annual Report, 1973 (Washington, D.C.: 1974), p. 25.

24. "The United States and the Multilateral Development Banks," pp. 55-56.

25. Gil, Latin American-United States Relations, pp. 238-46.

26. "The United States and the Multilateral Development Banks," pp. 67-68.

27. Ibid., pp. 63-64.

28. IDB, "Funds in Administration" (Office of the Financial Manager, April 22, 1974), pp. 4-5.

29. IDB, "General Guidelines on the Operating Policy of the Bank" (April 28, 1972), p. 29.

CHAPTER

# 2

## THE ROLE OF NATIONAL INTEREST AND DEPENDENCY

The role that national interest plays in the Inter-American Development Bank, while difficult to measure, must be analyzed if we are to understand the direction of policy formulation in the Bank. International organizations traditionally are established to achieve a structure that is intended to be "above" national politics and interests. This was certainly the impetus that inspired the United Nations. In most instances, however, international organizations have failed to reach a condition immune to national politics and interests. In the United Nations Charter, for example, the role of national interest is defined in Article 23 with the veto constitutionally held by the "Big Five" permanent members of the Security Council: China, France, the USSR, Great Britain, and the United States.[1]

Max Weber in his analysis of human activity concluded that interest was a central motivator of all human actions:

> Not ideas, but material and ideal interests, directly govern men's conduct. Yet very frequently the "world images" that have been created by "ideas" have, like switchmen, determined the tracks along which action has been pushed by the dynamic of interest.[2]

Interest, as Weber points out, is a prime mover in the actions of men, and in an international organization, the ideas, images, and constitutional boundaries of the organization act as "switchmen" or constraints in defining national interest within the institution. In the case of the Inter-American Development Bank, the constraints on national interest as expressed in foreign policy can be found in its history, organizational structure, constitution, its policies and pronouncements, and in the regional, historical, and global environment that define its activities. The internal debate and discussion of ideas within the organization also provide definition to the Bank's actions.

The patterning of national interest in the structure of the IDB, however, is quite complex, the result of a combination of internal as well as external factors. These factors, which may be the product of of the broad influence of national interest, such as U.S. public opinion or congressional pressure, also may be established as institutionalized agents of national interest within the Inter-American Development Bank, impinging on policy formation or the operations of the Bank. During the Bank's creation in 1959, the United States was instrumental in the IDB's adoption of the agreement that all decisions affecting the Fund for Special Operations (all concessionary funds) be subject to a two-thirds vote of the total voting power of the member countries.[3] Since the United States was to control approximately 40 percent of the total votes, this constitutional feature established a U.S. veto over soft loan monies in the Bank. Thus, the original push by the United States for a two-thirds vote on concessional funds, when adopted, provided an institutionalized vehicle of U.S. national interest in the form of a U.S. veto over soft loans, mitigating the necessity of U.S. direct involvement within the Bank. Before discussing the role of the direct leverage of national interest in the Bank, it is helpful to analyze the theoretical dimensions of national interest in that institution.

National interest is indeed a slippery concept, and its very elusiveness makes it an effective instrument of foreign policy. As Charles E. Hughes, a former U.S. secretary of state, has noted:

> Foreign policies are not built upon abstractions. They are the result of practical concepts of national interests arising from some immediate exigency of standing out vividly in some historical perspective.[4]

The concept of national interest must be disaggregated in order to be fully understood. National interest can influence the IDB in a number of areas: its structure, operations, development policies. Hans Morgenthau was one of the first to place it centrally in the political process. "The idea of interest," he commented, "is indeed the essence of politics and is unaffected by circumstance of time and place."[5]

While Morgenthau saw national interest as a key variable in the political relationship among nations, he failed to break the concept down into its various component parts. National interest is most often expressed in terms of the following concerns: political, economic, military, social, cultural, and psychological. Political interests are most often directed toward other nations or subnational units. National interest, however, operates on a multiplicity of levels, sometimes on different levels at the same time.

The levels on which the impact of national interest may be explicated are: the global, regional, national, or subnational. On the global level national political interest can be expounded, for example, in terms of imposing political sanctions on hostile governments, while economic interests on a global scale might be expressed by a "global" policy of trade reciprocity imposing economic sanctions such as boycotts, embargos, or tariffs on those nations that levy trade restrictions. Military national interest on a global scale might be experienced in a declaration of global or world war.

Social and cultural forms of national interest also are important and have had an important impact on nation-states, particularly during periods of imperialism or neoimperialism. This form of national interest expressed on a global scale can be found in such examples as the mass exportation of the U.S. lifestyle and ideas to many parts of the world since World War II. Earlier obvious examples of social and cultural forms of national interest were diffused by the French and the English on perhaps more of a regional level through their colonial empires. The impact of this form of national interest on neocolonial or colonial areas was intended to make them sympathetic to the imperialist powers, politically and commercially.

Another area of national interest is that expressed in psychological terms. On a global level one is reminded of the effects of psychological warfare during the Cold War. The psychological impact of national interest may be somewhat of a residual category in that it is most often the nontangible content of national interest. For example the threat of global or regional war or annihilation could often be used to bring about a particular psychological disposition favorable to the threatening nation.

All of these categories of national interest have operated on the various levels of global, regional, national, or subnational influence. The establishment of a sphere of influence such as that which the United States defined in Latin America in 1823 with the Monroe Doctrine, and the Roosevelt Corollary, or in Cuba with the Platt Amendment of 1904, provides prominent instances of the employment of national interest on the regional and national levels. The literature on dependency by such authors as Susanne Bodenheimer, Osvaldo Sunkel, Norman Girvan, and Theotino Dos Santos has defined the linkage between internal and external national interests and their impact on a particular nation's politics and economic development.[6] The dependency thesis provides a framework for exploring the impact of hegemonic national interest on the countries within a sphere of influence.

Linkages have been identified between the national interests of developed nations and the subnational units in developing countries such as the military, comprador classes (national classes of exporters), middle classes, and labor unions. These linkages have produced economic and political results favorable to the national interests of the developed countries, and have tended to thwart economic development and disaggregate or diffuse the bodies politic in the developing nations upon which these dominant national interests impinge. An example of this type of linkage between the developed and the developing country may be found in the economic assistance that the United States has given to rightwing military governments in Latin America, in return for their maintaining stability and a climate that is safe and attractive to foreign and, in particular, U.S. private investors. The economic support that the United States has given the Brazilian military government since 1964 is an instance of the linkage of U.S. national interests and a type of dependent development.[7]

While the above provides an overview of the substance of national interest, a discussion of the instruments of national interest reveals the parameters of the role of the Inter-American Development Bank in Latin America. U.S. national interest with regard to the IDB is primarily economic and may be reflected in an enumeration of foreign investments, trade, capital transfers, technological investments and transfers, the establishment of economic infrastructure, defensive investments such as investment in close proximity to cheap labor pools, cross-subsidization to increase vertical integration, transfer pricing, demand for inexpensive raw materials and resources, and other specific economic interests.*

The role of the IDB is that of a multilateral vehicle that assists in implementing these instruments of U.S. national interest. A specific definition of IDB assistance will be elaborated in Chapter 5 in the discussion of particular IDB projects in Costa Rica. My thesis therefore revolves around two sets of issues: that U.S. national interest has an impact on the Inter-American Development Bank and that the Inter-American Development Bank in turn mediates U.S. national interest, which has an impact on the process of Latin American development as I will demonstrate through specific IDB projects in Costa Rica.

---

*Cross-subsidization is the actual use by a conglomerate of monopoly profits earned in another industry to subsidize sales at a loss or at an abnormally low profit; by transfer pricing, multinational corporations often raise or lower prices on products they are sending to a subsidiary for tax reasons, many times at a loss of revenue to the host country.

The relationship of U.S. national interest and the role of the United States is specified further in Chapter 3; however, the actual theoretical impact of U.S. national interest via IDB on Costa Rican development can be further conceptually elaborated with the concept of dependency.

Theories of dependency focus on the external and internal linkages between the developed nations and developing nations that define development in the Third World. Simply stated, the growth, for instance, of the U.S. economy has an internal dynamic for expansion that has led to U.S. economic ventures in Latin America and other parts of the world in search of raw materials, markets, sources of cheap labor, tax benefits, or other economic benefits. This expansion has resulted in the economies of Latin America being linked with the economies of the United States, Japan, West Germany, and other developed nations and subject to the forces of those economies. In the case of Latin America, as is demonstrated in subsequent chapters, the United States remains the major trading partner and investor and it is upon the economy of the United States that Latin America is most dependent. This dependence is effected not only in terms of a drain on the economy through the repatriation of profits or unfavorable terms of trade, but additionally by the economic structures of the developed world that are replicated in the developing world. The thesis, therefore, of the dependency school is that the expansion of the developed world economic system into the Third World and Latin America fosters a type of development that leads to further underdevelopment. Osvaldo Sunkel, in an article entitled "Transnational Capitalism and Disintegration in Latin America," has described this process in the following manner:

> It becomes quite clear that external links and relationships have exercised a fundamental influence on the shaping of the structure of our system, and, therefore, on their functioning and outcome, as well as on the process of structural transformation. Nevertheless, the importance attached to these external links should not lead us to underestimate the existence of structures of underdevelopment internal to the system. Although external influences tend to prevail as main factors in the long term process of transformation, structural transformation is the product of the interaction between external and internal variables.[8]

The link between national interest and dependency, therefore, is that national interest, and particularly U.S. national interest in the case of Latin America, grows outward through various instruments or institutions (such as the Inter-American Development Bank), which in turn have an impact on the structure of Costa Rican development.

As mentioned above, the external factors of dependency or the instruments of U.S. national interest are: trade, foreign investment, demand for cheap raw materials and sources of labor, as well as markets. These external factors of dependency have an impact in terms of transforming the developing nations and effecting the process of national economic development. These external factors have an impact on the following internal factors: pattern of natural resource use; distribution of income and marginality among sectors of the population; political institutions, especially the state; on various sociopolitical groups and classes; and on specific policies followed by the government.

Sunkel shows how external factors can effect internal national development in describing the possible impact of the expansion of developed nations into Latin America:

> If demand remains constant during this process of technological substitution, an increase in investment in the modern sector would create idle capacity and unemployment, since the number of persons employed per unit of capital in the modern sector is less than in primitive activities. In this way it is conceivable that an increase in the rate of investment could lead to an increase in the rate of un- and underemployment and, therefore, of marginality. In fact, I would suggest that this is not just an extreme hypothetical situation, but is perhaps the best working hypothesis to explain the growing unemployment, underemployment and marginality in Latin America.[9]

Dependency, therefore, as in the above instance, leads to further dependency. In the case of IDB the external factors of dependency and U.S. national interests as I have defined them are implemented, at least partially, through the Bank and have an internal impact on Costa Rican development through the Bank's Costa Rican projects. (The "partial" impact of the IDB on Costa Rican development is because the Bank is only one of many multilateral and bilateral international organizations that act on behalf of U.S. national interests. An examination of IDB projects in Costa Rica will provide a description of the Bank's actual impact.)

Historically, the context of dependent relations between developed and developing nations in Latin America has been altered during particular time periods. Until about 1850 Latin America had a more or less mercantilistic relationship with Spain. The decline of Spanish power in Europe in the wake of the Napoleonic wars and the rise of

British power led to a period of laissez faire, or free trade liberalism in which Latin America traded primary agriculture and mineral commodities for manufactured goods at a comparative disadvantage. By 1930, however, with the Great Depression and the total collapse of the international political economy, the era of free trade was ebbing and laissez faire governments were falling in favor of regimes that increased government intervention in the economy to maintain high levels of economic growth and combat unemployment and inflation.

The 1930s to the present has been the era of neomercantilism, another form of dependency, in which the national state and the hegemonic state or developed nations have become increasingly linked in their effort to promote economic development. The postdepression era has been distinguished by two basic development strategies aimed at offsetting Latin American dependency on primary products. This was particularly important with the severe reduction in the price of primary products in the agricultural export sector during and after the Great Depression. The two alternatives offered were industrialization by invitation, and later during the 1950s industrialization via regional economic integration. Both alternatives were largely in response to the now famous Prebisch thesis, which advocated economic development via import substitution to defer national import demand. When import substitution through industrialization by invitation failed to promote economic development, the argument then became that import substitution must be accompanied by an expanded market and hence the idea of regional economic integration became the means to achieve an expanded national market base.[10] As a result of this latter joint effort on the part of Latin American governments and the United States, the various contemporary schemes of regional economic integration were born. These programs of regional integration are known under the various titles of CACM (Central American Common Market), LACM (Latin American Common Market), Caribbean Common Market, and the Andean group. Their impact on development, however, is just another stage in the history of dependency, as subsequent chapters will demonstrate.

The above discussion has defined the historical/ structural dimensions of dependency. Dependency in Latin America has resulted generally in the following types of economic configurations: stagnation in agricultural prices; sluggish growth of the industrial export sector; rapid growth of food imports; high commodity concentration of exports; high foreign exchange content of industrialization; growing fiscal deficit; increased foreign debt; stagnation in traditional mining and raw materials export prices; and an increased public sector role to resolve the above problems.[11] It is the contention of this study that the IDB as one of the multilateral lending agencies has contributed to some aspects of Latin American dependency. The linking of U.S.

TABLE 2.1

Paradigm: Global Framework of U.S. National Interests in IDB

| Global Instruments of U.S. Influence (ideas) | Vehicle | Implementation of Global Instruments through the IDB | |
|---|---|---|---|
| | | Washington IDB Response | Costa Rican IDB Response |
| Economic integration<br>Idea: Import substitution | IDB<br>Multilateral agencies to avoid confrontation with Latin American nations<br>OAS (Organization of American States)<br>World Bank<br>CABEI* | Institutionalize IDB as bank for integration<br>Foster integration loans<br>Technical assistance for integration<br>IDB internal changes<br>Fund subregional integration agencies such as CABEI | Fund infrastructure and integration projects<br>Fund CABEI*<br>Work with Central Bank, Ministry of Economy, and Industry<br>Work with OFIPLAN (National Planning Office) |

*Central American Bank for Economic Integration.
Source: Compiled by the author.

national interest through the Bank with IDB projects in Latin America, as will be demonstrated in the Costa Rican case study, has contributed to further dependency rather than alleviating Latin America's traditional dependency. In order to test this hypothesis, it is necessary to place the Bank center stage within the historical structural framework of Latin American dependency.

The Inter-American Development Bank can be placed in historical perspective within the stage of dependency through regional economic integration from 1960 to the present. The Bank's role in implementing regional economic integration within the context of U.S. national interest is outlined in Chapter 4. Table 2.1 illustrates in global terms the role of IDB in implementing regional economic integration.

TABLE 2.2

Paradigm: Direct U.S. Interest and IDB Relationship

| Specific U.S. Interests | Vehicle for Transmitting Influence to IDB | IDB Policy | Potential Impact on Costa Rica |
|---|---|---|---|
| Increased trade | U.S. Congress | Emphasize U.S. interest through development of infrastructure and productionist projects that favor U.S. interests | Increase foreign debt |
| Control of technology | U.S. State Department | Deemphasize social sector projects with low import component | Increase trade deficit |
| Foreign investment | NAC (National Advisory Council) | | Increase inflation |
| Source of cheap primary products | U.S. Commerce Department | | Increase dependence on few primary projects |
| Capitalist development | U.S. Agriculture Department | | Increase unemployment |
| U.S. repatriation of profits | Eximbank | | Force migration to urban areas |
| Secure and expanded markets | White House | | Increase service sector (marginality) |
| Cheap source of labor | Other government agencies | | Increase dependence on international lenders to service debt |
| Markets for capital and manufactured goods obsolete in United States | | | Increase role of state sector |
| Increased profits on pharmaceuticals | | | Distribute income in favor of middle classes |
| Investment opportunities for surplus U.S. capital | | | |

Source: Compiled by the author.

As Table 2.1 illustrates, the implementation of regional economic integration was accomplished by a number of international and national vehicles operating in Latin America, of which IDB was just one. The fostering of regional economic integration has, as subsequent chapters will illustrate, contributed to furthering Latin America's dependence upon the United States. Table 2.2, a second paradigm, offers a more specific framework describing the theoretical impact of IDB projects in fostering Latin American dependency. These projects are within the global historical framework described above in the dependency stages of regional economic integration. The paradigm that follows concretizes the three central questions of this study, which connects U.S. national interest, dependency, and the IDB. The questions are:

1. What is the impact of U.S. national interest on the IDB?
2. What is the Bank's impact on Costa Rican development?
3. What are the linkages between U.S. influence in the Bank and the Bank's impact on Costa Rican development?

Table 2.2, illustrating an analytical framework, addresses those concerns. It illustrates the theoretical relationship between U.S. national interest, IDB policies and projects, and their impact on Costa Rican development.

The discussions that follow within a historical/ institutional/ structural framework will analyze the role of U.S. national interest in the Inter-American Development Bank, the impact of U.S. national interest on the formulation of Bank projects in Latin America, and the impact of specific projects on Latin American development. The Costa Rican case study will provide a concrete illustration of the Bank's general role in Latin American development.

## NOTES

1. Inis L. Claude, Jr., Swords into Plowshares (New York: Random House, 1971), p. 141.

2. H. H. Gerth and C. Wright Mills, From Max Weber (New York: Oxford University Press, 1958), p. 280.

3. Inter-American Development Bank, "Agreement Establishing the Inter-American Development Bank," Washington, D.C., 1959, p. 7.

4. Charles A. Beard, The Idea of National Interest (Chicago: Quadrangle, 1966), p. 1.

5. Hans J. Morgenthau, Politics Among Nations (New York: Alfred A. Knopf, 1962), p. 8.

6. See the symposium issue ("Dependence and Underdevelopment in the New World and Old"), Social and Economic Studies 22, no. 1 (March 1973); K. T. Fann and Donald C. Hodges, Readings in U.S. Imperialism (Boston: Porter Sargent, 1971).

7. See Luigi R. Einaudi and Alfred C. Stepan III, Latin American Institutional Development, Changing Military Perspectives in Peru and Brazil (Santa Monica, Calif.: Rand, 1971).

8. Osvaldo Sunkel, "Transnational Capitalism and National Disintegration in Latin America," Social and Economic Studies 22, no. 1 (March 1973): 134.

9. Ibid., p. 143.

10. Norman Girvan, "The Development of Dependency Economics in the Caribbean and Latin America," Social and Economic Studies 22, no. 1 (March 1973): 1-33.

11. Ibid., p. 2.

# CHAPTER 3

# THE U.S. ROLE

While the Bank's historical development and structure produce certain constraints on its operations, its relationship to the U.S. government defines further the parameters of its actions. The United States seems to have a very special relationship to the Inter-American Development Bank. Unlike the other members of the Bank, who are responsible to their respective finance ministers, the U.S. representative is bound by the Bretton Woods Agreement Act, which stipulates that U.S. executive directors in international financial institutions must cooperate with the National Advisory Council on International Monetary and Financial Policies (NAC).[1] NAC is responsible for coordinating U.S. participation in all international lending institutions, both bilateral and multilateral, of which the United States is a member, such as the World Bank group, the Inter-American Development Bank, the Asian Development Bank, the International Monetary Fund, the Export-Import Bank, and the U.S. Agency for International Development (USAID).

The membership of NAC is composed of the secretary of the treasury, who acts as chairman; the secretary of state; the secretary of commerce; the chairman of the Board of Governors of the Federal Reserve System; and the chairman and president of the Export-Import Bank of the United States.[2] The NAC staff is housed in the U.S. Treasury, and the Treasury Department plays a central role in overseeing the daily activities of the IDB and other international financial institutions. NAC's basic mandate is to ensure that the international lending institutions under its jurisdiction comply with U.S. international monetary and financial policies, U.S. foreign policy, and U.S. commercial considerations. NAC reviews each loan document prior to its submission to the IDB Board and instructs the U.S. executive director how to vote.

NAC acts in reality as an advisory body for the secretary of the treasury, coordinating input from the respective member agencies and formulating a recommendation on the vote on each loan document. While NAC may act as a rubber stamp in its recommendation for approval of IDB loans, its influence on loans involving vital U.S. national interests can be decisive. In addition to priority of projects and technical feasibility estimates on IDB loan proposals, NAC oversees three particular special policy criteria:

1. Debt arrearage to the United States by the loan-requesting country.
2. Expropriations, nationalizations, or other serious investment disputes between U.S. investors and the loan-requesting country.
3. Problems of international narcotics control in the loan-requesting country.[3]

During the loan review process, U.S. influence is manifested indirectly when loan documents are redrafted to meet U.S. objections prior to being submitted for approval to the IDB Board. In certain instances the United States has abstained from voting on loans as a means of protest and has been effective in eliminating similar future proposals.[4] The three special policy criteria listed above have given the U.S. government, through the NAC, a singularly strong leverage in the Bank. If a loan-requesting country cannot meet these three special requirements, the U.S. executive director will be instructed by NAC to vote no. These special criteria are the result of U.S. congressional legislation and executive orders designed to persuade loan-requesting countries to adopt policies in accord with U.S. national interest. The potential threat of a U.S. veto on concessionary funds and U.S. control of 40.29 percent of the total votes for the approval of ordinary capital loans in the IDB require that member countries take the NAC loan criteria seriously.

A further elaboration of U.S. loan criteria is helpful to understand their impact on IDB policy. With regard to foreign debt arrearage, NAC policy states:

> Any delinquent payments on obligations owed the U.S. Government by the recipient country are of serious concern to the United States. Review of the efforts being made to collect such arrearages is an integral part of the USG loan appraisal process. Such arrearages cast doubt on the credit worthiness of a foreign government and on that government's ability to successfully implement both sound economic policies and projects supported by the international development banks. Unless special

> circumstances indicate otherwise, the National Advisory Council (NAC) follows the general policy of not recommending approval of international development bank loans and credits to governments in arrears in their official obligations to the U.S. Government until the particular foreign government either pays the arrearages in full or shows satisfactory evidence of its willingness to become current on its obligations to the United States.[5]

A presidential policy statement and the Gonzalez Amendment, which is attached to the 1972 IDB appropriation, both require the secretary of the treasury to instruct the U.S. executive director of the Bank to vote against any loan for the benefit of a country that has expropriated or nationalized U.S.-owned property. These statements provide the guidelines for NAC policy on expropriations. The NAC policy requires that the U.S. executive director vote against any loan or utilization of IDB funds for the benefit of any country that has:

1. Expropriated, nationalized, or seized ownership of U.S. property.
2. Taken steps to repudiate or nullify existing contracts or agreements with U.S. representatives.
3. Imposed or inforced discriminatory taxes or other assessments against any U.S. citizen, corporation, partnership, or association not less than 50 percent of which is owned by U.S. citizens.[6]

The daily implementation of the Gonzalez Amendment and the presidential policy directive are coordinated by the Council on International Economic Policy, part of the White House staff, which reports its findings to NAC and recommends appropriate action. NAC in turn makes recommendations to the U.S. delegate in the IDB.

The third area of special consideration in the NAC review of IDB loan documents is narcotics control. The Rangel Amendment, added to the IDB Act in 1972 by the U.S. Congress, forms the basis for the NAC criteria on narcotics control, imposing very specific narcotic regulations on loan-requesting nations. NAC policy states:

> The various Bank Acts, as amended in March, 1972, require the U.S. Executive Director at each institution "to vote against any loan or other utilization of the funds of the Bank for the benefit of any country with respect to which the President has made a determination, and so notified the Secretary of the Treasury, that the government of such country has failed to take adequate steps to prevent narcotics, drugs and other controlled substances

> produced or processed, in whole or in part, in such country, or transported through such country, from being illegally within the jurisdiction of such country to United States Government personnel or their dependents, or from entering the United States unlawfully. Such suspension shall continue until the President determines that the government of such country has taken adequate steps " . . . to prevent such sale or entry of narcotics, drugs and other controlled substances.[7]

These special criteria for loan approval by NAC are quite distinct; however, they do not define all the policy constraints that establish the NAC and U.S. government position toward the Bank. Under the aegis of U.S. foreign policy, additional areas of national interest via NAC have an impact on IDB loan operations. NAC guidelines on the role of foreign policy considerations are quite concise:

> Participation in the international development banks presupposes a certain degree of insulation of Bank activities from the individual bilateral concerns of member countries.
>
> The Articles of Agreement of each of the Banks contain provisions which restrict the political activity of the Banks and their officers and affirm the exclusion of political considerations from the decisions of the Bank. Nonetheless, U.S. support for a Bank loan must be consistent with U.S. foreign policy concerns.[8]

This NAC policy guideline makes it evident that IDB loans will be recommended for approval, disapproval, or revision based on U.S. foreign policy considerations. What these foreign policy considerations are and how they impinge upon the IDB provides insight into the role of U.S. national interest in the Bank.

Some observers have argued that multilateral institutions like the IDB are more politically impartial and therefore further removed from the influence of national interest than bilateral organizations.[9] Others have refuted this view. John White in his study of regional development banks commented:

> Most multilateral agencies, for instance, claim that their operations have the "advantage" of being free of political considerations. If all that is meant is that institutions do not have foreign policies in quite the same way as foreign governments, then it is a truism. If anything more is meant, then it is false. Quite apart from the patent

> absurdity of characterizing the UN system as a nonpolitical system, it is reasonable to ask what kind of a frame of reference it is, and whether it is an "advantageous" one, that can exclude the political content of choices in development policy.[10]

White's remarks support evidence on the role of U.S. foreign policy considerations in the IDB. U.S. foreign policy and national interest influence Bank policy in a number of ways. U.S. policy interests within the Bank are composed of a number of factors: economic, political, national security, and humanitarian. The desire to bring about economic development in Latin America within a specific capitalist direction is certainly part of U.S. concern in the Bank. Other economic interests also are evident. In addition to a broad concern for economic development, macroeconomic considerations are part of U.S. national interest. In assessing a loan-requesting country's past performance, NAC considers the following: monetary and fiscal policies; the effectiveness of a country's financial institutions; the role of private savings on the country's economic development; and the capability of the requesting government to finance needed public sector investments. If any of these areas do not meet U.S. standards, a bank loan may be held up until the country adopts the appropriate policy or provides the necessary institutional reform.[11] As a result of these NAC policy guidelines the U.S. government has the opportunity to exert indirect influence to shape the internal domestic economic policies and structures of an IDB loan recipient country toward compatibility with U.S. national interests. A number of U.S. government spokesmen have noted that international lending institutions can promote development compatible with U.S. national interests. Secretary of State William Rogers, in testimony before the Senate Committee on Appropriations in 1974, said:

> Also important to us is the role these institutions play in promoting a Western oriented economic philosophy in the developing world. In their loan appraisals and operating policies, they encourage growth of free markets, sound fiscal and monetary policies, careful foreign exchange management, and maximum international movement of goods, services, and capital.[12]

Under Secretary of the Treasury Paul A. Volcker commented on the contributions that the multilateral banks make to private investment:

> There is close to $25 billion of U.S. investment in developing countries, yielding over $4 billion annually in return flows. Assistance from the [multilateral banks] helps build and keep a healthy environment for this important U.S. investment.[13]

The maintenance of U.S. national economic interests in the developing world is perceived by most U.S. officials as a high priority. In discussion with NAC staff and in reviewing NAC policies and the statements of high U.S. officials, it is obvious that prime emphasis is given to U.S. national economic interests in the IDB and all international lending institutions.[14]

Some U.S. officials have voiced concern that the United States may not be getting its fair share in a dollar return on its subscription to the international lending institutions. They also have claimed these institutions have been a drain on the U.S. balance of payments. Table 3.1 illustrates, however, that development banks do not have a negative impact on the U.S. balance of payments; instead, it shows that foreign aid can reap a substantial return. These figures indicate that rather than a balance of payments deficit, the United States has a net payments surplus of $2,673.5 million from its involvements in the banks.

The Inter-American Development Bank's contribution to this surplus may be attributed to a number of factors. One obvious factor is that the U.S. contribution to the Fund for Special Operations is tied to procurements in the United States. Another factor tending to offset a negative balance of payments is that IDB headquarters are in Washington, D.C., and a considerable operational cost is spent in the United States. Interest on IDB bonds floated in the U.S. capital market contributes to net dollar surplus from the Bank. The "fair share," however, that the United States receives in its percentage of procurement from U.S. suppliers of the IDB provides the greatest support. In 1973 the U.S. Treasury reported that the U.S. percentage of the share of procurement for the IDB was 33 percent for ordinary capital and 69 percent of the Fund for Special Operations. Tables 3.2 and 3.3 illustrate the impact of U.S. procurement in the IDB's ordinary capital and Fund for Special Operations on the United States balance of payments; they show that the United States has not suffered economically by its subscriptions to the IDB.[15] In addition to the direct dollar return from the IDB, the United States benefits from the Bank's development of infrastructure and industrial projects. These projects provide investment opportunities in Latin America for American businessmen. The U.S. Department of Commerce's Bureau of International Commerce provides a monthly status report of the IDB's activities and a biweekly periodical, Commerce Today, in which IDB

TABLE 3.1

Balance of Payments Between the United States and the Banks, Cumulative: Inception to 1973

| Outflow and Inflow | Millions of $ |
| --- | --- |
| U.S. payments to the banks | |
| World Bank Group subscriptions | 1,460.2 |
| Inter-American Bank subscriptions | 964.8 |
| Asian Bank subscriptions | 55.3 |
| World Bank bond sales in United States | 2,492.0 |
| Inter-American Bank bond sales in United States | 423.2 |
| Asian Bank bond sales in United States | 42.0 |
| WBG earnings on investments in United States | 1,284.0 |
| IDB earnings on investments in United States | 221.3 |
| ADB earnings on investments in United States | 39.1 |
| Total U.S. payments to banks | 6,991.9 |
| Bank payments to the United States | |
| World Bank Group U.S. procurement | 4,391.0 |
| Inter-American Bank U.S. procurement | 733.0 |
| Asian Bank U.S. procurement | 12.5 |
| WBG interest to U.S. bondholders | 1,308.0 |
| IDB interest to U.S. bondholders | 149.7 |
| ADB interest to U.S. bondholders | 7.0 |
| WBG administrative expenses in United States | 617.9 |
| ADB administrative expenses in United States | 16.5 |
| WBG net long-term investments in United States | 2,094.0 |
| IDB net long-term investments in United States | 68.5 |
| ADB net long-term investments in United States | 82.0 |
| IDB administrative expenses in United States | 184.3 |
| Bank payments to the United States | 9,664.4 |
| Net U.S. payments surplus | 2,673.5 |

Source: U.S. House of Representatives, Committee on Foreign Relations, The United States and the Multilateral Development Banks, 93rd Congress, 2nd Session (March 1974), pp. 148-49.

TABLE 3.2

Estimated Effects of IDB Ordinary Capital Transactions on the U.S. Balance of Payments, 1960-72
(millions of dollars)

| | Inception through 12/31/65 | Calendar Year 1966 | 1967 | 1968 | 1969 | 1970 | 1971 | 1972 | Inception through 12/31/72 |
|---|---|---|---|---|---|---|---|---|---|
| 1. U.S. subscriptions[a] | 75 | 37.5 | 37.5 | | | | | | 150.0 |
| 2. Net sales of bonds and loan participations in United States | 215 | 3.1 | 86.8 | 73.6 | 5.1 | 79.5 | 13.7 | 16.0 | 423.2 |
| 3. Investment income earned by IDB in United States | 343 | 14.8 | 18.1 | 21.3 | 29.1 | 34.6 | 28.8 | 24.3 | 205.3 |
| 4. U.S. payments to IDB | 324.3 | 55.4 | 142.4 | 94.9 | 24.0 | 114.1 | 15.1 | 8.3 | 778.5 |
| 5. IDB-financed goods bought in United States[b] | 62.9 | 19.0 | 22.4 | 43.0 | 20.6 | 33.6 | 24.6 | 28.6 | 254.7 |
| 6. Interest paid by IDB to U.S. bondholders and purchasers of participations | 18.1 | 10.6 | 11.9 | 15.5 | 19.9 | 19.3 | 27.1 | 27.1 | 149.5 |
| 7. IDB administrative expenses in United States[c] | 27.2 | 8.5 | 9.3 | 8.0 | 8.4 | 9.6 | 10.6 | 11.0 | 92.6 |
| 8. Net investment in long-term U.S. assets[d] | 101.0 | 81.0 | 105.6 | 50.0 | 38.4 | 2.2 | 224.0 | 4.5 | 68.5 |
| 9. U.S. receipts from IDB (items 5 through 8) | 209.2 | 119.1 | 149.2 | 116.5 | 10.5 | 60.3 | 161.7 | 62.2 | 565.3 |
| 10. Balance on "liquidity basis" (items 9 minus 4) | 115.1 | 63.7 | 6.8 | 21.6 | 13.5 | 53.8 | 176.8 | 53.9 | 213.2 |
| 11. Net investment in U.S. short-term assets and government securities[e] | 120.7 | 27.5 | 16.8 | 20.6 | 8.8 | 58.9 | 205.3 | 6.7 | 322.1 |
| 12. Balance on "official reserve transactions" basis (items 10 plus 11) | 5.6 | 36.2 | 10.0 | 1.0 | 4.7 | 5.1 | 28.5 | 47.2 | 108.9 |

[a]Total U.S. subscriptions net of amounts held by IDB in nonnegotiable, non-interest-bearing notes received from the United States on account of its own subscription.

[b]Partly estimated.

[c]Includes payment for real estate and mortgages amortization.

[d]Net changes in IDB holdings in certificates of deposit issued by U.S. banks with maturities of more than 12 months.

[e]Demand deposits, short-term certificates of deposit issued by U.S. banks, and U.S. Government obligations.

Source: National Advisory Council, Annual Report (Washington, D.C., July 1, 1972-June 30, 1973), p. 200.

TABLE 3.3

Estimated Effects of IDB Funds for Special Operations Transactions on the U.S. Balance of Payments, 1960-December 31, 1972
(millions of dollars)

| Item | $ Millions |
|---|---|
| 1. U.S. subscription: | |
| Total subscription | 2,910.0 |
| Less: amount not yet received in cash | 2,095.2 |
| Total amount received | 814.8 |
| 2. Investment income earned by IDB in United States | 16.0 |
| 3. U.S. payments to IDB[a] | 830.8 |
| 4. IDB-financed goods bought in United States via direct purchases | 168.1 |
| 5. IDB-financed goods bought in United States via special letters of credit | 310.2 |
| 6. Interest paid by IDB to U.S. purchasers of participations | .2 |
| 7. IDB administrative and technical assistance expenses in United States[b] | 91.7 |
| 8. U.S. receipts from IDB (items 4 through 7) | 570.2 |
| 9. Balance both on "liquidity basis" and "official reserve transactions" basis (item 8 - 3) | 260.6 |

[a]Excludes $35,000,000 of dollar participations in loans of the Fund for Special Operations sold to the Social Progress Trust Fund.

[b]Partly estimated.

Source: National Advisory Council, Annual Report (Washington D.C.: July 1, 1972-June 30, 1973), p. 201.

bid announcements are regularly published. While figures are not available to illustrate direct IDB stimulation of U.S. investments in Latin America, Table 3.4 provides an overall clue suggesting the trade surplus that the United States has accrued in Latin America.

U.S. participation in the IDB, as can be seen from the above discussion, has been to the benefit of the United States both economically and politically. Volcker, the U.S. Undersecretary of the

Treasury for monetary affairs, commented on the tradeoff for U.S. subscription in the development banks at Senate hearings:

> We have significant opportunities to shape policies and operations of the international institutions at an early state, and my observation is that when we set out to achieve a given objective we have a high prospect for ultimate means . . . . But this influence will inevitably and quickly erode if we are not willing to put up our fair share of resources.[16]

TABLE 3.4

U.S. Balance of Payments with Latin America, 1961-74
(millions of dollars)

| Year | Exports | Imports | Balance |
|---|---|---|---|
| 1961 | 3,523 | 3,178 | +345 |
| 1962 | 3,323 | 3,381 | -58 |
| 1963 | 3,264 | 3,450 | -186 |
| 1964 | 3,832 | 3,524 | +308 |
| 1965 | 3,788 | 3,675 | +113 |
| 1966 | 4,231 | 3,970 | +261 |
| 1967 | 4,126 | 3,853 | +273 |
| 1968 | 4,600 | 4,288 | +411 |
| 1969 | 4,869 | 4,214 | +655 |
| 1970 | 5,695 | 4,779 | +916 |
| 1971 | 5,667 | 4,881 | +786 |
| 1972 | 6,471 | 5,772 | +699 |
| 1973 | 8,921 | 7,827 | +1,094 |
| 1974 | 14,504 | 13,678 | +836 |

Source: U.S. Department of Commerce, Overseas Business Reports, OBR 68-31 (May 1968), p. 17; OBR 73-44 (August 1973), pp. 3, 29; OBR 75-38 (September 1975), pp. 3, 29.

## DIRECT U.S. INVOLVEMENT IN IDB ACTIVITIES

Hard evidence of direct U.S. influence in the Bank is difficult to document, although the NAC policy criteria do establish some obvious objectives. In a Government Accounting Office report to the U.S. Congress in 1972, a number of illustrations of U.S. direct influence did surface. The report noted that on a number of occasions the United States had been successful in delaying loans to countries that had expropriated U.S. property. In addition, the report noted that U.S. officials had been successful in stopping an attempt by Latin Americans to move IDB headquarters from Washington to Latin America.[17] Loans to Bolivia and Peru also were held up because of expropriation of U.S. investments. As the GAO report states:

> In seeking to avoid open confrontations with the Latin American members, U.S. officials have worked quietly behind the scenes to keep IDB management from submitting loan proposals to the board of Executive Directors for approval, and in this manner, have been able to delay loan proposals for several months.[18]

The above accurately describes the "low profile" U.S. influence in the Bank. Treasury Undersecretary for International Affairs Charles Walker commented in 1971 on the U.S. attitude toward expropriations:

> There is a real question whether you are creating a climate attractive to private investment when the entrepreneurs are fearful whatever they develop is going to be taken over even with adequate compensation. In the case of the Peruvian situation, in the case of the Bolivian loan, in the case of the Guyanan loan, all of which we have abstained in connection with, I think it is going too far to say that is simply an extension of U.S. foreign policy, but I would say that it is within the context of the new look in foreign economic policy and would defend it vigorously on that basis.[19]

In Chile, the application of U.S. economic sanctions via the IDB in reprisal for the Allende government's expropriation of U.S. interests has been described by James F. Petras and Morris Morley's The United States and Chile.[20] A study of U.S.-Chilean relations by the House Subcommittee on Inter-American Affairs reported in 1973 that "neither the Inter-American Development Bank nor the World Bank had granted new credits to Chile since Allende assumed the presidency."[21] The IDB Statement of Loans, 1973, provides evidence that from the time Allende took office in December 1970 until December 31, 1973, no loans were approved out of ordinary capital and only two loans were approved in 1971 from concessionary sources, both for the expansion of the private universities at Valdivia and Santiago.[22] These economic sanctions against Chile represent a clear pattern of direct U.S. influence in the Bank. In light of the report of the Senate Subcommittee on Multinational Corporations in 1974, Multinational Corporations and United States Foreign Policy, U.S. influence via the IDB toward Chile appears to be part of a global strategy to support political alignments and economic interests compatible with the U.S. outlook.[23]

The case of Chile, the statements of Treasury Undersecretary Walker on Peru, Bolivia, and Guyana, and the confidential GAO report on the use of "low profile" methods in the IDB all document instances in which the United States has used its influence in the Bank to further the U.S. national interest.

Another area of concern to the U.S. government is export financing. While U.S. officials have strongly supported the need for creating a healthy climate for foreign investment, they have consistently opposed programs to finance Latin American exports. Such programs could contribute to economic development and the capital surplus necessary for industrialization in Latin America.[24]

U.S. participation, therefore, has imposed severe constraints on IDB activities. Not only does the United States attempt to have funding withheld from Latin American nations that do not meet its requirements in expropriation policy, debt arrearage, and narcotics control, but it also imposes limitations in other areas. These loan criteria can also be used to affect economic and political affairs in the recipient country, or to exert leverage to bring about a climate attractive for U.S. investment, as appears to have been the case in Chile and Peru. It is also apparent that the specific tied nature of the Fund for Special Operations resources, demanding purchases from U.S. suppliers, is another instance of U.S. influence to support national economic interests. The tied nature of this aid sometimes forces recipient countries to make purchases at uncompetitively high prices and to undertake projects that may not be in their national economic interest. U.S. ability to thwart programs that would develop export industries in Latin America has undermined Latin America's economic development and protected U.S. national interest in maintaining a favorable trade balance.

The above analysis defines some of the U.S. constraints on the Bank's activities. In the following chapters, these parameters affecting Bank action will become clearer within the context of the U.S. role in the Inter-American system and the historical roles of the IDB and the United States in Costa Rica.

## NOTES

1. U.S. House of Representatives, Committee on Foreign Relations, "The United States and the Multilateral Development Banks," 93rd Congress, 2nd Session (March 1974), p. 141.

2. National Advisory Council on International Monetary and Financial Policies, *Annual Report* (Washington, D.C.: July 1, 1972-June 30, 1973), pp. 1-2.

3. National Advisory Council, *Manual of Procedures and Policy Criteria Employed by the United States in the Appraisal of Financial Committments of the International Lending Institutions* (Washington, D.C., March 1973), p. 27.

4. The direct influence of the U.S. government was confirmed in interviews with NAC officials and the U.S. delegate in the IDB in July 1974. This pattern of U.S. involvement is also reported in "The United States and the Multilateral Development Banks," pp. 112-14.

5. *Manual of Procedures and Policy Criteria*, pp. 27-28.

6. Office of the White House Press Secretary, "Policy Statement: Economic Assistance and Investment Security in Developing Nations," January 19, 1972; Gonzalez Amendment, *Congressional Record*, "Expropriation Policy," January 19, 1972, pp. H105-6.

7. *Manual of Procedures and Policy Criteria*, p. 31.

8. Ibid., p. 32.

9. Robert E. Asher, *Development Assistance in the Seventies: Alternatives for the United States* (Washington, D.C.: Brookings Institution, 1970), p. 131.

10. John White, *Regional Development Banks: The Asian, African, and Inter-American Development Banks* (New York: Praeger, 1972), p. 15.

11. *Manual of Procedures and Policy Criteria*, p. 34.

12. U.S. Senate Committee on Appropriations, *Foreign Assistance and Related Programs Appropriations, Fiscal Year 1974*, 93rd Congress, First Session, Part I (April 9, 1973), pp. 474-75.

13. Ibid., p. 401.

14. This view was apparent in interviews with National Advisory Council officers and U.S. Treasury Department staff, Washington, D.C., August 1974, in the report of "The United States and the Multilateral Development Banks," pp. 129-31, and *Manual of Procedures and Policy Criteria*, pp. 33-34.

15. "The United States and the Multilateral Development Banks, pp. 150-54.

16. *Foreign Assistance and Related Programs Appropriations*, p. 405.

17. General Accounting Office, Confidential Report to the Congress, *The U.S. System for Appraising and Evaluating Inter-*

American Bank Projects and Activities, B-161470 (August 22, 1972), p. 21.

18. Ibid., pp. 42-43.

19. U.S. House of Representatives, Committee on Banking and Currency, To Authorize the United States to Provide Additional Financial Resources to the Asian Development Bank and the Inter-American Development Bank, 92nd Congress, First Session (October 26, 1971), p. 139.

20. See James F. Petras and Morris Morley, The United States and Chile (New York: Monthly Review Press, 1975), for an in-depth analysis of the response of U.S. national interest to Chilean expropriations and Salvador Allende; see table, p. 167 of same.

21. U.S. House of Representatives, Subcommittee on Inter-American Affairs, Committee on Foreign Affairs, United States-Chilean Relations, 93rd Congress, First Session (October 26, 1971), p. 139.

22. Inter-American Development Bank, Statement of Loans (Washington, D.C., 1974), pp. 20, 21, 79.

23. See Senate Subcommittee on Multinational Corporations, Committee of Foreign Relations, Multinational Corporations and United States Foreign Policy, 93rd Congress, March 20, 21, 22, 27, 28, 29 and April 2, 1973, Parts I and II on The International Telephone and Telegraph Company and Chile, 1970-71.

24. To Authorize the United States, p. 152.

CHAPTER

# 4

# THE BANK'S RELATIONSHIP TO U.S. FOREIGN POLICY

While the Inter-American Development Bank functions technically as an international lending institution, the Bank in fact is an integral part of the international political system and responds to political and historical currents. The U.S. position in the Bank is critical, for its national interest is in the economic development of Latin America and dominant Bank membership provides another forum for the exercise of U.S. foreign policy. The previous chapter demonstrated some of the means by which U.S. membership has affected the Bank's policies and structure. A discussion of U.S. foreign policy goals and their relationship to the IDB provides a macro-level overview within which to consider the historical orientation of the IDB as an aspect of U.S. foreign policy.

There were general sectoral changes in funding allocation from high social content in 1962 (with 7 percent infrastructure, 45 percent urban water supply, and 34 percent agricultural and industrial funding) to high infrastructure content in 1974 (with 52 percent economic infrastructure, 30 percent agricultural, industrial, and mining, and only 12 percent for social infrastructure). This illustrates a dramatic shift in IDB's priorities through its short history.[1] This shift, as well as other IDB policy changes, can be explained to some extent as alignment with, and outgrowth of, U.S. foreign policy. The U.S. role in the IDB is intimately associated with U.S. policies toward Latin America. One illustration is the overall parallelism of the Bank's historic policy concerns with U.S. foreign policy interests.

In July 1975 the assistant secretary of state for Latin America, speaking before the Subcommittee on International Development Institutions of the House Banking, Currency, and Housing Committee, requested increased U.S. participation in the IDB. He connected U.S. foreign policy objectives with interest in the IDB:

> The Inter-American Development Bank (IDB), since its establishment in 1959, has been a principal component of our Latin American policy. It is a key symbol—and living expression—of continuing hemispheric cooperation for a better life for the peoples of Americas . . . . Such growth, I must add, contributes to international economic stability as well as to immediate U.S. investment and trade objective. In our interdependent world our national interests are served by development which reaches all nations.
>
> There is no better illustration of such interdependence than our economic relationships with Latin America. Over several recent years, about 13 percent of our exports of $8.9 billion annually, has been sold in Latin American markets making up more than a third of their total imports. In turn, we have imported tropical products and raw materials from Latin America whose cost would be greater if secured outside the hemisphere. Our balance of trade with the region has traditionally been favorable, a measure of the high level of demand for the intermediate and capital goods imputs absorbed by the region as it grows.[2]

The above passage provides a general view of the IDB as an instrument of U.S. foreign policy. At the hearings for the 1975 funding for the Inter-American Foundation, which is partially funded by the IDB, Rep. Otto Passman, chairman of the Committee on Appropriations, speaking before the Subcommittee on Foreign Operations and Related Agencies, succinctly stated his view of the relationship of the international lending organizations to U.S. foreign policy: "It does not matter what they are. We are not going to support any organization, or foundation or program that is contrary to our own policy."[3]

Passman's view, while not representing an official U.S. foreign policy position, places an informal constraint on policy making within agencies such as IDB, which depend on the U.S. Congress for a majority of their financial support. A review of IDB policy objectives and U.S. foreign policy toward Latin America presents a revealing and often parallel pattern.

In the wake of the Cuban Revolution of 1959, the United States was forced to reassess its Latin American policy. Until that juncture, U.S. policy had sanctioned trade liberalization and private investment as the engines of growth for Latin America. The fall of Cuba to the "Communists" posed a security threat to the United States, unleashing fears that other unstable nations in Latin America would follow the Cuban model. Central America, particularly because of the region's strategic location as the gateway to the Panama Canal, was a concern and heightened the U.S. desire to maintain friendly relations. Hence, the United States through the Alliance for Progress provided strong support to any program that might strengthen Central American governments against destabilizing "Communist" movements and increasing social and political unrest.

One U.S. scheme to achieve political and economic objectives in Central and South America was regional economic integration. The United States seized upon economic integration as a means to achieve its political objectives of stabilizing the area after Castro's 1959 success, and to expand U.S. markets within Latin America while shoring up that region's weak and unstable national economies. Plans of economic integration had been put forth in the 1950s by Dr. Raul Prebisch, the noted Argentine economist, and the United Nations Economic Commission for Latin America. These early attempts at economic integration, however, were squelched by U.S. opposition.[4] The threat that Cuba posed to the traditional U.S. method of diplomacy, one that advocated trade liberalization while ignoring economic and social conditions, encouraged the United States to reassess quickly its negative position toward economic integration. By the time the Charter of Punta del Este was signed in 1961, inaugurating the Alliance for Progress, U.S. policy toward Latin America had undergone major revisions. President John F. Kennedy, in proposing the Alliance for Progress to the U.S. Congress, commented:

> We must support all economic integration which is a genuine step toward larger markets and greater competitive opportunity. The fragmentation of Latin American economies is a serious barrier to industrial growth. Projects such as the Central American Common Market and free trade areas in South America can help to remove these obstacles.[5]

U.S. support for economic integration did not begin, however, with the Kennedy administration. A joint communique from President Dwight D. Eisenhower and President José María Lemus of El Salvador in 1959 was one of the first steps to publicize U.S. support for economic integration. This statement was endorsed enthusiastically by the U.S. Congress and for President Kennedy and later President Lyndon B. Johnson became a central theme of U.S. foreign policy toward Latin America. In 1963, at the conclusion of the San José

Conference, President Kennedy and the presidents of the Central American countries issued a joint communique that reaffirmed Kennedy's earlier pledge for integration:

> The President of the United States is impressed by the determination of the Presidents of the Central American Republics to move as rapidly as possible toward the integration of the economies of their countries, and of their intention to formulate a regional economic development plan within which their national plans would be coordinated, and he believes that the coordination of the respective monetary, fiscal, economic and social policies is a great step toward the achievement of the goals set forth in the Charter of Punta del Este. The President of the United States is prepared to offer the greatest cooperation in the preparation and implementation of the regional and national development projects of Central America and Panama and declares that his government will intensify its joint efforts with the governments and appropriate regional organizations in order to extend to them increased technical and financial assistance.[6]

In 1967 President Johnson renewed the U.S. pledge in support of economic integration. In April of that year Johnson joined the Latin American heads of state at Punta del Este, Uruguay, to urge the creation of a Latin American common market. From that meeting came the Declaration of American Presidents, which committed the Latin American governments to the creation of a Common Market for Latin America by 1985. The U.S. vision of economic integration indeed was far-reaching, as is evident from a portion of President Johnson's address to the Latin American Presidents:

> In my message to the Congress . . . I recommended increased financial assistance to your countries in the areas covered by the declaration before me: economic integration, multinational projects, agriculture, education and health. This represents my convictions and foreign policy today.
>
> I have already made my position clear to my Congress and people: If Latin America decides to create a Common Market, I shall recommend a substantial contribution to a fund that will ease the transition into an integrated regional economy.[7]

Thus, the United States, employing carrot and stick diplomacy, encouraged Latin American governments to adopt regional integrationist policies and programs. According to a U.S. government policy document, the attitude of the United States was based on the belief that regional integration would achieve the following objectives: improve the social and economic conditions in Central and South America; provide the basis of unity on the Central American isthmus; and facilitate the expansion and liberalization of trade as well as the increased flow of investment capital.[8]

The rhetoric of U.S. foreign policy has changed from one of overt confrontation and intervention, as in the Bay of Pigs in Cuba in 1961 and the U.S. Marines intervention in the Dominican Republic in 1965, to a strategy of low profile via economic sanctions and the diplomacy of credit restrictions in the 1970s with the Nixon and Ford administrations. Economic integration, however, has remained a cornerstone of U.S. foreign policy in Latin America. The implementation of economic integration presently is most complete in Central America and the Caribbean, while a common market is being projected for the rest of Latin America by 1980. There are four integration schemes presently operating in Latin America: the Latin American Free Trade Association (LAFTA), created in 1960 by the Treaty of Montevideo, whose members are ten South American countries and Mexico; the Central American Common Market (CACM), established by the Treaty of Managua in December 1960, which comprises the five Central American countries; the Andean group, established by the Cartagena Agreement in May 1969, that proposes to accelerate integration among the countries of the Andes; and the Caribbean Free Trade Association (CARIFTA), established by the Treaty of St. John in April 1968 and transformed into the Caribbean Economic Community (common market) in July 1973.[9]

## LINKAGE WITH U.S. FOREIGN POLICY

The involvement of IDB in regional economic integration was clear from the beginning. As a result of the Charter of Punta del Este the Bank was officially linked to the integration process. In accordance with the provisions of Title III of the Charter, the IDB became "the principal financial agent of Latin American integration by reason of its direct action or by its contribution to the Central American Bank for Economic Integration (CABEI) to SIECA and to LAFTA."[10] The simultaneous establishment of the Central American Common Market, the Latin American Free Trade Association, and the IDB and its U.S.-funded Social Progress Trust Fund pinpoints the beginning of a parallelism that allowed the Bank a central role in the integration process. This is consistent with IDB's own interpretation of the Establishing Agreement for the Bank:

> the function set forth in the Agreement is that of cooperating with the member governments to orient their development policies toward a better utilization of their resources, in a manner consistent with the objectives of making their economies more complementary and of fostering the orderly growth of foreign trade. This clearly shows that the fundamental purpose of promoting development is to be pursued collectively and that the Bank must find policies, rules, and procedures that will make its activities consistent with the regional integration process, in which it is involved, because for the Bank, since its establishment, integration and development have been the inseparable terms of one binomium . . . . The Bank is not solely a forum for integration but that a series of institutional decisions adopted by it and its technical cooperation operations and its financing of multinational projects fully justify the IDB as the Bank of Integration.[11]

The United States had extensive involvement in advocating economic integration as a cornerstone of the Inter-American system and the Alliance for Progress in the early 1960s, and commanded the dominant role in shaping IDB policy, utilizing the Bank as an instrument for implementing regional economic integration in Latin America, particularly within the Central American republics. The Bank and other international organizations offer the United States the advantage of influencing internal economies and political structures of other nations to integration without coming into direct confrontation with any particular nation. Secretary of State William Rogers indicated in his 1972 foreign policy report: "The multilateral approach has enabled the United States to share with other industrialized countries and has encouraged recipient countries to make hard economic decisions as a condition for aid."[12]

One of the conditions of IDB loan assistance became, in the 1960s, its relationship to economic integration. One U.S. official, when asked in 1967 by a Central American diplomat if U.S. aid would depend on the adoption of an integration plan, commented: "naturally the United States would offer to give greater assistance to those countries which advance toward greater integration with their neighbors."[13] The funds that the United States proposed for economic integration were to be administered by the IDB rather than a regional organization like the Central American Bank for Economic Integration (CABEI), which is limited in its membership to nations participating in the integration agreement.[14] The United States further ensured its hegemony both at the international level with IDB and at the regional level with CABEI by its capacity to approve or disapprove the CABEI executive vice president. This position is critical and is similar to the vice president of the IDB, who has a veto power over all Fund for Special Operation loans.[15] The Inter-American Development Bank, therefore, provided the ideal forum at the international level, and at the regional level with CABEI to implement the U.S. formula for economic integration.

The development of that formula involved the Inter-American Development Bank at the regional and national level in the creation of a number of integrationist plans and institutions. From the outset, IDB in conjunction with the U.S. government was involved in shaping integrationist strategy for Central America. The Bank's efforts were only one component of the multifaceted U.S. approach to institutionalizing its plan for economic integration in Central and South America. The United States also employed two other international vehicles. Initially, on the international level, the Organization of American States provided one forum for the discussion of economic integration. The actual implementation of those discussions, however, was to be carried out by the Permanent Secretariat for Central American Economic Integration (SIECA), an OAS regional organization that has been dependent on substantial funding from the United States channeled through the various international lending organizations.

In 1962 the U.S. portion of funding in SIECA was well over 50 percent and it remained as high as 40 to 50 percent into the 1970s. The conduits for U.S. funding to SIECA were the Regional Organization for Central America and Panama (ROCAP), a USAID organization, and the IDB. Both ROCAP and IDB, therefore, gave the United States decided leverage in shaping plans and future institutions for economic integration in Central America. All initial projects and experts contracted by SIECA using ROCAP and IDB funds had to be approved by those agencies. Therefore, the U.S. government could influence SIECA's role in the formulation of integration policies for Central America by its veto power over projects funded by ROCAP and the IDB.[16] According to one high ROCAP official interviewed in 1967, U.S. influence increased as the integration process progressed:

> Formerly our assistance was confined to statistics and customs harmonization studies, and there was not much possibility for leverage in these areas. Now that they [SIECA] are in a financial bind, we are getting into other areas. Here ROCAP can, and we intend to, exercise more overall strategic leverage by earmarking funds and insisting on their setting priorities.[17]

Clearly the direct influence of the United States through its control of ROCAP and its substantial influence in IDB allowed for the shaping of integrationist strategy in Central America to U.S. aims.

Another important vehicle for institutionalizing economic integration in Central America is CABEI, the Central American Bank for Economic Integration. CABEI, even more than SIECA, was dominated by the United States. In its formative stage in 1961, CABEI relied heavily on USAID and on IDB officials for technical assistance, even in such sensitive areas as personnel. CABEI therefore never really achieved autonomous status as a Central American institution; it became dependent on USAID, AID-ROCAP, and IDB for its continued existence. In the initial years of its development this support even included the Bank's administrative overhead, which gave the United States ample leverage for exercising policy constraints on integration formulas. A study of CABEI in 1969 concluded that of its $250 million resources, $215 million or 86 percent were from external sources—about three-fourths from the United States and the Inter-American Development Bank, and the other one-fourth from supplier credits granted by some Western Euorpean countries and Mexico.[18] The substantial influence of the United States, and the United States via the IDB, is revealed specifically in Table 4.1, outlining foreign loans to CABEI.

The heavily tied nature of the loans to CABEI is shown in Table 4.1. IDB loans, as noted earlier, are informally tied to the United States by tying loan purchases to IDB member countries, which means that experts and capital goods most likely come from the United States with its monopoly over capital goods and technology. This fact provides the United States with additional input in the formulation of economic integration by CABEI in Central America. The influence of the Inter-American Development Bank and its linkage with U.S. foreign policy in the economic integration of Central America, however, is just one component of IDB's efforts to institutionalize the integrationist strategy.

At the international level, IDB was designated as the primary bank for economic integration. The integrationist mission of the IDB was clearly envisioned in 1960, at the first Board of Governors meeting in El Salvador. The president of El Salvador, in his inaugural address, pointed to the coincidence of the establishment of IDB and the revitalization of the integrationist movement in Latin America:

> the Inter-American Development Bank is uniquely significant in the history of Pan Americanism, not only in terms of immediate aid for the solution of the most anguishing problems of underdevelopment but also for what it means as a concrete measure that could lead to a strengthening of the programs directed

TABLE 4.1

Foreign Loans to CABEI through September 1976

| Source of Loan | Year | Use | Tied | Repayment Period (years) | Annual Interest Rate | Amount of Loan ($ millions) |
|---|---|---|---|---|---|---|
| To CABEI Ordinary Fund | | | | | | |
| AID-598-001 | 1962 | industrial and agricultural development | yes | 15 | 4 | 5 |
| AID-596-002 | 1963 | feasibility studies | yes | 40 | 2 | 2.5 |
| AID-596-004 | 1964 | industrial projects | yes | 40 | 2 | 10 |
| AID-596-010 | 1970 | export and tourism industries | yes | 40 | 3 | 30 |
| IDB-33/SF-CA | 1963 | industry, infrastructure | no[a] | 20 | 4 | 6 |
| IDB-50/SF-CA | 1965 | industry, infrastructure | no[a] | 20 | 4 | 8.2 |
| IDB-93/SF-CA | 1966 | preinvestment studies | no[a] | 20 | 4 | 3 |
| IDB-152/OC-CA | 1967 | industry, telecommunications | no[a] | 18 | 6.25 | 10 |
| Banco de Mexico | 1966 | industry | yes | 10 | 6 | 5 |
| Dollar Bonds, 1976 | 1966 | economic development | no | 10 | 5 | 1 |
| Consortium of Italian Banks | 1967 | industrial development | yes | 8 | 5.9 | 0.225 |
| Netherlands Investment Bank | 1967 | industry | yes | 19 | 6.5 | 1.3 |
| Bank of America | 1966 | industry | no | 2 & 5 | 6.5 | 1.35 |
| Bank of America | 1970 | industry, tourism, exports | no | 7 | 1 over prime | 5 |
| Bank of America | 1972 | industry, tourism, exports | no | 7 | 1 over prime | 2 |
| Bank of America (cooperative financing) | 1971 | industry | yes | 7 | 1 over prime | 2 |
| Morgan Guaranty Trust Co. | 1966 | industry | no | 4.25 | 6.5 | 1.43 |
| Morgan Guaranty Trust Co. | 1970 | industrial projects | no | 4 | 1 over prime | 3 |
| Union Bank of Switzerland | 1967 | industrial projects | yes | 9.5 | 7.25 | 1.74 |
| Consortium of Swiss Banks | 1967 | industrial projects | yes | 5, 8 & 10 | 6.25–7.5 | 4.6 |
| Syndicate of Belgian Banks | 1968 | industrial projects | yes | 3, 5 & 7 | 6.2 | 5 |
| Bank of London & South America | 1968 | industrial and feasibility studies | yes | 5 & 7 | 5.5 & 7 | 7.2 |
| U.S. Eximbank 2653-CA | 1970 | industrial projects | yes | 7 | 6 | 1.5 |
| U.S. Eximbank (cooperative financing) | 1971 | industrial projects | yes | 7 | 6 | 2 |

| | | | | | | |
|---|---|---|---|---|---|---|
| Export Bank of Japan | 1969 | telecommunications | yes | 15 | 6.5 | 6.4 |
| Export Bank of Japan | 1970 | industrial projects | yes | 8 | 6.5 | 5 |
| Spain, Dollar Bonds | 1966 | industry, studies, services | yes | 8 | 5.75, 6,25, & 6 | 1.3 |
| Tecniberia (Spain) | 1970 | services, goods, and ships | yes | 3-8 | 7 & 7.5 | 3 |
| Kreditanstalt Bank | 1970 | capital goods, public and private services | yes | 30 | 4 & 5.5 | 3.3 |
| Manufacturers Hanover Trust | 1971 | industry, agriculture, tourism | no | 4 | 1.5 over prime | 3 |
| Manufacturers Hanover Trust | 1972 | industry, agriculture, tourism | no | 4 | 1 over Eurodollar | 1 |
| Wells Fargo Bank | 1972 | economic development | no | 5 | 1.25 over London interbank rate | 5 |
| Central National Bank of Chicago | 1972 | economic development | | | 1 over London interbank rate | 1 |
| Total Ordinary Fund | | | | | | 148[b] |
| To CABEI Integration Fund (infrastructure) | | | | | | |
| AID-596-L-006 | 1965 | infrastructure | yes | 40 | 2.5 | 35 |
| AID-596-L-007 | 1968 | infrastructure | yes | 40 | 2.5 | 20 |
| AID-596-L-008 | 1969 | infrastructure | yes | 40 | 2.5 | 30 |
| IDB-8/ CD-CA | 1967 | infrastructure | yes | 50 | 1.25 + 0.75 | 2.6 |
| IDB-132/SF-CA | 1967 | infrastructure | yes | 30 | 3.25 + 0.75 | 11.5 |
| IDB-284/SF-CA | 1971 | infrastructure | yes | 30 | 3.25 + 0.75 | 20 |
| Total Integration Fund | | | | | | 119[b] |
| To CABEI Housing Fund | | | | | | |
| AID-596-L-003 | 1963 | housing | yes | 40 | 0.75 | 10 |
| Federal Home Loan Bank of Boston | 1970 | housing | no | 24.5 | 8.125 | 5 |
| Federal Home Loan Bank of New York | 1970 | housing | no | 25 | 8.125 | 5 |
| Total Housing Fund | | | | | | 20[b] |
| Total all funds | | | | | | 287[b] |

Note: This chart does not include technical assistance grants to CABEI or to other CACM agencies such as SIECA.

[a]Tied to purchases from IDB/ IMF members.

[b]Figure not exact due to rounding.

Source: Susanne Jonas (Bodenheimer), "Masterminding the Mini-Market: U.S. Aid to the Central American Common Market," North American Congress on Latin America 7, no. 5 (May-June 1973): 9.

to the establishment of a great economic and financial community in the Americas.[19]

In the 15 years since the first Board of Governors meeting the IDB has played a prominent part by its internal adoption of institutional decisions on integration and its implementation of those decision throughout Latin America. This study has demonstrated that the United States played a substantial role in shaping the internal institutional decisions in the Inter-American Development Bank to determine the shape of integration for Latin America. The timing of IDB's establishment, the substantial internal influence of the United States in the IDB organization, and the linkage of the Bank with other U.S.-sponsored organizations in the formulation of regional integration projects in Latin America suggest that the similarity between IDB's strategy for economic integration and U.S. foreign policy is more real than apparent. The Bank's programs and policies in many respects parallel U.S. foreign policy in Latin America.

## INSTITUTIONALIZATION OF ECONOMIC INTEGRATION

The Inter-American Development Bank is one of several international organizations implementing the largely U.S.-oriented policies of regional economic integration, which promise increased investment and export opportunities for U.S. business. The IDB as one agent of this integration process has implemented a number of internal organizational decisions assisting in designing the direction and structure of regional economic integration in Latin America. (See Chapter 8 for a more specific elaboration of the institutionalization of U.S. influence.) The Bank management has institutionalized the integration strategy within the IDB's organizational structure and has adopted a number of integrationist policies, which exert external constraints on its activities in Latin America. One such decision was the establishment in 1965 of the Office of Integration Advisor, which links the Bank more directly with other integration agencies. Through this office the Bank endeavors to devise formulas at the regional and national level to support regional economic integration as the basic instrument of social and economic development in Latin America. Currently, as a result of the Bank's increased interest in integration, the Office of the Integration Advisor has been transformed to the Office of the Deputy Manager for Integration of the Economic and Social Development Department of the IDB.

Another IDB effort to institutionalize integration was the establishment of the Institute for Latin American Integration (INTAL), which began operations in August 1965. INTAL functioned as a research vehicle assisting countries in overcoming legal, economic, and social problems dealing with integration. INTAL is also instrumental in training staff personnel concerned with integration from both the public and private sector in Latin America. In 1967, for instance, over 2,000 persons from Bank member countries participated in training programs and seminars dealing with integration.[20] INTAL, located in Buenos Aires, Argentina, serves a vital role in the recruitment and socialization of personnel as well as in providing the technical instrument for implementing IDB's program of integration in Latin America.

But the paramount factor in IDB's importance in the integration of Latin America involves its policies influencing the funding priorities. The decision in 1966, at the seventh annual meeting of the Board of Governors held in Mexico, established a Preinvestment Fund for Latin American integration and gave the integration process a high priority in IDB's funding schedule. The Preinvestment Fund was designed to finance projects that would accelerate Latin American integration by mobilizing additional external financing. The emphasis of the Preinvestment Fund predisposed Latin American governments to develop highly integrationist-oriented projects in order to be assured of continued and increased IDB funding. Of the priority areas to be financed by the fund, special emphasis was given to the following categories: infrastructure; the development of multinational zones; the regionalization of basic industries; multinational exploitation of natural resources; and studies aimed at better investment possibilities.

The establishment of these specific priorities and the fund itself grew out of a larger decision on the part of the Inter-American Committee on the Alliance for Progress (CIAP) in August 1965. This landmark decision resulted in negotiations to obtain support from governments of the hemisphere and their external financial institutions for establishing a revolving fund to finance projects and feasibility studies related to regional economic integration. The importance of that CIAP decision was later compounded in November 1965 by the decision of the foreign ministers of the LAFTA member countries, who encouraged IDB to establish a preinvestment fund for Latin American integration. The Second Special Inter-American Conference, which met the same year in Rio de Janeiro, also advocated special priority for multinational projects to accelerate economic integration.[21] Not only was regional economic integration provided a high priority within the Inter-American Development Bank but additionally the emphasis on integration was orchestrated throughout the Inter-American Development Bank but additionally the emphasis on integration was orchestrated throughout the Inter-American system.

The institutionalization of regional economic integration is most vividly expressed in an analysis of IDB's country loans through IDB-sponsored subregional banks and technical-administrative integration agencies. The total amount of such lending as of December 31, 1974, was $1,023.3 billion, which is part of the total of $2,304.4 billion mobilized by IDB's integration projects.[22] This amount, however, does not include the substantial investments from private resources that integration projects have stimulated through their expansion of commercially attractive markets and the development of economic infrastructure. An example of the multiplier effect of integrationist activity is the attraction of some $200 million of foreign private capital through creation of the Central American Common Market in the 1961-65 period.[23]

Inter-American Development Bank loans that have traditionally supported integration projects may be divided into three basic categories: (1) infrastructure, including transportation, energy, telecommunications, industry, agriculture, and advanced and technical education; (2) technical assistance, including feasibility and preinvestment studies as well as integration of related training and research; and (3) the financing of capital goods. The largest loans for integration have been granted to the infrastructure sector, as is evident in Table 4.2, which outlines the IDB's integration loans in 1961-74.

Of the Bank's cumulative lending of $7.4 billion to the end of 1974, over $1 billion or 14 percent can be specifically designated integrationist by its association with national projects to directly benefit neighboring countries or whole regions.[24] Projects of a more limited nature within national boundaries, but having an infrastructure emphasis, however, do contribute indirectly to regional economic integration. It should be noted that in 1961-74 the Bank's sectoral lending averaged the following percentages for infrastructure: agriculture, 23 percent; industry and mining, 15 percent; electric power, 21 percent; and transportation and communications, 17 percent. Using a broad interpretation of economic infrastructure, over three-fourths of IDB loans have been skewed toward infrastructure, indirectly supporting integration.[25]

On the regional level IDB has used a number of intermediary organizations to facilitate integrations. Tables 4.3 and 4.4 illustrate IDB's regional lending and program for financing intermediary development institutions, which in turn subcontract to various national integration projects in Central and South America.

The intermediary regional projects of CABEI are some of the projects in which the linkage between the United States and the Inter-American Development Bank was established above. The impact of the regional organization, the Atlantic Community Group for the Development of Latin America (ADELA), a multinational investment

TABLE 4.2

IDB Support for Economic Integration, 1961-74

| Activity | Bank Support | Total Cost ($ thousands) |
|---|---|---|
| Projects with multinational impact | | |
| Transportation | 474,100 | 959,800 |
| Electric power | 238,100 | 704,300 |
| Telecommunications | 19,800 | 42,200 |
| Industry and tourism | 62,000 | 108,700 |
| Agriculture | 68,900 | 213,500 |
| Education | 4,900 | 18,900 |
| Export financing program | 108,300 | 160,000 |
| Studies and preinvestment | | |
| Sectoral | 11,800 | 16,500 |
| General | 400 | 400 |
| Transportation | 5,300 | 7,900 |
| Communications | 1,300 | 4,600 |
| Electric power | 3,500 | 6,100 |
| Industry | 2,500 | 4,300 |
| Agriculture | 6,900 | 12,300 |
| Border and multinational | 1,100 | 3,800 |
| Training and research | 11,600 | 26,100 |
| Institutional research | 2,800 | 15,000 |
| Total | 1,023,300 | 2,304,400 |

Source: Inter-American Development Bank, Fifteen Years of Activity 1960-1974 (Washington, D.C., December 1974), p. 81.

company that represents 54 of the largest U.S. corporations for 50 percent of its capital subscription, offers an illustration of the linkage between the U.S. government, the IDB, and private foreign investment capital in the economic integration of Latin America. The primary role of ADELA has been to generate investment opportunities for multinational corporations desiring to penetrate Latin America. ADELA works closely with the other international development agencies such as the International Finance Corporation, the Agency for International Development, and the Inter-American Development Bank. In 1968 ADELA's annual report discussed its

TABLE 4.3

Regional IDB Loans for Economic Integration
($ thousands)

| Borrower | Year | Industry No. | Industry Amount | Industry Total Cost of Projects | Electric Power No. | Electric Power Amount | Electric Power Total Cost of Projects | Education No. | Education Amount | Education Total Cost of Projects | Total Loan | Total Total Cost of Projects |
|---|---|---|---|---|---|---|---|---|---|---|---|---|
| ADELA Investment Company | 1966 | 1 | 8,043 | 54,280 | — | — | — | — | — | — | 8,043 | 54,280 |
| Panamerican Health Foundation | 1970 | — | — | — | — | — | — | 1 | 2,000 | 8,500 | 2,000 | 8,500 |
| Joint Technical Commission | 1973 | — | — | — | 1 | 79,367 | 432,000 | — | — | — | 79,367 | 432,000 |
| of Salto Grande | 1974 | — | — | — | 1 | 95,000 | 297,715 | — | — | — | 95,000 | 297,715 |
| Total | | 1 | 8,043 | 54,280 | 2 | 174,367 | 729,715 | 1 | 2,000 | 8,500 | 184,410 | 792,495 |

Source: Inter-American Development Bank, Fifteen Years of Activity 1960–1974 (Washington, D.C.: December 1974), p. 79.

TABLE 4.4

IDB Lending for Regional Projects in Central America
through the Central American Bank for Economic Integration
($ thousands)

| Sector | Year | Ordinary Capital Resources No. | Ordinary Capital Resources Amount | Ordinary Capital Resources Total Cost of Projects | Fund for Special Operations No. | Fund for Special Operations Amount | Fund for Special Operations Total Cost of Projects | Social Progress Trust Fund No. | Social Progress Trust Fund Amount | Social Progress Trust Fund Total Cost of Projects | Other Resources No. | Other Resources Amount | Other Resources Total Cost of Projects | Total No. | Total Amount | Total Total Cost of Projects |
|---|---|---|---|---|---|---|---|---|---|---|---|---|---|---|---|---|
| Agriculture | 1973 | — | — | — | 1 | 6,800 | 15,400 | — | — | — | — | — | — | 1 | 6,800 | 15,400 |
| Industry | 1963 | — | — | — | 1 | 6,004 | 9,004 | — | — | — | — | — | — | 1 | 6,004 | 9,004 |
| | 1964 | — | — | — | 1 | 8,200 | 13,600 | — | — | — | — | — | — | 1 | 8,200 | 13,600 |
| | 1967 | 1 | 7,009 | 45,787 | — | — | — | — | — | — | — | — | — | 1 | 7,009 | 45,787 |
| Transportation and | 1967 | — | 3,002* | 19,623 | 1 | 11,500 | 13,000 | — | — | — | 1 | 2,813 | 3,342 | 2 | 17,315 | 35,965 |
| Communications | 1970 | — | — | — | 1 | 20,000 | 25,000 | — | — | — | — | — | — | 1 | 20,000 | 25,000 |
| Education | 1962 | — | — | — | — | — | — | 1 | 2,902 | 10,410 | — | — | — | 1 | 2,902 | 10,410 |
| Preinvestment | 1966 | — | — | — | 1 | 3,000 | 4,300 | — | — | — | — | — | — | 1 | 3,000 | 4,300 |
| | 1972 | — | — | — | 1 | 4,000 | 5,300 | — | — | — | — | — | — | 1 | 4,000 | 5,300 |
| Total | | 1 | 10,011 | 65,410 | 7 | 59,504 | 85,604 | 1 | 2,902 | 10,410 | 1 | 2,813 | 3,342 | 10 | 75,230 | 164,766 |

*Assigned to a communications project in a loan devoted primarily to industrial credit.

Source: Inter-American Development Bank, Fifteen Years of Activity 1960–1974 (Washington, D.C.: December 1974), p. 79.

> close relationships with the Inter-American Development Bank (IDB) and with International Finance Corporation (IFC). In addition to the $10 million long term loan granted by IDB to ADELA for financing small and medium range projects which are not within IDB's direct reach, IDB has made parallel loans to larger projects in which we have invested. With IFC we have an increasing number of joint projects including joint sponsorship of very large investments. With both institutions there exists a continuous contact and free exchange of information so as to avoid duplication of effort in the areas of development and evaluating investment opportunities.[26]

The Inter-American Development Bank's integration efforts, in conjunction with U.S. bilateral development agencies and U.S. development policies, have tended to open up the Latin American region to external private investment. From the institutional standpoint, the Central American Common Market is the most complete system of regional economic integration. In addition to the secretariat (SEICA) and the Central American Bank for Economic Integration (CABEI), a number of specialized agencies such as ICAP, the Central American Institute for Public Administration, have been established to assist in the public administrative and technical aspects of regional economic integration. The other schemes for integration in Latin America and the Caribbean, while less complete, promise the development of a Latin American common market and the expansion of the Caribbean Common Market (comprised of Barbados, Guyana, Jamaica, and Trinidad and Tobago), which should open up the region to further foreign investment opportunities. Furthermore, infrastructure loans that are the backbone of development through integration favor investments that tend to be most attractive to foreign investors by providing expanded markets for capital and other manufactured goods.

## INVESTMENT LOANS FOR INTEGRATION

Loans for integration emphasize economic infrastructure. Infrastructure loans along with those for technical assistance, preinvestment studies, and the exportation of capital goods provide the basic economic overhead necessary to attract external investment within the integrated region.

Loans for highways have been the most common type of infrastructure loan. Sizable loans also have been granted in the electric energy field, such as the $80 million Salto Grande hydroelectric project in 1972, a joint venture between Argentina and Uruguay. Another important sector receiving financing from IDB for integration is telecommunications. The Bank has been instrumental in assisting in the expansion of the telecommunications systems between Bolivia and Brazil, and within Chile and Central America.

The industrial sector, while it has not received the highest percentage of loans for regional infrastructure, remains an important sector. To assist in the establishment of the industrial infrastructure necessary for integration, the IDB has channeled development loans for industrial purposes through subregional banks and intermediary mechanisms. For instance, CABEI received $14.2 million and ADELA received $8.5 million for industrial purposes as of December 1973. Only a small percentage of IDB's integration funds, amounting to less than 10 percent, are channeled through subregional banks. The vast majority of IDB's loans for regional integration are funded directly by the Bank (see Table 4.2).

Export financing is yet another facet of the integration process sponsored by the Bank. By December 1973 over $100 million had been advanced for export financing. However, the impact of this program is limited to exports of capital goods. Most countries in Latin America do not have the capacity to manufacture capital goods and import such goods from abroad, to be used in consumer-oriented light manufacturing and heavy industry. The impact of export financing has been nil and should concentrate in the future on intermediate goods like shoes and not capital goods.

Technical cooperation and training remain the smallest area in IDB's support for regional integration. As of December 1973 technical assistance amounted to only $37.6 million. Preinvestment studies for integration also have been an area of minimal financing but with considerable impact. A total of $11.8 million in global preinvestment loans had been granted for preinvestment projects as of December 1973, of which $7 million was granted to CABEI. The breakdown of IDB preinvestment financing of integration projects approximates its overall loan priorities for the following categories: infrastructure, 58 percent; industrial projects, 16 percent; agriculture, 19 percent; and 7 percent to integrated studies for identifying multinational projects. In the infrastructure sector, over 51 percent of financing has been for transportation studies, especially highway studies necessary for the development of land communications for effective integration of Latin American national economies. The channeling of Latin American preinvestment funds through CABEI allows IDB considerable influence on the direction of integration and development.[27]

For the future, IDB plans to continue its integration efforts through subregional financing agencies. An IDB integration report elaborated on this strategy of forging closer links with subregional financing agencies:

> Until very recently, the only institution of this kind was the Central American Bank for Economic Integration, for the establishment of which in 1960 the IDB made an effective contribution and through which it has so far channeled US $75.2 million. As a result of the establishment of the Andean Development Corporation, the Caribbean Development Bank and the proposed financial agency of the River Plate Basin, the situation with respect to the financing of integration as it existed during the 1960's is undergoing a radical change. The establishment of such agencies completes a pyramidal financial structure, the base of which consists of national cooperation, above which are subregional agencies already mentioned and, at its vertex, regional institutions such as the Inter-American Development Bank or world institutions such as the International Bank for Reconstruction and Development or the United Nations Development Programs.[28]

The elaboration of the regional integration institution allows IDB considerably more leverage to transform the region using subregional units which follow its strategy of development through integration. In IDB's view:

> The subregional schemes, therefore, are not final arrangements, but instruments in the process of convergence which the Presidents of the Americas called for in 1967 and which the Bank will do everything in its power to promote.[29]

The process of development through integration, as is evident from the above discussion, imposes a pattern of development on Latin America that increasingly has stressed infrastructure. As noted at the beginning of this chapter, IDB's sectoral loans in infrastructure had increased from a low of 7 percent in 1962 to 54 percent in 1974.[30] Analysis clearly points to the IDB's emphasis on development through integration as having an overriding impact on the increase in infrastructure projects in Latin America.

## THE UNITED STATES, THE BANK, AND INFRASTRUCTURE PROJECTS

The relationship between infrastructure, integration, and development, and IDB's lending programs, emphasize another conjuncture of interests between the Bank and U.S. foreign policy. In hearings before the Subcommittee on Foreign Operations and Related Agencies considering the 1975 appropriations for the IDB, the relationship of foreign assistance, infrastructure, and foreign policy was discussed by John Porges, the U.S. executive director of the IDB:

> One of the other advantages, and I believe there are several . . . is that the infrastructure we have helped build in the underdeveloped countries has been a requisite for U.S. foreign investment, and U.S. investment abroad has brought a return which has helped our balance of payments. During the period when our balance of payments was not positive, this was a very important item and it still is today, now that our balance of payments has turned the corner. So the return on this capital, which was made possible by infrastructure and by stable economic and political systems is part of the advantage to the United States. I think too that we are a country that imports a tremendous amount of natural resources. Our copper, oil, tin and so on, come from the less developed countries. If we don't have stable political situations in these countries, it may very well be that we will be unable to obtain these essential raw materials.[31]

The development of infrastructure, as Porges noted, is to the advantage of the U.S. national interest. Thus, the IDB integration projects discussed above all provided positive benefits for the U.S. national economic interest. Direct U.S. involvement in infrastructure development as a facet of foreign policy is clearly discerned also in the role of the U.S. Export-Import Bank. An official history of the Eximbank noted, "in addition to its contribution to the foreign trade of the United States, the Export-Import Bank has served often as an instrument of U.S. foreign policy."[32] A 1974 study of the Export-Import Bank commented:

> Aid alone cannot provide all the infrastructure assistance needed by business interests; the Eximbank must be called upon to help mold the economies of other countries into forms complimentary to U.S. efforts and investments.[33]

The similarity in the approach to development between the U.S. Export-Import Bank and the IDB with its heavy investment in infrastructure adds weight to the argument that the IDB is acting in the interest of U.S. foreign policy. Chapter 3 noted that the Bank responded favorably to U.S. foreign policy concerns in relation to specific expropriations in Bolivia, Chile, and Peru. The expropriation issue has been noted as the most manifest alignment of U.S. foreign policy and the IDB. However, the consistent alignment of the Bank and U.S. foreign policy since the early 1960s in attempting to integrate Latin American economies, while not as obvious as the expropriations issue, has a continuing and far more significant impact on development and the opening up of the region to foreign investors. Integration has expanded Latin America's national markets to a regional market basis and offered tax benefits and duty exemptions to attract foreign investors. Infrastructure investments, which have no cost to the foreign investor, provide the transportation, communications, and necessary economic overhead for regional integration, thus expanding market opportunities. The advantages of integration have been several to foreign investors and to the U.S. government. The integration of Central and South America has provided expanded markets for U.S. goods, particularly capital goods, and this in turn has contributed to a favorable U.S. trade balance with Latin America, as is evident in Table 3.4.

Regional economic integration has provided investment opportunities for U.S. firms as well as for other multinational corporations. Additionally, economic growth through economic integration is considered by the U.S. government as a prerequisite for continued stability in the region, while at the same time allowing substantial profits to be repatriated. The role of the United States in Central America is particularly illustrative of the role of U.S. foreign investment. In the initial years of the Central American Common Market, 1961-65, U.S. business invested over $200 million, most of which was used to buy out existing industries and to finance new economy of scale industries that could operate within the newly enlarged marketplace.[34] Central America, therefore, provides a prominent instance of the United States turning development through integration to its economic and political advantage.

The following chapters examine the role of the Inter-American Development Bank in a specific Central American Common Market country, Costa Rica. IDB's role in Costa Rica illustrates in concrete terms the costs and benefits of the Bank's alignment with U.S. national interest and the impact of this alignment on Costa Rican development.

## NOTES

1. U.S. House Committee on Foreign Relations, The United States and the Multilateral Development Banks, 93rd Congress, 2nd Session (March 1974), p. 33.

2. U.S. Department of State, Bureau of Public Affairs, news release, "U.S. Participation in the Inter-American Development Bank" (July 29, 1975), pp. 1-2.

3. U.S. House of Representatives, Hearings Before a Subcommittee of the Committee on Appropriations, Foreign Assistance and Related Agencies Appropriations for 1975, 93rd Congress, 2nd Session (1974), p. 223.

4. Robert Edwin Denham, "The Role of the U.S. as an External Actor in the Integration of Central America," Journal of Common Market Studies 7 (1968-69): 199-205.

5. Ibid., p. 205.

6. James D. Cochrane, The Politics of Regional Integration: The Central American Case, Tulane Studies in Political Science, vol. 12 (New Orleans: Tulane University, 1969), p. 206.

7. Ibid., p. 207.

8. Ibid., p. 208.

9. Inter-American Development Bank, Office of the Deputy Manager for Integration, IDB and Its Relations with the Latin American Integration Process (Washington, D.C., December 1973), annex 3, p. 3.

10. Ibid., p. 4.

11. Ibid., pp. 12-13.

12. The United States and the Multilateral Development Banks, p. 124.

13. Denham, "The Role of the U.S.," p. 209.

14. Ibid., p. 213.

15. See Susanne Jonas (Bodenheimer), "Masterminding the Mini-Market: U.S. Aid to the Central American Common Market," North American Congress on Latin America 7, no. 5 (May-June 1973): 8. See Chapter 8 of the present study for a further elaboration of the U.S. role in Central America.

16. Ibid., p. 6, and Interview with a high ranking USAID official revealed that ROCAP was instrumental in also setting up CABEI throughout Central America, San José, Costa Rica, April, 1975.

17. Ibid., p. 7.

18. Isaac Cohen Orantes, Regional Integration in Central America (Lexington, Mass.: Lexington Books-D. C. Heath, 1972), p. 60.

19. Inter-American Development Bank, Proceedings, First Meeting of the Board of Governors (San Salvador, El Salvador, February 3-16, 1960), p. 10.

20. Inter-American Development Bank, Annual Report, 1967 (Washington, D.C.), p. 156.

21. IDB and Its Relations With the Latin American Integration Process, pp. 20-24.

22. Inter-American Development Bank, Fifteen Years of Activities, 1960-1974 (Washington, D.C., December 1974), p. 81.

23. Miguel S. Wionczek, "Latin American Integration and United States Economic Policies," in International Organization in the Western Hemisphere, ed. Robert W. Gregg (Syracuse, N.Y.: Syracuse University Press, 1968), p. 129.

24. Fifteen Years of Activities, p. 80.

25. Inter-American Development Bank, Annual Report, 1974 (Washington, D.C., April 1975), p. 33.

26. Hector Melo and Israel Yost, "Funding the Empire: Part 2, The Multinational Strategy," North American Congress on Latin America 4, no. 3 (May-June 1970): 14.

27. These figures assist in defining the Bank's impact on Latin American integration and are drawn from IDB and Its Relations With the Latin American Integration Process, pp. 25-33.

28. IDB and Its Relations with the Latin American Integration Process, p. 49.

29. Ibid., p. 52.

30. IDB, Annual Report, 1974, p. 33.

31. Foreign Assistance and Related Agencies Appropriations for 1975, p. 468.

32. Hawthorne Arey, History of Operations and Policies of Export-Import Bank of Washington (Washington, D.C.: Export Import Bank, 1953), p. 55.

33. Mary Helen Boyer, "The Eximbank, Exports for Empire," North American Congress on Latin America 8, no. 7 (September 1974): 26.

34. Wionczek, "Latin American Integration," p. 129.

# PART II

# THE CASE OF COSTA RICA

CHAPTER

# 5

# DEVELOPMENT ASSISTANCE TO COSTA RICA

Costa Rica provides a specific illustration of the politics and projects of the Inter-American Development Bank in Latin America. Costa Rica is by no means typical of all other Latin American countries. With a per capita gross domestic product of $645.30 in 1973 and an annual rate of growth of total GDP (gross domestic product) in 1960-73 of 6.3 percent, Costa Rica enjoys one of the higher standards of living in Latin America.[1] In spite of Costa Rica's small geographic size, approximately 19,653 square miles, and with a population in 1973 of 1,915,000 (projected to reach 2,476,000 by 1980), on a per capita base in the 20-year period between 1947 and 1967, Costa Rica was the second highest recipient of foreign aid in Latin America.[2] The U.S. government was responsible for about one-half of the foreign assistance to Costa Rica.[3] Costa Rica therefore seems an appropriate example for considering the impact of the external assistance programs and policies of the Inter-American Development Bank.

IDB aid to Costa Rica has been substantial, providing some $89.45 million between 1961 and June 1974.[4] This concentration of aid in a relatively small country provides a ready opportunity to analyze the impact of Bank programs. The density of aid plus the relatively easy access to travel around the countryside made Costa Rica attractive for research on the Bank's role in a Latin American context.

The total weight of external assistance from the IDB, the World Bank (the International Bank for Reconstruction and Development), and USAID between 1961 and June 1974 reached $314.42 million. Of this total the Inter-American Development Bank contributed $89.45 million, approximately one-third.[5] With the new Arenal Hydroelectric Dam Project, which commenced construction in 1976 with an IDB cost

TABLE 5.1

Loans to Costa Rica by IDB, IBRD, and USAID, 1961–June 1974
(in millions of U.S. dollars)

| Sector | IDB | | IBRD | | USAID | | Total | |
|---|---|---|---|---|---|---|---|---|
| | Amount | Percent | Amount | Percent | Amount | Percent | Amount | Percent |
| Industry and mining | 15.63 | 17.5 | 2.88 | 2.0 | 9.98 | 12.5 | 28.49 | 9.0 |
| Agriculture | 17.73 | 19.8 | 12.00 | 8.2 | 41.55 | 52.0 | 71.28 | 22.7 |
| Public health | 7.60 | 8.5 | — | — | 6.43 | 8.0 | 14.03 | 4.5 |
| Urban development and housing | 7.10 | 7.9 | — | — | 5.47 | 6.9 | 12.57 | 4.0 |
| Transportation and communications | 27.50 | 30.7 | 73.25 | 50.5 | 9.20 | 11.5 | 109.95 | 35.0 |
| Energy | 6.48 | 7.3 | 49.30 | 34.0 | 4.80 | 6.0 | 60.38 | 19.3 |
| Education, science, and technology | 4.87 | 5.5 | 6.20 | 4.3 | — | — | 11.07 | 3.5 |
| Preinvestment, and technical assistance | 2.54 | 2.8 | 1.40 | 1.0 | 1.45 | 1.8 | 5.39 | 1.7 |
| Export financing | — | — | — | — | — | — | — | — |
| Tourism | — | — | — | — | — | — | — | — |
| Other | — | — | — | — | 1.06 | 1.3 | 1.06 | 0.3 |
| Total | 89.45 | 100.0 | 145.03 | 100.0 | 79.94 | 100.0 | 314.42 | 100.0 |

Source: IDB, Costa Rica, Estrategia (Confidentia) 1975–1977 (Department of Economic and Social Development, Washington, D.C., October 25, 1974), p. 23.

component of $50.5 million, the share of IDB's financial investment in Costa Rica will increase dramatically. The Bank's contribution, when broken down by sectors and compared with the loans of the USAID and the World Bank, provides additional depth to the significance of IDB's financial assistance. Table 5.1 lists the loans of IDB, USAID, and the World Bank from 1961 to June 1974.

The Bank tended during the period 1961-74 to emphasize transportation and communications (30.7 percent), agriculture (19.8 percent), and industry and mining (17.5 percent), while the World Bank stressed transportation and communication (50.5 percent) and particularly energy (34 percent). USAID stressed agriculture at 52 percent with industry and mining at 12.5 percent, and transportation and communications at 11.5 percent. As a result of the passage of the 1973 Foreign Assistance Act, USAID was specifically mandated to give exclusive priority to the following areas containing a high social impact component: agriculture, nutrition, basic education (nonuniversity), population, and rural health.[6] USAID's recent emphasis on agriculture can be explained to some extent by these new guidelines; however, a change in other sectors is not evident at this time.

A comparison of the project priorities of IDB and the World Bank reveals that IDB has traditionally made heavy investments in infrastructure and production projects in Costa Rica, while the World Bank has placed particular emphasis on energy in addition to the traditional infrastructure projects in transportation and communications. One highly placed Costa Rican official said in an interview that the IDB's recent interest in energy has been spurred largely by a competitive spirit with World Bank energy projects, particularly the hydroelectric project.[7] A review of the sectoral lending of all international lenders in Costa Rica reveals a pattern that emphasizes infrastructure and production over projects of high social content.

A review of current IDB projects in Costa Rica provides a more complete understanding of the Bank's commitment by sector. In industry and mining, IDB has a number of important projects. Two initial industrial projects for Costa Rica were approved in 1962. The first was a loan for the installation of a cement factory at a cost of $2.8 million. The second industrial loan in 1962, a loan of $3 million for industrial development credits, was more typical of the IDB pattern in Costa Rica. Since this original industrial credit loan in 1962, several other programs of industrial credits have been sponsored by the Bank. Two recent industrial credit loans, one in 1970 for $2.2 million of ordinary capital lent at the commercial rate of 8 percent, and another of $3 million from the Fund for Special Operations (soft loan capital) lent at an annual interest of 3.25 percent, extended the IDB's commitment to industrial development through the concept of a global loan for small industries. The global loan provides a lump sum grant to a local national institution, in the latter case the Banco de Costa Rica (an autonomous public institution established by the National Banking System Act of September 1953), which in turn provides lines of industrial credit to infant industries within Costa Rica, especially in the Meseta Central (Central Plateau). The program called for earmarking approximately 60 percent of the loan resources to finance consumer goods industries using a high proportion of national resource The balance of the loan (40 percent) is to be used for intermediate or capital goods producing industries.

The Bank's justification for these programs was to maintain the high rate of growth in Costa Rica's industrial sector and to assist the government in meeting its goal of establishing and expanding industries that use a high percentage of national raw materials and generate export products. In addition, the IDB was influential in supporting programs of industrial development to facilitate Costa Rica's involvement with the Central American Common Market. The importance of the Central American Common Market may be drawn from the fact that in 1963-67 approximately 83 percent of the increase in Costa Rican industrial exports were shipped to that market.[8]

In the agricultural sector, Bank loans also have been mostly for agricultural credit. The Bank's first agricultural loan to Costa Rica was a livestock development program. This $3 million loan was subcontracted through the Banco Nacional de Costa Rica, an autonomous national bank that is also an integral part of the national banking system. The original line of credit for livestock development was continued in 1972 with an IDB loan for an amount equivalent to $6 million, together with a Banco Nacional de Costa Rica contribution equivalent to $2.5 million. This was in the form of a global loan for subloans to about 1,000 small and middle-scale livestock producers. The interest rate on this loan was nonconcessionary at 8 percent, with up to 14 years to pay. In addition, recipients were required to make an aggregate contribution of up to 15 percent of the total cost of the loan. The loans allowed purchase of all necessary livestock development resourc (such as cattle, equipment, and infrastructure) except land.[9] The program was aimed at middle-level farms with a capitalization of less than $60,000, and subloans were not to exceed $40,000.

The rationale for the Bank's agricultural program was the lack of diversity in Costa Rica's agricultural exports, notably its dependence on coffee and bananas and the sluggishness of these products in recent years on the international commodities markets. In addition, Costa Rica needed to develop extensive unexplored areas outside the Central Plateau, especially on the West Coast in Guanacaste Province. Livestock production seemed to provide an opportunity for additional foreign exchange as well as a means of developing the hinterland.[10]

Transportation and communications traditionally represented the Bank's largest investment, with agriculture and industry running a close second and third. With the recent $50.5 million funding of the Arenal Hydroelectric project, transportation and communications projects are now the second most heavily funded. Transportation, communications, and the hydroelectric energy project continued overwhelmingly to represent infrastructure as IDB's top priority. The Bank's transportation projects have provided $27.5 million, primarily for access or feeder roads to the interior. The main highway through Costa Rica is the Pan American Highway, which runs north to south through the entire country. Most other roads are either dirt or gravel or are in very poor condition. Good secondary roads are certainly necessary so that goods and agricultural products can be transported to San José, the central distribution point. The most recent IDB project in this sector was a $16 million loan in 1974 for the construction of light secondary roads totaling 126 kilometers. This loan was made directly to the Republic of Costa Rica through the Public Works and Transportation Ministry at a concessional rate of 2 percent. This project is fairly typical of IDB's transportation projects in Costa Rica and is compatible with the Bank's basic philosophy that infrastructure is a necessary primary investment to induce long-term industrial and agricultural development.

The Bank has placed much lower priority on housing, health and sanitation, and education. The IDB traditionally has deemphasized areas with a high social component in favor of infrastructure and productivity projects throughout Latin America, and in Costa Rica. From 1961 to June 1974 in Costa Rica, health commanded 8.5 percent of IDB total loan resources while urban development and housing as well as education received only 7.9 and 5.5 percent, respectively. The recent funding of the $50.5 million Arenal Hydroelectric project has brought the IDB's infrastructure and productionist projects to a new high level, with industry and mining at 11 percent, agriculture at 12.6 percent, transportation and communications at 19 percent, and energy clearly moving into a dollar priority position with 36 percent of the total IDB allocation in Costa Rica. On the other hand, projects with a stronger social component have been further deemphasized with health dropping to 0.054 percent, housing at 0.05 percent, and education receiving the lowest allocation at 0.035 percent. In Costa Rica, as in other parts of Latin America, the IDB clearly has been moving away from the traditionally conceived social projects. The focus is on projects that will have a long-term impact on development rather than those that might have an immediate impact on social and economic problems.

The argument is constantly offered that infrastructure projects literally have paved the way for further development. Highways and

TABLE 5.2

Current IDB Costa Rican Projects

| Number | Borrower | Executor | Objective | Contract Date | Amount ($ million) |
|---|---|---|---|---|---|
| 196/OC | BCR | BCR | Industry | 9/4/70 | 2.2 |
| 274/OC | ICE | ICE | Energy | | 50.5 |
| 215/SF | Republic of Costa Rica | Ministry of Transportation | Roads | 4/24/69 | 7.5 |
| 239/SF | Republic of Costa Rica | Ministry of Agriculture | Agriculture | 12/4/69 | 2.5 |
| 255/SF | BCR | BCR | Industry | 9/4/70 | 3.3 |
| 273/SF | ICE | ICE | Energy | 12/15/70 | 3.8 |
| 281/SF | SNAA | SNAA | Sanitation | 1/25/71 | 6.3 |
| 308/SF | Republic of Costa Rica | Ministry of Education | Education | 12/2/71 | 3.5 |
| 323/SF | BNCR | BNCR | Agriculture | 5/11/72 | 6.0 |
| 335/SF | Republic of Costa Rica | OFIPLAN | Preinvestment | 11/20/72 | 2.3 |
| 386/SF | Republic of Costa Rica | MOPT | Roads | 3/4/74 | 16.0 |
| 405/SF | Republic of Costa Rica | ITCO | Education | 9/2/74 | 3.3 |

Key: BNCR — Banco Nacional de Costa Rica
BCR — Banco de Costa Rica
ICE — Instituto Costarricense de Electricidad
SNAA — Servicio Nacional de Acueductos y Alcantarillados
MOPT — Ministerio Obras Públicas y Tranportes
ITCO — Instituto de Tierras y Colonización
OFIPLAN — Oficina de Planificación

Source: IDB, "Detalle de los Préstamos Otorgados A Costa Rica" (internal memo).

byways are necessary to open up the hinterland for industrial development; and industrial growth goes hand in hand with the need for more infrastructure in communications and an ever-increasing demand for more energy. Implicit in this argument is the position that long-range planning and projects keyed to future industrial development will far outweigh any benefits from short-range social projects. The costs and benefits of this approach in Costa Rica are, however, a matter of question. In order to assess that problem, one must measure IDB's actions against social and economic conditions and place Bank projects within the context of U.S. national interest and the Costa Rican national interest. Bank projects in Costa Rica are listed in Table 5.2.

## U.S. NATIONAL INTEREST AND COSTA RICAN DEVELOPMENT

The above overview of IDB projects begins to establish a pattern within which to test the following theoretical questions: What is the impact of U.S. national interest on the IDB? What is the impact of the IDB on Costa Rican development? What are the linkages between U.S. influence in the IDB and the Bank's impact on Costa Rican development?

The theoretical dimensions of these questions were explored in Chapter 2. While the linkages between U.S. national interest and the Bank were defined and discussed in Chapters 3 and 4, it now remains to connect specific IDB Costa Rican projects with specific U.S. national interests or Costa Rican national interests in order to comment further upon the direction of policy within the Bank. Table 5.3 offers a paradigm to enumerate specific U.S. national interests, link them to specific IDB policies, and project their impact on Costa Rican development.

The general relationship outlined in the paradigm in terms of the impact of specific Bank projects and their impact on Costa Rican development is elaborated further in Chapter 6. In order to concretize the assertions linking U.S. national interest and IDB projects, the following empirical evidence should be noted. Chapter 4 demonstrated that the Bank, along with the other international lending organizations, made a substantial positive contribution to the U.S. balance of payments surplus. The net U.S. payment surplus generated by the international lending organizations was $2.673.5 millions. It is therefore in the national economic interest of the United States to support international assistance agencies like IDB. The IDB's role in generating this balance of payments surplus can be examined through its projects in Costa Rica and Latin America.

U.S. trade with Latin America provided a balance of payments surplus in 1964-74 and assisted the United States in offsetting its trade deficit from other parts of the world (see Chapter 3, Table 3.4). The IDB and the other international lending agencies assisted the U.S. national interest by financing development projects in Latin America that stimulate trade and a positive U.S. balance of payments. Projects that reflect heavily tied terms or a heavy infrastructure or production component provide trade opportunities for U.S. exporters in Latin America. The Bank's emphasis on infrastructure and production projects also provides investment opportunities to U.S. foreign investors through specific productionist venture projects. Table 5.4 provides an overview of U.S. foreign investment in Latin America by country and major sector, 1961-69.

As Table 5.4 demonstrates, U.S. investments to Latin America increased dramatically during the 1960s. I believe that IDB through

TABLE 5.3

Paradigm: Impact of U.S. Interests via IDB on Costa Rican Development

| Interests | IDB Policy and Projects | Impact on Costa Rican Development |
|---|---|---|
| U.S. interests<br>Stabilize area<br>Control technology<br>Increase trade<br>Foreign investment<br>Source of primary products at cheap price<br>Capitalist development<br>U.S. repatriation of profits<br>Secure and expanded markets<br>Cheap source of labor<br>Market for capital and manufactured goods that are obsolete in U.S.<br>Increased profits on pharmaceuticals<br>Investment opportunities for surplus capital | Infrastructure and productions policy such as (projects):<br>Livestock development<br>Industrial credits<br>Roads<br>Hydroelectric project<br>Social projects having a low import component | Capital inflation<br>Increase foreign debt and debt service<br>Increase trade deficit<br>Force non-economy-of-scale businesses out of business<br>Loss of tax revenue due to industrial incentives and lowering of tariffs<br>Increase inflation<br>Increase Costa Rican dependence on a few primary products<br>Create increased unemployment<br>Force migration to urban area in search of jobs that could not be found<br>Increase service sector<br>Increase Costa Rican dependence on international lenders to service debt<br>Redistribute income in favor of middle-class groups and away from lower-income groups |

<u>Source</u>: Compiled by the author.

U.S. Private Direct Investments in Latin America, 1961-69, Net Capital Outflows
(in millions of dollars)

| | 1961 | 1962 | 1963 | 1964 | 1965 | 1966 | 1967 | 1968 | 1969 | Total |
|---|---|---|---|---|---|---|---|---|---|---|
| By country | | | | | | | | | | |
| Mexico | 45 | 25 | 24 | 95 | 99 | 19 | -4 | 63 | 93 | 459 |
| Panama | 12 | -23 | 31 | 28 | 20 | 28 | 3 | 72 | 84 | 255 |
| Other Central America[a] | -1 | 7 | 28 | 34 | 26 | 47 | 62 | 24 | 36 | 263 |
| Argentina | 104 | 96 | 19 | 16 | 16 | -13 | 62 | 36 | 61 | 397 |
| Brazil | 7 | 14 | -8 | -189 | -6 | 87 | 39 | 80 | 64 | 88 |
| Chile | b | 13 | 14 | 8 | 23 | -4 | 24 | 79 | -137 | 20 |
| Colombia | -7 | 21 | -1 | 28 | 11 | 28 | 20 | 34 | 36 | 170 |
| Peru | 14 | 14 | -5 | 10 | 55 | 34 | 61 | 24 | 1 | 208 |
| Venezuela | (2) | -199 | -35 | -59 | -93 | -50 | -92 | 26 | -20 | 542 |
| Other Latin America[c] | (2) | (2) | (2) | 17 | 24 | 15 | 14 | 40 | 53 | 163 |
| Total | 173 | -32 | 69 | -12 | 176 | 190 | 189 | 477 | 271 | 1,501 |
| By major sector | | | | | | | | | | |
| Mining and smelting | 32 | -7 | -6 | -8 | -13 | 6 | 8 | 127 | -87 | 52 |
| Petroleum | 30 | -111 | -80 | -13 | -80 | -69 | -27 | 97 | 57 | -196 |
| Manufacturing | 77 | 115 | 106 | 97 | 211 | 131 | 159 | 218 | 158 | 1,272 |
| Other | 33 | -30 | 49 | -88 | 58 | 123 | 49 | 36 | 143 | 373 |
| Total | 173 | -32 | 69 | -12 | 176 | 190 | 189 | 477 | 271 | 1,501 |

[a]Includes Costa Rica, El Salvador, Guatemala, Honduras, and Nicaragua.

[b]Combined in other industries.

[c]Includes Bolivia, Dominican Republic, Ecuador, Haiti, Paraguay, and Uruguay.

Source: U.S. Congress, House Committee on Foreign Affairs, Development Assistance to Latin America 1961-1970, 92nd Congress, 1st Session (Washington, D.C., April 14, 1971), p. 18.

TABLE 5.5

U.S. Direct Investment Position Abroad, 1974
($ millions)

| Investment | Amount: All Industries |
|---|---|
| Developed countries | |
| Europe | 54,808 |
| Japan | 3,337 |
| Australia, New Zealand, and South Africa | 6,572 |
| Canada | 28,378 |
| Developing countries | |
| Latin America and Caribbean | 19,620 |
| Africa | 2,223 |
| Middle East | 2,129 |
| Asia and Pacific | 2,729 |

Source: U.S. Department of Commerce, Survey of Current Business (Washington, D.C., October 1975), pp. 52-53.

its emphasis on infrastructure and production has contributed to this increase of U.S. investment in Latin America. This more direct connection between IDB projects and U.S. economic interest will be demonstrated in specific Bank projects in Costa Rica.

Another indication of the importance of U.S. national economic interest in Latin America is the role of multinational corporations in Central America. The Guatemalan economist Gert Rosenthal has estimated that the capital inflow to Central America from multinational corporations during the period 1960-71 increased by 344 percent, while capital outflows rose to 982 percent.[11] The positive impact of this capital outflow for the U.S. economy is evident in the fact that U.S. direct private investment in Central America in 1961-69 has averaged in excess of 75 percent of the total foreign investment (see Chapter 8). U.S. direct private investment in Latin America and the Caribbean equaled $19,620 million in 1974.[12] Table 5.5 illustrates the importance of Latin America to U.S. investment interests in the developing world.

Trade is another area in which Latin America dominates U.S. economic interest, especially in relationship to the developing world. Table 5.6 illustrates the importance of U.S. exports to Latin America in 1969-74. Latin America, as the table illustrates, continues to be a major U.S. trading partner that has contributed positively to the U.S. balance of payments. It is no wonder, then, that U.S. participation in the international development banks has focused on the Inter-American Development Bank. U.S. voting power in the Bank, and financial support to the Bank, far outweigh U.S. support to the Asian Development Bank or the African Development Bank.[13]

The paradigm in Table 5.3 suggests links between U.S. economic national interest and specific Bank projects. These in turn suggest the linkages between U.S. influence and the IDB's impact on Costa Rican development.

By analyzing specific IDB projects in Costa Rica one can assess their relevance to U.S. national interests and Costa Rican national interests. Costa Rican projects fall into the following categories: industrial credit; agricultural credit (livestock development); roads; energy (largely the Arenal Hydroelectric project); sanitation; pre-investment; and education. The actual impact in cost/benefit terms of specific projects is provided in Chapter 4. Taking the projects one by one, Table 5.7 outlines the advantages to the United States and Costa Rica.

As the table indicates, some projects serve U.S. economic interests more than others, while others are to the advantage of Costa Rica. While IDB projects in education and sanitation are of little advantage to the U.S. economic interests and provide some

TABLE 5.6

U.S. Exports to Major World Areas, 1969-74
($ millions)

| | Year | | | | | |
|---|---|---|---|---|---|---|
| Area | 1969 | 1970 | 1971 | 1972 | 1973 | 1974 |
| Canada | 9,137 | 9,079 | 10,365 | 12,415 | 15,104 | 19,932 |
| Europe | 12,392 | 14,463 | 14,178 | 15,361 | 21,359 | 28,639 |
| European Economic Community | 9,663 | 11,298 | 11,141 | 11,900 | 16,745 | 22,069 |
| Japan | 3,490 | 4,652 | 4,055 | 4,963 | 8,313 | 10,679 |
| Australia, New Zealand, and South Africa | 1,460 | 1,683 | 1,737 | 1,580 | 2,432 | 3,769 |
| Latin America | 4,869 | 5,695 | 5,667 | 6,464 | 8,921 | 14,504 |
| Near East | 1,344 | 1,423 | 1,816 | 1,954 | 3,041 | 5,557 |
| East and South Asia | 3,495 | 4,029 | 4,047 | 4,373 | 6,600 | 9,196 |

Source: U.S. Department of Commerce, Overseas Business Reports, OBR 75-38 (Washington, D.C., September 1975), pp. 2-3.

TABLE 5.7

Specific IDB Projects and Their Cost/Benefit Advantage for Costa Rica and the United States

| IDB Project | U.S. Interests | Costa Rica Interests |
|---|---|---|
| 1. Industrial credit | increased trade opportunities, especially for capital goods; expanded markets | opportunities for elite; limited employment opportunities due to labor-extensive nature of technical industry |
| 2. Livestock development | cheap source of beef; opportunity to sell capital goods like tractors | opportunities for large landowners to sell beef and offset balance of payments; increased unemployment in rural areas and external dependence for basic grains |
| 3. Energy: Arenal project | creates infrastructure for foreign investment; trade opportunities for capital goods | lower dependence on petroenergy |
| 4. Roads | trade opportunities for U.S. equipment; infrastructure for integration | access and public service jobs as well as large public expenditures |
| 5. Sanitation | limited U.S. trade advantage | good for public works sector; definite public need |
| 6. Preinvestment | U.S. can impose its economic interest through OFIPLAN (Costa Rican Planning Office) | source of public sector jobs and advanced technical assistance |
| 7. Education | little advantage to United States | good technical training; public need to upgrade skills |

Source: Compiled by the author.

positive social benefit to Costa Rica, projects in livestock development, energy, preinvestment, roads, and industrial credit are very much to the economic national interest of the United States. The livestock development project provided a cheap source of beef, which was exported to the United States, and also provided trading opportunities for U.S. investment. (Equipment for the livestock development project had to be bought from an IDB member country and the United States is the only member country that is a major manufacturer of farm equipment.) The industrial credit program provided trading opportunities for U.S. exporters of capital goods. The Bank's road and energy projects, while providing increased market opportunities for capital goods, also had the added advantage to U.S. national economic interests of providing some of the necessary economic infrastructure (such as roads, electricity, and communications) to make Costa Rica increasingly attractive to foreign investment, which in Costa Rica is about 75 percent U.S.-dominated (see Chapter 8). The Inter-American Development Bank preinvestment program also was to the advantage of the United States in that it provided for a loan to OFIPLAN, the National Planning Office, which gave U.S. economic interests direct access to shaping of Costa Rica's future development projects.

The above describes the area of economic advantage to U.S. national interest. The following chapter details the advantages and disadvantages of these projects in terms of Costa Rican national interest and elaborates further on some of the economic advantages to the United States. It is important to note, however, that each of the IDB projects benefit specific groups in Costa Rica. The groups that benefit are by and large the same groups that support the government development plan, which in many ways is more advantageous to U.S. national economic interests than to those of Costa Rica. A discussion of who benefits from IDB projects and the process that supports Costa Rican development strategy will be found in Chapters 6 and 7.

## BANK MISSIONS AND PLANNING

In addition to IDB's present projects, a number of tentative loan projects were proposed as a result of a recent IDB mission in Costa Rica. The Bank mission plays a key role in the formulation of future projects to be submitted to the IDB's Washington office for final approval. There seem to be three general varieties of Bank missions: (1) technical missions, (2) project development missions, and (3) project review and evaluation missions. Of the three, the first two are perhaps most important in establishing IDB's priorities and programs.

TABLE 5.8

Tentative Program of Loans for Costa Rica, 1975-77
(in millions of U.S. dollars)

| | Sector | Tentative Amount |
|---|---|---|
| Projects for 1975 | | |
| 1. Banco Anglo Costarricense: fisheries project | agriculture | 13.1 (9.5 FOE[a] + 3.6 OC[b]) |
| 2. SNAA: sewer project to San José | public health | 11.0 FOE |
| 3. Caja Costarricense de Seguro Social: rural health centers | public health | 17.0 FOE |
| 4. BCR: Global Industrial III | industry | 10.0 OC |
| 5. FONAPE: credit for education | education | 5.0 FOE |
| Total 1975 | | 56.1 |
| Possible projects for 1976-77 | | |
| 6. MAG: animal sanitation | agriculture | 4.0 FOE |
| 7. SNAA: rural water supply | public health | 7.0 FOE |
| 8. UCR: regional university centers | education | 6.0 FOE |
| 9. IFAM: agricultural market | agriculture | 5.0 FOE |
| 10. Ministerio de Educación Pública: vocational education | education | n.a.[c] FOE |
| 11. MAG: irrigation (El Arenal-Tempisque) | agriculture | 10.0 FOE |
| 12. ICE: Energy II (Boruca) | energy | n.a. |
| 13. ICE: rural electrification | energy | n.a. |
| 14. CODESA: large global industry | industry | n.a. OC |
| 15. MOPT: rural roads | transportation and communication | n.a. FOE |
| 16. BNCR: global agricultural credit | agriculture | n.a. FOE |
| 17. ICE: geothermal energy | energy | n.a. OC |

[a]Fund for Special Operations.
[b]Ordinary Capital.
[c]Not available.

Key:

| | |
|---|---|
| SNAA | Servicio Nacional de Acueductos y Alcantarillados |
| BCR | Banco de Costa Rica |
| FONAPE | Fondo Nacional para la Educación |
| MAG | Ministerio de Agricultura y Ganadería |
| UCR | University of Costa Rica |
| IFAM | Instituto de Fomento y Asesoría Municipal |
| ICE | Instituto Costarricense de Electricidad |
| CODESA | Costa Rican Development Corporation |
| BNCR | Banco Nacional de Costa Rica |

Source: OFIPLAN, Estudios en Ejecución (San José, Costa Rica, December 31, 1974), pp. 1-4.

The typical mission is made up of representatives and technical specialists from the Washington office who meet with Costa Rican government and agency officials from the concerned ministries to establish program priorities. The Costa Rican office is largely a checkpoint operation that has primary responsibility for coordination of IDB activities but plays second fiddle to the IDB missions in the establishment of future programs. The Bank mission officials usually also meet with other international agency officials in Costa Rica such as USAID, World Bank, United Nations, and OAS officials, especially when inter-agency coordination on a particular project is anticipated. Some of the tentative IDB projects anticipated by IDB missions as of January 1975 are listed in Table 5.8.

Project proposals that are submitted to a Bank mission and deemed worthy of consideration are usually developed further by IDB officials and technical specialists into a formal proposal in the IDB's Washington office, and at the appropriate time submitted to the IDB Board of Directors for funding consideration. The missions, therefore, remain a dominant instrument of IDB planning.

## NATIONAL PLANNING IN COSTA RICA

On the Costa Rican national level, planning is conducted by a multiplicity of vehicles. By statute, OFIPLAN (the National Planning Office) is charged with the responsibility. In fact, however, while OFIPLAN does generate a large quantity of vital information and has come forth under the direction of Minister of Planning Oscar Arias Sánchez with a plan for national development for 1974-78, it ignores Costa Rica's future development needs.[14] This national plan is presented in four parts: diagnostic, productive section, strategy, and global plan. The public section is meant to be the prime instrument to measure all national priorities and future development projects. Conversations with several Bank officials in Costa Rica implied that OFIPLAN's plan for national development was indeed the guideline that the IDB followed. In fact, however, this is far from the truth. OFIPLAN's national plan for 1974-78 is largely a paper tiger that is circumvented by the informal national planning process. While OFIPLAN remains the legislated agency of national planning, almost all national agencies in Costa Rica have their own planning instrument. For instance, the Ministry of Agriculture has its own planning office and currently the country's vice president, Dr. Carlos Manuel Castillo, plays an important role in national planning, which tends to overshadow OFIPLAN's role. The recent attempt to coordinate a basic grains program for Costa Rica clearly illustrates the conflict in the planning

TABLE 5.9

OFIPLAN Studies for Possible Future IDB Funding in Costa Rica

| Infrastructure | Productionist | Social |
|---|---|---|
| Improvement of Pacific railroad | Alcoa Aluminum plant Pérez Zeledon* | Design of aqueducts and sanitation system |
| Design of two bridges in the project Carretera El Robe-Caldera | Geological study for cement plant | New structure for FONAPE and dollar credit program to IDB* |
| Design of administrative building and warehouse in Puerto Caldera | Preinvestment studies for promotion sector | Study of education facilities in the countryside |
| Irrigation system in Guanacaste* | Study tourist development beaches south of Bahia Culebra | |
| Cement plant in Punta de Pudra | Study for the establishment of a solar salt plant in Guanacaste | |
| Study of needed projects in municipal and regional development | Line of credit for promotion sector | |
| Design of two bridges | Animal sanitation | |
| Study for improvement of Atlantic Railroad | Prevention of tuberculosis and bracelosis bovina in animals | |
| Study for the utilization of the water for the Arenal hydroelectric project* | | |
| Dredging of Puerto Caldera | | |

*Projects that Bank officials felt would certainly be funded directly by IDB.

Source: OFIPLAN, Estudios Completados y Proyectos Resultantes, Parts 1A, 1B, 1C, 1D (San José, Costa Rica: 1975), p. 1.

process. It was the vice president's office that was coordinating the basic grain program, not OFIPLAN.[15]

The decentralized nature of the national planning effort in Costa Rica allows IDB a greater impact on national development priorities than might otherwise be the case. In the absence of a unified national plan, IDB and the other international agencies establish their own priorities independently or are able to influence the national planning process by default. In 1972 IDB granted a $2.3 million loan to OFIPLAN for a preinvestment fund, whose object was to develop viable projects for future Bank funding. OFIPLAN, using IDB funds, subcontracts with various national agencies to develop projects for possible IDB funding. Thus IDB, through its grant to OFIPLAN, establishes a direct linkage into the national planning process. For example, using Bank funds, OFIPLAN subcontracted for the following projects: with the Ministry of Economy, Industry, and Commerce for a study to develop a plan for the development of an Alcoa aluminum plant and hydroelectric station in Pérez Zeledon; with Nacional Electric Service for an irrigation system in Guanacaste Province in the watershed of the Arenal hydroelectric project; as well as a study to be conducted by the Costa Rican Development Corporation for the installation of a cement plant.[16] An evaluation of the remainder of the studies in progress or completed is shown in Table 5.9.

As is evident from the information presented above, only a few of the projects funded through OFIPLAN by IDB's planning grant fall into the social development category. The three that do are of limited social impact and at a cost of only $18,800, clearly demonstrating IDB's low priority for such projects. Of 21 studies listed as part of the Bank's planning grant in Costa Rica, all but three emphasized a definite infrastructure and production orientation. This, of course, has been the pattern of IDB's ongoing projects in Costa Rica and throughout Latin America.

It is important to note, however, that with the Bank planning loan 335/SF to OFIPLAN there is a direct tie between IDB and the Costa Rican government that allows IDB a more effective influence. The direction of IDB influence is toward infrastructure and production. Projects of high social content are left in the wake of economic development that benefits upper-class groups, who have the economic wherewithal to participate in the Bank's image of economic development.

IDB's insertion into the Costa Rican planning process also suggests the possible indirect involvement of the U.S. government. It was established in Chapter 3 that the United States is quite influential in determining the outcome of specific IDB projects. The extent to which the United States has exercised its influence in Costa Rica's development is, however, open to speculation. One has to be impressed with the overwhelming impact of all forms of external assistance through international missions and agencies, and the impact that specialists have on determining the direction of Costa Rica's development strategy. The ability of the IDB to influence not only the formal planning process through OFIPLAN but the informal process through its OFIPLAN subcontracts to individual Costa Rican government agencies allows IDB and the U.S. government a strong potential position from which to shape Costa Rica's development strategy.

## PRIORITIES AND DEVELOPMENT STRATEGY

The 1974-78 national plan developed by OFIPLAN proposes a number of components for the initial development strategy. It emphasizes the need to export newly discovered resources and to decentralize the Costa Rican economy away from the Meseta Central to the local regions, especially in the central valley. In addition, the plan proposes that the gap between social classes, especially rich and poor, be closed and that the economy reduce its dependency on external resources while maintaining a 7.5 percent rate of growth per annum. The plan also stresses the need to expand agricultural production for export to offset balance of payment deficits, as well as the need for capital for industrial development and the exploitation of natural resources.[17]

Comparing the pattern of overall external assistance to Costa Rica from 1961 to June 1974 with the proposed 1974-78 national plan, the following patterns are evident. During this period IDB, USAID, and the World Bank bestowed upon Costa Rica some $318 million. The World Bank was the principal contributor with $145 million, while the IDB and USAID contributed $89 million and $80 million, respectively. All these international lending agencies concentrated on infrastructure projects. Industry and agriculture constituted a total of approximately one-third. The social sector received about 12 percent of the total loan commitment. While the national plan does give some emphasis to narrowing the gap between rich and poor, the IDB, USAID, and the World Bank have not provided priority assistance to the social area. For the period 1975-79, the World Bank will continue to fund Costa Rica with approximately $32 million per year for about six projects. For the period 1974-75, the World Bank considered three projects that included: a highway project between Limón and San José, a project of agricultural credit for $10 million and part of the Arenal hydroelectric project in conjunction with the Inter-American Development Bank. Clearly World Bank projects for the immediate future will continue to stress infrastructure and production. In line with this pattern, the World Bank is now considering an aluminum smelting plant for $43 million and a hydroelectric plant for $36 million to assist Costa Rica in the exploitation of its extensive bauxite resources.

USAID, as a result of the mandate of the Foreign Assistance Act of 1973, approaches the social guidelines of the national plan more than the World Bank or IDB. In the first half of 1974, USAID approved a $7.9 million loan for rural development.[18] However, all the international lending agencies discussed above have a history of funding heavily in the direction of infrastructure and production projects, which tend to favor U.S. economic interest in trade and foreign investment. Whether USAID will break with this pattern remains to be seen.

## FACTORS INFLUENCING THE BANK'S DEVELOPMENT STRATEGY

The specific strategy of the Inter-American Development Bank is influenced by a number of factors. For the past decade, IDB (according to its Costa Rican strategy document) has viewed itself in the role of promoting production by providing the necessary infrastructure. In this regard IDB has authorized funds to Costa Rica in the following categories: 45 percent to agriculture, industry, and mining; 24.5 percent to transportation, communications, and energy; and approximately 17 percent for health and education. IDB strategy for the future tends to mirror the past, with the exception that additional emphasis is being provided to energy infrastructure and the financing of internal natural resources projects.[19] As part of its strategy for 1975-77, the Bank proposes to increase investment to local projects that contribute to regional development and utilize a higher percentage of manual labor. The IDB also proposes to offer technical assistance to strengthen the real estate tax system in Costa Rica, as a means of offsetting the ever-increasing external debt (which almost doubled to $534 million in 1974 with annual payments running at $54 million or 11 percent of the total external debt[20]) and the balance of payment deficits of $270 million (which increased 124 percent from the previous year[21]).

The IDB also views part of its technical assistance role as offering assistance to CODESA (the Costa Rican Development Corporation) and the institutional strengthening of the Export Promotion Center, in order to increase the production of exports and to enhance Costa Rica's much diminished dollar reserves.[22]

Recognizing that the agricultural sector is the Costa Rican economy's motor for growth through agricultural exporting, IDB plans to continue a high percentage of its expenditures to this sector. Most IDB growth in this area will emphasize rural infrastructure and credit to increase agricultural production. In terms of infrastructure, the Bank has designated the drainage and irrigation system of the Arenal project in the northern zone of the country as of prime importance. Based on future projections, IDB will continue to give priority to livestock development projects through credit and technical assistance to health and research programs to improve the quality and quantity of livestock. The Bank also plans to consider projects in forest development in the provinces of Alajuela and Heredia, located in the north.

The IDB strategy document for 1975-77 also outlines the following areas of concentration.[23] In transportation, the IDB will continue to concentrate on the construction of roads that help integrate the central plateau and the rural countryside. In the energy sector the IDB plans to emphasize hydroelectric and geothermal electric plants, as well as research to offset the cost of generated energy and the inflated cost of petroleum. The IDB also anticipates a need to expand the rural electrification program and to study the need for the interconnection with the national electric systems of Panama and Nicaragua. Industrial projects continue to maintain a high priority for the IDB. However, a great deal of industrial financing will come from internal national resources, with CABEI (Central American Bank for Economic Integration), the Inter-American Development Bank, and the World Bank providing the necessary infrastructure. However, the IDB will continue to advance industrial credit loans through the national lending system to small local industries, particularly in the central valley.

Tourism in recent years has become an increasing interest of the IDB. However, it has yet to develop a specific program to develop tourism to offset Costa Rica's trade deficit. In education, the IDB will confine its loans largely to the development of vocational education in order to expand the skilled work force. Health, like education, will continue to receive a low priority, with the Bank involved in some marginal programs for the development of hospitals and rural health centers.

Clearly, IDB plans for the future tend to reflect past efforts in infrastructure and production. One must question the extent to which the Bank's continuity in aims meets Costa Rica's complex and ever-changing social and economic development needs. The following chapter assesses the Bank's role in meeting Costa Rica's needs.

## NOTES

1. IDB, Economic and Social Progress in Latin America, 1973, annual report (Washington, D.C.: 1974), p. 176.

2. Ibid., p. 176.

3. Howard I. Blutstein, et al., Area Handbook for Costa Rica (Washington, D.C.: Government Printing Office, July 18, 1969), pp. 216-17.

4. IDB, Costa Rica, Estrategia (Confidencial) 1975-1977 (Department of Economic and Social Development, Washington, D.C., October 25, 1974), p. 22.

5. Ibid., p. 22.

6. Interview no. 1, San José, Costa Rica, USAID Mission, April 4, 1975.

7. Interview no. 21, San José, Costa Rica, April 25, 1975.

8. IDB Loan Document, Loan to the Banco de Costa Rica, Industrial Development Program (March 31, 1970), pp. 1-10.

9. IDB Loan Document, Loan to Banco Nacional de Costa Rica, Livestock Development Program (December 14, 1971), pp. 1-7.

10. Banco Nacional de Costa Rica, Manual de Instrucciones para los sub-préstamos destinados al financiamiento parcial de proyectos de desarrollo del sector agropecuario, mediante el uso de fondos obtenidos por medio préstamo 323 SF/CR del Banco InterAmericano de Desarrollo y de Fondos propios del Banco Nacional (San José, Costa Rica: 1975), p. 3.

11. Richard T. Barnet and Ronald E. Müller, Global Reach: The Power of the Multinational Corporations (New York: Simon and Schuster, 1974), p. 161.

12. U.S. Department of Commerce, Survey of Current Business (Washington, D.C., October 1975), pp. 52-53.

13. U.S. House Committee on Foreign Affairs, The United States and the Multilateral Development Bank, 93rd Congress, 2nd Session (March 1974), p. 125.

14. Presidencia de la República, Oficina de Planificación, Plan Nacional Desarrollo, 1974-1978 (San José, Costa Rica, November 1973).

15. Interview, Instituto Interamericano de Ciencias Agricolas, San José, Costa Rica, February 1975.

16. OFIPLAN, Estudios en Ejecución, Cuadro 1-B (San José, Costa Rica, December 31, 1974), p. 1.

17. Estrategia 1975-1977, pp. 6-9.

18. Ibid., pp. 11-12.

19. Ibid., p. 14.

20. Ibid., p. 2.

21. American Embassy, Annual Economic Report, Costa Rica (San José, Costa Rica, January 17, 1975), p. 2.

22. Costa Rica's dollar reserves fell sharply in 1974 mainly because of a 56 percent increase in imports. Net reserves were only $21 million in September 1974 and by the end of the year had recovered

$38.5 million. The United States is Costa Rica's major trading partner. (Ibid., pp. 5-6).

23. Estrategia 1975-1977, pp. 19-21.

CHAPTER

# 6

# THE BANK'S IMPACT ON COSTA RICA'S SOCIAL AND ECONOMIC CONDITION

Costa Rica ranks relatively high in comparison to the rest of Latin America with a per capita gross domestic product of $645.30 in 1973, a total gross domestic product growth of 6.3 percent in 1960–73, and a 3 percent per capita growth during the same period. However, analysts of the social and economic environment of Costa Rica should not be complacent with this country's plight, as the relative statistical success of the Costa Rican economy does not paint an accurate picture of the desperate condition of large numbers of its people.

Recent economic and social progress has been shattered by an extremely high rate of inflation. In March 1975 a local San José newspaper reported that Costa Rica had the highest rate of inflation in Central America. This article indicated that Costa Rica had a rate of inflation of 28.1 percent as compared to the other Central American countries: Guatemala, 23.5 percent; Honduras, 15.1 percent; Nicaragua, 13.1 percent; with El Salvador's rate not available. The report added that price controls and other anti-inflationary measures adopted have not had a significant impact in inhibiting the inflationary spiral. Salaries of Costa Rican workers have, moreover, fallen behind prices to the extent that there has been a sizable loss in real buying power.[1]

Costa Rica's total dependence on foreign oil as a nonproducing nation has made further inroads into relative prosperity. With a domestic oil production rate of zero, Costa Rica increased domestic consumption 10.9 percent in 1970–73. The impact of these economic pressures can be seen in the price of gasoline in Costa Rica of approximately one dollar per gallon, the highest price in all Central America.[2] In addition, Costa Rica is economically dependent on its major trading partner, the United States, which supplies approximately one-third of imports. The Costa Rican economy is highly dependent on exports, particularly of agriculture products such as coffee, sugar, bananas, rice, and livestock, which alone make up 30 to 40 percent of the GNP for foreign exchange. So any change in prices or the quantity exported to the United States can have devastating repercussions.[3]

As a result of inflationary pressures and the increasing burden of balance of payment deficits, which rose from a deficit of $120.8 million in 1973 to $270.0 million in 1974 and was expected to worsen further in 1975, Costa Rica was experiencing during 1975 a period of economic stagnation and retrenchment. During the final months of 1974, credit restraints were imposed to reduce imports. The Costa Rican government regulated sales on credit of 31 articles either imported or with a high content of imported material. Sales of dollars to the public were regulated and interest rates on time accounts in dollars and other foreign currencies were made competitive in an attempt, in particular, to halve the outflow of dollars. Net reserves had fallen to a low of $21 million in September 1974, compared to $60.3 million at the end of 1973. Other fiscal pressures were brought on by the loss of revenues from the collection of import levies, the result of a 1970 law providing a tax exemption for industrial incentive. Additionally, by October 8, 1974, the external public debt of the central government, including interest charges, had risen to $122.1 million, equaling about 23 percent of the current account receipts of the balance of payments.[4]

Beyond the dollar crunch and the trade deficit, inflation was Costa Rica's most serious domestic economic problem. The increase in petroleum prices by OPEC (Organization of Petroleum Exporting Countries) heightened Costa Rica's dollar outflow by $30 million, inflated the price of goods made from petroleum, and resulted in increased energy prices affecting power costs. This was an extremely important factor for Costa Rican agriculture, which depends on fertilizer, a petroleum product. The impact of high petroleum prices was mitigated somewhat in 1975 by a scheme under which Venezuela would lend back to Costa Rica at 8 percent interest roughly half of what it pays for oil (for development purposes).[5]

Agriculture composed the largest percentage of the Costa Rican export capacity of $350.4 million in 1973 and $425.0 million in 1974. Table 6.1 illustrates Costa Rica's substantial dependence on the export of primary agricultural products. While agriculture remains currently the principal sector, generating 22.7 percent of the gross domestic product, industry commanded a healthy 15.7 percent of the gross domestic product in 1973. This figure reflects a giant expansion in articles for export, which showed 39 percent growth.

Tourism is another activity that has witnessed a rapid growth in recent years with the number of visitors reaching 246,825 in 1973,

TABLE 6.1

Exports of Major Agricultural Products

| | 1973 | Estimate 1974 | Projected 1975 | Percent Change 1974 | Projected Percent Change 1975 |
|---|---|---|---|---|---|
| Coffee | | | | | |
| Value (million $) | 94.0 | 120.0 | 105.0 | 28 | -11 |
| Volume (metric tons) | 72.9 | 82.5 | 70.0 | | |
| Bananas | | | | | |
| Value | 96.2 | 92.5 | 118.5 | -4 | +28 |
| Volume | 1171.8 | 1030.0 | 1185.0 | | |
| Beef | | | | | |
| Value | 31.6 | 34.5 | 30.9 | 9 | -13 |
| Volume | 20.4 | 26.0 | 26.0 | | |
| Sugar | | | | | |
| Value | 13.6 | 22.0 | 75.0 | 62 | +241 |
| Volume | 112.1 | 76.6 | 100.0 | | |

Source: American Embassy, Annual Economic Report (San José, Costa Rica, January 17, 1975), p. 5.

an increase of 22 percent over 1972. The Costa Rican government has great hopes for tourism and is actively encouraging businessmen to invest in the hotel industry. Areas that currently are economically depressed but have great natural beauty, such as Bahía Culebra in Guanacaste Province, are being considered for tourist development.

A significant factor in the growth of various sectors of the economy is the distribution of credit by the Central Bank. Historically, the Central Bank has channeled the greatest share of credit to farming, livestock, and industrial activities. In 1973 these areas accounted for about 75 percent of the total credit allocated by the Central Bank. Sectorally these may be broken down as follows: livestock, 30.2 percent; farming, 22.9 percent; and industry, 21.6 percent. The credit weight has shifted more recently. By September 1974, especially with the rise in cost of imported raw materials and the demand by foreign exporters for cash payment for many intermediate and capital goods, industry had replaced farming as the second highest recipient of credit.[6]

TABLE 6.2

Employment, by Occupation
(percentages)

| Occupation Sector | 1963 | 1973 | 1978 |
|---|---|---|---|
| Agriculture | 49.7 | 37.1 | 33.5 |
| Mining and industry | 11.7 | 11.8 | 12.8 |
| Construction | 5.5 | 6.5 | 7.9 |
| Basic services | 9.8 | 4.9 | 5.0 |
| Commerce | 9.9 | 13.5 | 14.9 |
| Services | 18.4 | 26.2 | 25.9 |

Source: United Nations Development Program to Costa Rica, La Situación Socio-Economíca En Función del Plan Nacional de Desarrollo (San José, Costa Rica, February 1975), p. 15.

These recent economic difficulties have had a severe impact on the population. While macroeconomic analysis indicated a relatively high rate of growth and prosperity (6.3 percent gross domestic product and 3.0 percent gross domestic product per capita in 1960–73), a microeconomic view of the impact of the economy on social conditions in Costa Rica reveals a harsher reality.

The 1973 census listed the population at 1,889,109, with approximately 40 percent urban and 60 percent rural. By 1978 the population is projected to reach 2,164,914, with urban and rural population leveling out at 41.6 and 58.4 percent, respectively. In 1973 the work force was composed of 607,000 individuals or 32.1 percent of the population. The unemployment rate in 1973 was 7.1 percent.[7] Table 6.2 illustrates the breakdown of the population by occupation.

In analyzing the pattern of employment in Costa Rica, the agricultural sector, although growing smaller, remains the dominant sector because of the country's dependence on exports of primary agricultural products. Most other sectors have maintained relative stability, with the next most dynamic change in the service sector, slightly over 8 percent increase in 1963-73. This is important to note in considering Costa Rica's development because the growth of the service sector throughout the rest of Latin America has been synonymous with marginal employment. Therefore, the growth of the service sector or marginal employment may suggest the failure of the development program to improve the human condition.

The distribution of income provides another measure. A rough estimate can be discerned from the fact that in 1971 the lowest 50 percent of the population received 20.9 percent of the total family income or an average $74 per month, while the top 5 percent received 22.8 percent of the total family income or an average family income of $808 per month.[8] Clearly, the gap between rich and poor remains wide. The 1973 census indicates the general employment trend, as shown in Table 6.3.

The census material reveals a continuing high level of unemployment and marginality, which is reflected in low income levels. Using 1973 census materials again, the plight of the Costa Rican worker is illustrated in Figure 6.1.

Comparing the 1971 to 1973 figures for the distribution of income, one does not find any marked improvement. In fact, given the current rate of world inflation, the cost of energy, and Costa Rica's ever-increasing trade deficit, the prospect for the future is not favorable. A recent mission by the World Bank group projected an unfavorable employment pattern for 1970-90 (see Table 6.4).

The growth of unemployment and underemployment can be explained not only by the external factors effecting the Costa Rican economy but also by internal economic factors. Costa Rica as an agriculturally oriented economy has a high rate of underemployment due to the seasonal nature of such crops as coffee, tobacco, and

TABLE 6.3

General Employment Trend
(percentages)

| | Economically Active Population | Unemployed | Underemployed* |
|---|---|---|---|
| Costa Rica | 48.0 | 7.3 | 5.3 |
| By region | | | |
| Atlantic | 53.0 | 7.6 | 5.2 |
| Pacific South | 48.6 | 6.0 | 5.1 |
| Pacific North | 46.6 | 8.0 | 11.0 |

*Defined as less than 33 weeks per year.

Source: Instituto de Fomento y Asesoría Municipal, "Regional Overview of Acción International Canton Reports and Studies," unpublished papers (San José, Costa Rica, 1975), p. 11.

FIGURE 6.1

Distribution of Income in Costa Rica, 1973

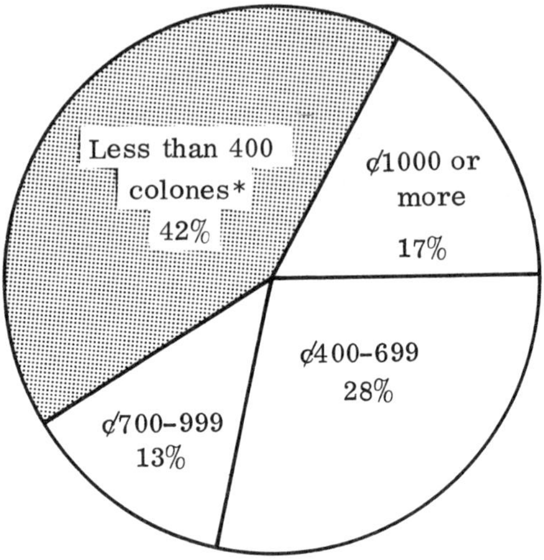


*1 dollar = 8.54 colones; ¢ = colones

Source: Instituto de Fomento y Asesoría Municipal, "Regional Overview of Acción International Canton Reports and Studies," unpublished papers (San José, Costa Rica, 1975), p. 11.

TABLE 6.4

Projection of Possible Levels of Unemployment, 1970-90

| | | | | Annual Growth Rate (percent) | |
|---|---|---|---|---|---|
| | 1970 | 1980 | 1990 | 1970-80 | 1980-90 |
| Population (thousands) | 1729 | 2225 | 2822 | 2.5 | 2.4 |
| Labor force (thousands) | 535 | 750 | 991 | 3.4 | 2.8 |
| GDP (dollars) | 850 | 1438 | 2457 | 5.4 | 5.5 |
| Employment (thousands) | 508 | 658 | 862 | 2.6 | 2.7 |
| Unemployment (thousands) | 27 | 92 | 129 | 13.0 | 3.4 |
| Underemployment (percent) | 5.1 | 12.3 | 13.0 | | |

Source: International Bank for Reconstruction and Development, Economic Report of Costa Rica, vol. 1 (Latin America and Caribbean Regional Office, March 15, 1974), p. 9.

bananas. The recent lack of growth in the agricultural sector also has created higher levels of unemployment and forced many agricultural workers to migrate to urban areas in search of jobs. A policy of increased credit to industry, a continuing policy of the Central Bank, as well as the Industrial Incentive Program of 1970, has tended to redistribute income away from the agricultural sector and agricultural workers toward the industrial middle classes. While the share of income of the top 5 percent of the population fell from 35 percent to about 23 percent, the share of the middle 60 percent of the population increased from 34 to 44 percent in 1961-71.

However, in spite of this redistribution in favor of the middle sectors, the relative position of the poorest 20 percent of the rural population has improved little. The poorest portion accounts for around 5.4 percent of the total income and its average income is only 27 percent of the national average. This sector in 1971 had a yearly family income of $751 and a per capita income of approximately $96. By and large, the income of rural workers tends to be 45 percent less than their counterparts in urban areas. In the countryside throughout Costa Rica the system of land tenure also contributes to the income disparity. A 1963 land tenure survey indicates that fewer than 4 percent of the farms in Costa Rica held over half of the land, while the smaller 43 percent of the farms held less than 3 percent of the land.[9] Although a land reform agency, ITCO (Instituto Nacional de Tierras y Colonizaje), has been established, its effectiveness has been virtually nil and the inequities in the land tenure system persist.

## ROLE OF THE CENTRAL AMERICAN COMMON MARKET

Another explanation for the failure to redistribute income levels or to lower underemployment and unemployment is the relative failure of the Central American Common Market to contribute to the expansion of the Costa Rican economy. CACM, while opening the door for foreign investors to Costa Rica and the Central American markets by lowering national tariff barriers and by creating various tax incentive programs, weakens the Costa Rican economy. It increases its vulnerability to balance of payment deficits with other member market countries and creates a loss of foreign exchange necessitated by the increased purchases of capital and finished goods for Common Market industrial projects. Table 6.5 illustrates, in particular, the unfavorable terms of Costa Rica's trade with CACM neighbors.

CACM also contributed to the penetration of the Costa Rican economy by numerous foreign investors who tended to repatriate their profits, depriving Costa Rica of necessary investment capital for development. A rough estimate of industrial financing in Costa Rica

TABLE 6.5

Costa Rica: Trade with CACM Countries, 1965–71
(millions of U.S. $)

| | 1965 | 1966 | 1967 | 1968 | 1969 | 1970 | 1971 |
|---|---|---|---|---|---|---|---|
| Exports, f.o.b. | 18.3 | 25.2 | 26.9 | 36.2 | 37.7 | 46.1 | 47.1 |
| Guatemala | 4.3 | 4.7 | 5.6 | 8.0 | 8.8 | 11.1 | 15.4 |
| El Salvador | 4.7 | 6.1 | 6.1 | 8.6 | 8.7 | 10.5 | 11.5 |
| Honduras | 3.0 | 4.4 | 4.4 | 6.1 | 7.8 | 11.6 | 4.8 |
| Nicaragua | 6.3 | 10.0 | 10.8 | 13.5 | 12.5 | 12.9 | 15.4 |
| Imports, c.i.f. | 14.7 | 23.2 | 34.2 | 48.8 | 51.2 | 68.7 | 76.5 |
| Guatemala | 5.3 | 9.1 | 11.3 | 15.8 | 17.6 | 21.5 | 27.1 |
| El Salvador | 4.8 | 7.7 | 12.3 | 16.0 | 14.2 | 20.1 | 21.5 |
| Honduras | 1.4 | 2.0 | 3.2 | 5.2 | 5.8 | 7.1 | 1.6 |
| Nicaragua | 3.2 | 4.4 | 7.4 | 11.8 | 13.6 | 19.9 | 26.3 |
| Trade balance | 3.6 | 2.0 | -7.3 | -12.6 | -13.5 | -22.6 | -29.4 |
| Guatemala | -1.0 | -4.4 | -5.7 | -7.8 | -8.8 | -10.5 | -11.7 |
| El Salvador | -0.1 | -1.6 | -6.2 | -7.4 | -5.6 | -9.6 | -10.0 |
| Honduras | 1.6 | 2.4 | 1.2 | 0.9 | 2.0 | 4.5 | 3.2 |
| Nicaragua | 3.1 | 5.6 | 3.5 | 1.6 | -1.1 | -7.1 | -10.9 |

Source: International Bank for Reconstruction and Development, Economic Report of Costa Rica, vol. II (Latin American and Caribbean Regional Office, March 15, 1974).

breaks down as follows: 40 percent foreign investors, 25 percent financial intermediaries, and the remaining 35 percent for internal financing, equity investment, and loans from private noninstitutional investors. The overall pattern is one of low debt equity and a large participation of foreign investors. Therefore, CACM industrial investment was marginally effective in contributing to economic development and improving the human condition in Costa Rica. These industrial projects on the whole exacerbated the balance of payment deficit; cost the national government needed tax revenues due to the industrial incentives for foreign investment, which increased from $9 million in 1962 to $579 million in 1971, a level four times the total contribution of international lending to Costa Rica in 1960-70; and created few positions in the labor market because of their low labor intensity.[10]

The cost of economic development has been great, therefore, not only in its negative impact on the Costa Rican economy and in terms of lower rates of real growth, but additionally in the cost of underemployment and unemployment, which continue to be high. While there have been some shifts in income distribution, the effect has been in favor of the middle sector and to the disadvantage of lower-income groups, which comprise the majority of the population. Within this context the Inter-American Development Bank has been a prime mover in a sector of Costa Rican development along with the other international lending agencies. What has IDB's impact been on Costa Rican development?

## IDB PROJECTS IN COSTA RICA

The Inter-American Development Bank's efforts in Costa Rica through the 1960s, as indicated in the previous chapter, emphasized economic infrastructure and productionist projects. Projects of a high social content or impact, on the other hand, were given a significantly lower priority in IDB funding in Costa Rica and other parts of Latin America. Table 6.6 gives an overview of Bank projects in Costa Rica.

### Agricultural Sector

By sector, in 1961-74, some 82.3 percent of IDB funding in Costa Rica was directed toward economic infrastructure and production-oriented projects.[11] By analyzing IDB's specific development effort in individual projects, the impact of IDB's choices becomes more discernible. Bank projects in agriculture are important to Costa Rica, whose economy has been oriented largely around the exportation of

TABLE 6.6

IDB Lending for Projects in Costa Rica, 1961-74

| | Number | Amount (dollars) |
|---|---|---|
| IDB resources | | |
| Ordinary capital | 7 | 66,020,000 |
| Fund for Special Operation | 16 | 65,491,000 |
| Social Progress Trust Fund | 6 | 11,700,000 |
| Total | 29 | 143,211,000 |
| By sector | | |
| Agriculture and fishing | 7 | 17,729,000 |
| Industry and mining | 6 | 15,591,000 |
| Transportation and communication | 3 | 27,500,000 |
| Sanitation | 2 | 7,600,000 |
| Housing and urban development | 2 | 7,100,000 |
| Education | 3 | 8,170,000 |
| Preinvestment | 3 | 2,540,000 |
| Total | 29 | 143,211,000 |

Source: IDB, Fifteen Years of Activities 1960-1974 (Washington, D.C., December 1974), p. 44.

primary agricultural products. Loans to the agricultural sector have the potential of making a critical difference. Of the total contribution to the agricultural sector, the vast majority of funds have been channeled into livestock development projects and rural credit—with the credit provided for the cattle industry.

As recently as February 1975 the Bank lent Costa Rica $13.5 million to develop and improve cooperative fisheries and industrial fishing along the northwest Pacific Coast. This loan is unique to Costa Rican agricultural development programs because of its approach. It was also the first loan to be extended by the Bank from the $500 million Venezuelan Trust Fund. The loan will be used largely for the acquisition of 50 small boats for coastal water fishing for domestic consumption, for a support ship, and for the construction of a port and terminal building, and the purchase of mobile sales vehicles and freezers.[12]

Other IDB loans to the agricultural sector amount to some $17.7 million and reflect the more dominant pattern of the IDB agricultural assistance through its livestock development programs. IDB loans to the agricultural sector since 1961, however, have been oriented to the cattle development or infrastructure for the cattle industry. Possible exceptions to that basic funding pattern would be a loan of $1 million in 1964 for the development of cooperatives; $1.3 million to ITCO (Instituto Nacional de Tierras y Colonizaje) in 1965 for agriculture infrastructure and equipment; and a loan in 1969 to the Ministerio de Agricultura y Ganadería for the development of extension services. The latter fund is used for the construction of buildings throughout the country for the rural extension service. With the possible exception of the infrastructure loan to ITCO, the other two IDB loans provide support to the IDB's livestock development program.

The Bank's initial investment in livestock development in Costa Rica came in November 1961, with a grant of $3 million for renovation of pastures, purchase of livestock and equipment, and infrastructure. This grant was supplemented in 1966 by a $400,000 loan. The investment went mostly to western Costa Rica, with 48 percent allocated to Guanacaste Province, 19 percent to Alajuela Province, 14 percent to Puntarenas Province, and 3 percent to the Province of San José. In 1965 IDB also made $5.2 million in loans through the BNCR (Banco Nacional de Costa Rica), the agency responsible for all livestock development projects. The purpose was to fund livestock and other agricultural items and to advance credit to reclaim land damaged by the eruption of the Irazú Volcano, which was active from March 1963 until December 1964. These initial livestock development efforts were followed in 1972 by a $6 million loan, also funneled through the Banco Nacional de Costa Rica (BNCR).

The aim of these programs in livestock development is to continue and expand earlier programs by providing credit to 1,000 small and medium ranches, 90 percent of which would be located in the Guanacaste, Puntarenas, and Meseta Central regions. The program guidelines require that the borrowers' total agricultural assets not exceed $60,000 and that each borrower raise 15 percent of the total value of the loan in equity. Loans may not exceed $40,000, with interest of 8 percent. The program, therefore, was tailored to farmers with sufficient land for cattle production (land could not be purchased with the credit). This program is applicable to only a small percentage of the agricultural population. Since one can still purchase considerable land in Costa Rica for $60,000, most of the farms that I visited as part of this project were sizable. The program, then, would seem to contribute little to Costa Rica's sizable low-income agricultural population, especially since cattle production is of low labor intensity.

IDB's justification for the heavy emphasis on livestock development is primarily that the production and exportation of meat will offset Costa Rica's declining terms of trade. Prior to the consideration of this program in 1972, the Costa Rican balance of payments was adversely affected in 1970 by a substantial 40 percent growth in the volume of imports as a result of a high level of economic activity. The trade deficit in that year nearly doubled to $110 million from 1969. Cattle production, which made up 30 percent of the Costa Rican farm production, had allowed a 300 percent increase in the exportation of beef in 1960-69, providing a means of lessening the trade deficit. At the time, IDB also anticipated that Costa Rica would continue to share in the increased demand for meat in the U.S. market, which was expanding at 4 percent per annum.[13]

To some extent, IDB estimations for beef production have been borne out with 9 percent increase, from $31.6 million in 1973 to $34.5 million in 1974. However, production was expected to fall off in 1975 by as much as 13 percent due to inflation and new restrictive U.S. beef import quotas.[14] The Bank's anticipated production has been met, at least in the short run, although the future for beef looks less promising. At the microeconomic level in the countryside, the impact of IDB's livestock development program is more difficult to assess.

One recent concern over the priority given to livestock development by IDB and the Costa Rican government is the effect that this has on the cultivation of basic grain for national consumption. By basic grain is meant staples such as beans, rice, and corn, which in the last two years have been in such short supply that they have had to be imported. The northern and southern Pacific areas are major producers of beans, rice, and corn, accounting for 59 percent, 76 percent, and 56 percent, respectively, of national production. Credit for livestock development, therefore, has diminished the production of basic grains in this area and lessened the number of hectares under cultivation.[15] Table 6.7 illustrates the movement away from the production of basic grains in 1967-72. While the production of most agricultural products was on the increase in Costa Rica in 1967-72, the production of basic grains declined. The increased credit available to the cattle industry seems a probable factor in the decline in the production of beans, rice, and corn. In 1967-72 the area devoted to basic grain declined from 147,000 hectares to 90,000 hectares as the cattle industry converted land for livestock production.[16] By 1974 the situation in basic grains had become critical, resulting in domestic shortages and further pressures on the balance of trade due to the necessity to import basic grains from neighboring Central American countries. In 1974, therefore, the government of President Daniel Oduber commenced a basic grain program, a major thrust of the administration, to offset this national shortage.

To some extent, obviously, the IDB approach to agricultural development has contributed to Costa Rica's basic grain shortages.

TABLE 6.7

Value of Agricultural Production in Costa Rica
(millions of colones; 1 dollar = 8.54 colones)

| | 1967 | 1968 | 1969 | 1970 | 1971 | 1972 |
|---|---|---|---|---|---|---|
| Coffee | 379 | 351 | 404 | 366 | 426 | 373 |
| Bananas | 220 | 312 | 396 | 454 | 497 | 535 |
| Sugar | 68 | 71 | 86 | 86 | 88 | 91 |
| Beef | 163 | 176 | 188 | 193 | 213 | 228 |
| Cotton | 15 | 11 | 5 | 1 | — | — |
| Tobacco | 7 | 7 | 6 | 7 | 8 | 8 |
| Beans | 17 | 12 | 17 | 11 | 7 | 6 |
| Corn | 37 | 37 | 35 | 20 | 22 | 18 |
| Rice | 69 | 73 | 61 | 64 | 74 | 63 |
| Hogs | 17 | 18 | 29 | 24 | 24 | 24 |
| Milk | 136 | 142 | 149 | 185 | 188 | 192 |
| Eggs | 62 | 66 | 70 | 92 | 100 | 108 |

Source: USAID, Programa de Desarrollo Rural 1975-1978, Documento de Antecedentes para el Préstamo AID-55-T-025 entre el Gobierno de la República de Costa Rica y el Gobierno de los Estado Unidos de America (San José, Costa Rica, November 1974), p. 1.

Charges may be leveled at IDB for not anticipating the diminished growth of the basic grain sector, which became a clear pattern in 1967-72 during the second phase of the livestock development project and, additionally, for fostering agricultural development that depended on one primary product. Certainly the economic development literature abounds warnings of the disastrous consequences for developing countries dependent on a few agricultural products subject to wide commodity price fluctuations. Therefore, by not financing a more diversified program of agricultural development, the Bank contributed to Costa Rican dependence on a few crops subject to international price fluctuations and the need to import other agricultural products, thus increasing the trade deficit.

IDB also seems to have failed to consider the impact of its efforts on the agricultural sector of Costa Rica's labor force, particularly in the provinces of Guanacaste, Alajuela, and Puntarenas. In these provinces, the expansion of the labor-extensive cattle industry contributed few new jobs. As a matter of fact, there is some evidence that the marginality of the work force increased, resulting in increased

TABLE 6.8

Costa Rican Employment Situation, 1973

| Region | Economically Active Population | Unemployed | Underemployed* |
|---|---|---|---|
| Total | 48.0 | 7.3 | 5.3 |
| Atlantic Watershed | 53.0 | 7.6 | 5.2 |
| Southern Pacific | 48.6 | 6.0 | 5.0 |
| Northern Pacific | 46.6 | 8.0 | 11.0 |

*Less than 33 weeks per year.

Source: Instituto de Fomento y Asesoría, "Regional Overview of Acción Internacional Canton Reports and Studies," unpublished papers (San José, Costa Rica, 1975), p. 11.

migration to San José and the Meseta Central in search of employment. Agricultural workers make up about 60 percent of the work force in Pacific North and 70 percent in Pacific South. Therefore, fluctuations in agricultural production are critical to employment patterns. Table 6.8 illustrates the current employment situation in the northern and southern Pacific cattle-producing provinces.[17]

Table 6.8 illustrates that of the two cattle-producing areas in the southern and northern Pacific, it is the Pacífico Norte that bears the highest burden of unemployment (8.0 percent) and underemployment (11.0 percent). It is interesting to note that the same region is responsible for 40 percent of national cattle production, while the Pacífico Sur and the la Vertiente Atlántico only produce 12 percent and 6 percent, respectively, of the national output. Therefore, the increase in cattle production in the Pacífico Norte would appear to have had a negative impact on the labor force.[18]

Interviews in those three regions also indicated that the population believes work opportunities have declined in the last five years, particularly in the Pacific North during the significant period of livestock development. In the Vertiente Atlántica, 23 percent of the communities felt there was less work than five years ago, while in the Pacífico Sur and Pacífico Norte the figure rose to 33 percent and 43 percent, respectively. In the Pacífico Norte, only 24 percent of the communities felt there was more work in 1975 than five years before. Reasons given for the decline in employment varied. In the Pacífico Sur, 23 communities or 50 percent mentioned the mechanization of agriculture as a reason why farmers were hiring fewer workers, and eight communities or 17 percent specifically mentioned the increase in cattle production with its low labor requirement as an explanation for the lower labor demand. In the Pacífico Norte, the impact of cattle production was more apparent. Twenty-five communities or 48 percent mentioned the increase in livestock production and its low labor intensity as a prime reason for the erosion of the agricultural work force. In the Pacífico Norte 18 communities or 35 percent also listed the mechanization of agriculture as a major force in the decline of the labor force.[19]

The low labor intensity of livestock development also has been a factor in the increasing migration from the Pacífico Norte and Pacífico Sur to urban areas such as San José and the Meseta Central. Lack of employment and low wages provide sharp pressures to induce rural-urban migration in search of permanent or seasonal employment. Figure 6.2 illustrates relative monthly salary levels.

Wage pressure has clearly been greatest for the cattle-producing region of the Pacífico Norte, where 63 percent of the work force earn less than 400 colones/month and another 20 percent earn between 400 and 699 colones/month. Wages in the Pacífico Sur are also low, with 49 percent of the population earning less than 400 colones/month and another 22 percent earning between 400 and 699 colones. These pressures are certainly an impetus for emigration from the Pacífico Norte and Pacífico Sur, which remains the highest in Costa Rica. In the Pacífico Norte and Pacífico Sur, 69 percent and 58 percent, respectively, of the communities reported significant out-migration. Despite the Pacífico Norte's high out-migration, 43 percent of the communities reported no seasonal in-migration. The 1973 census reported that the Pacífico Norte with 8 percent of total out-migration had the lowest percentage of population in residence for five years or more, nearly half the figure for all of Costa Rica, which was 15 percent.

The Pacífico Norte, with 40 percent of the national production of cattle, remained by labor standards one of the most backward areas, with workers forced to migrate in search of decent employment. The Pacífico Sur, with 18 percent of the cattle production, continues to be a depressed area. It is evident that the Bank's livestock development efforts, especially in the Pacífico Norte, have not benefited the agricultural workers. Indeed, livestock development, particularly in the Pacífico Norte, appears to have had a negative impact, contributing to the unemployment and marginality of the work force.

On the national level, it has been suggested that livestock development priorities may have contributed to the trade deficit by increasing the basic grain shortages. Additionally, the declining world price of beef and the shrinkage of the U.S. beef quota for Costa Rica suggests that the Bank's priority agricultural programs should be reconsidered in terms of a more diversified program.[20]

FIGURE 6.2

Monthly Salaries of Workers in Costa Rica
(in colones or ¢; $1 = ¢8.54)

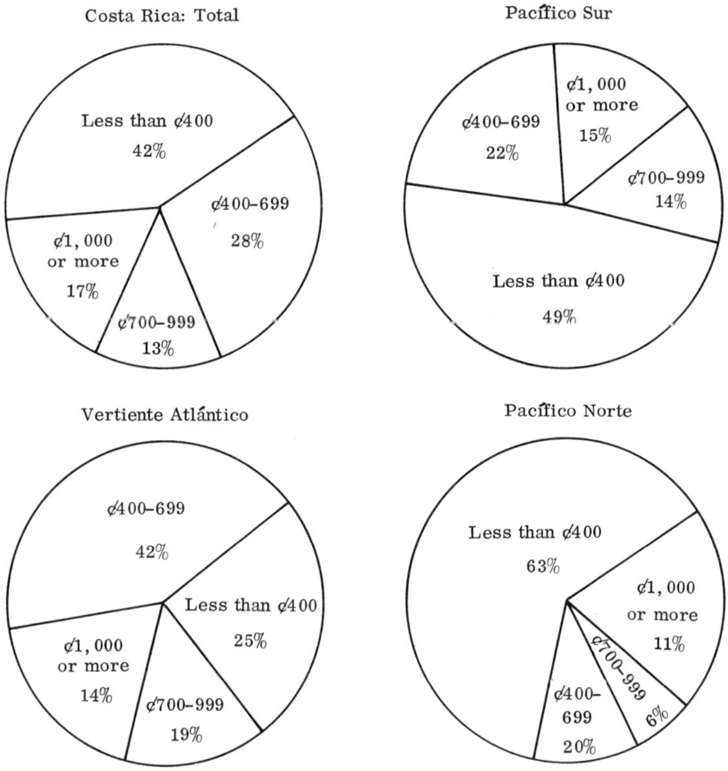


Source: Instituto de Fomento y Asesoría, "Regional Overview of Acción Internacional Canton Reports and Studies," unpublished papers (San José, Costa Rica, 1975), p. 29.

## Industrial Sector

Since 1961 the Bank contribution to the industrial sector in Costa Rica has totaled some $15,591,000 distributed among six development projects.[21] Industrial development assistance is viewed by IDB as an "engine of growth," a means of minimizing Costa Rica's dependency on a few agricultural export products.

All of IDB's industrial development loans have been global loans that granted lines of credit to industrial projects through a local lending institution. The sole exception was a $2.8 million loan for installation of a cement plant. The other IDB loans were global, providing subloans through the Banco de Costa Rica, a local national bank. The loan priorities are tailored largely to the guidelines of the Costa Rican Planning Office (OFIPLAN) and to those of the Central Bank. OFIPLAN's strategy for industrial development proposed preferences for industries offering an immediate possibility of alleviating the pressure on the balance of payments. OFIPLAN set forth two priorities to that end. The first was to increase the capacity of existing domestic industry and export production based on natural resources. The second, based on the familiar import substitution model, recommended the development of new plants to produce intermediate and consumer goods that were being imported. The Central Bank also laid down some rather stringent requirements to the banks composing the national banking system, instituting the following priorities for industrial credit:

1. Industrial projects must use at least 50 percent raw materials of national origin.
2. At least 30 percent of industrial production must be oriented toward exports achievable in a few years.
3. Added value must account for 40 percent of total value and wages for 10 percent.
4. At least 50 percent of the total production must be represented by Costa Rican inputs.[22]

While these guidelines do provide some rather rigid standards, the policing of these standards seems to be a much more difficult area. Little available evidence indicated that the standards were upheld.

The IDB cited similar priorities for an industrial development loan program:

1. To increase the rate of economic growth and employment.
2. To improve internal organization of companies and the quality of personnel.

3. To decentralize industry, thus bringing new areas into Costa Rica's productive economy.

4. To increase Costa Rican participation in the Central America Economic Integration Program.

5. To increase import substitution and export development.[23]

The extent to which these goals have been accomplished will be seen in the program evaluation that follows.

The IDB's industrial development projects call for a global loan program with credits destined for small and medium industrial producers in the private sector. Program credit resources have been broken down as follows: 60 percent to industries producing consumer goods (such as textiles, foodstuffs, furniture, garments, footwear, and miscellaneous industries); and 40 percent to industries producing intermediate and capital goods to replace imports and supply foreign markets (such as leather, chemicals, basic metals, nonmetallic mineral products, metal products, and transportation).

Interest rates on the various development loans vary. The most recent were granted with an annual rate of 6.5 percent from the Fund for Special Operations (IDB soft loan window) and 10.5 percent on ordinary capital loans. In addition, Banco de Costa Rica would add 2 percent to cover the cost of operating the program.

With the industrial loan program, IDB hoped to sustain Costa Rica's relatively high rate of economic growth in 1960-68, which exceeded 6 percent per annum. During the same period, gross industrial production increased at a rate of 10.6 percent, exceeding the general economy. Since 1968, however, this rate has not been sustained. By 1973 gross national production had leveled off at 5.5 percent; in recent years, internal-external economic pressures have eroded economic growth further.[24] Costa Rica faces a situation of economic stagnation in which low growth is being undermined by an increasing trade deficit, unfavorable terms of trade with other CACM members, the loss of import revenues due to CACM agreements, and the increasing burden of servicing an external debt of $122.1 million, which represents 23 percent of the current receipts of the Costa Rican balance of payments.[25]

It is debatable whether IDB's industrial development programs have met its own objectives and those of OFIPLAN and the Central Bank. By and large, available statistics provide only a means of measuring project success on a macroeconomic level. At that level, however, one can observe that IDB's efforts were not alone sufficient to tip the balance in Costa Rica's increasing demand for imports, particularly from the United States. By 1974 the Costa Rican trade deficit had reached $270 million, an increase of 124 percent over 1973, and in 1975 this deficit was expected to increase significantly. While the increased cost of oil accounted for approximately $30 million of the deficit, consumer spending, particularly for imported goods, also was a factor. This forced the government to institutionalize credit restrictions and increase sales taxes to stem the outflow of dollar reserves, which reached a low point of $21 million in September 1974.[26] At least on the macroeconomic level, therefore, IDB's impact in offsetting the trade deficit through import substitution, export development, and the use of national raw materials is difficult to assess, but it seems less than satisfactory.

One of the IDB's goals was the redistribution of industrial development projects throughout Costa Rica. The vast majority of projects have tended to be located in the Meseta Central surrounding San José. Of the global loans for industrial development granted by the IDB, 262 subloans were made in the San José area while only 34 subloans were made outside of San José, allowing $11.778 million of the total $13.778 million to go to the San José area. Clearly, IDB's goal of redistributing wealth away from the Meseta Central San José area has fallen short.[27]

Certainly an essential goal for Costa Rican economic development, both for industrial expansion and to improve the human condition, is to alleviate the trade deficit. The development rhetoric of OFIPLAN, the Central Bank, IDB, and the other international lending agencies has constantly recommended industrial development emphasizing exports to offset the growing trade deficit and ease the burden of domestic inflation and unemployment. This burden has increased through the 1970s and is projected to worsen in the 1980s.[28] The 1973 Costa Rican census clearly demonstrates that, in spite of the efforts of IDB and other international lending agencies, Costa Rica's trade deficit with CACM continues to drain resources, to the tune of $132,121,753 in 1973. The trade deficit with the United States, Costa Rica's major trading partner, expanded 14 times in 1969-73 from a surplus of $3,202,928 in 1969 to a deficit of $45,485,348 in 1973.[29] IDB and the other international development agencies have not been able to alleviate Costa Rica's ever-increasing trade deficit and may, in fact, be contributing to it by increasing Costa Rica's debt service and the need to import capital and other goods for industrialization. These last two factors have contributed a major portion of the trade and debt deficit, and will be discussed in Chapter 9.

One very large industrial project currently on the drawing boards is the exploitation of bauxite and the development of an aluminum industry in Costa Rica's central valley. The Inter-American Development Bank and other international lending agencies have already shown an interest in funding various aspects of this project, and IDB has funded a preinvestment study of bauxite use through OFIPLAN. The project, slated for some $300 million investment in

TABLE 6.9

Projected Balance of Payments
Including Aluminum Project 1975-90
(in millions of dollars)

| | 1975-80 | 1980 | 1981 | 1990 |
|---|---|---|---|---|
| Export of goods | 545 | 1,164 | 856 | 1,752 |
| Import of goods | -692 | -1,175 | -870 | -1,732 |
| Resource balance | -147 | -11 | -14 | -20 |
| Factor income net | -62 | -183 | -143 | -242 |
| Transfers net | 11 | 15 | 13 | -17 |
| Current account balance | -198 | -179 | -143 | -205 |
| Private capital, net | 109 | 71 | 64 | 40 |
| Medium and long-term loans to the public sector, net | 98 | 119 | 83 | 181 |
| Other capital, net | -2 | -2 | -2 | -2 |
| International reserves, net | -7 | -9 | -2 | -14 |

Source: International Bank for Reconstruction and Development, Economic Report of Costa Rica, vol. 1 (Washington, D.C.: Latin America and the Caribbean Regional Office), p. 91.

an agreement between the Costa Rican government and Alcoa, is hailed by many as essential to national development. The Bank's interest in the program is primarily that it will relieve the trade deficit and provide employment opportunities. In fact, however, current estimates by the World Bank indicate that even by 1990 the aluminum project will not solve the Costa Rican balance of payments problem, as illustrated in Table 6.9.

It is evident from Table 6.9 that, in spite of the aluminum development program, Costa Rica will be running a considerable trade deficit at least through 1990. In fact, the head of one development assistance agency in Costa Rica said in an interview that at least initially, because of the low grade of the Costa Rican bauxite which makes it nonprofitable to smelt at current world aluminum prices, bauxite will be imported to Costa Rica for smelting in the first few years of operation.[30] Costa Rican ore has only 31 percent bauxite content while world prices demand 61 percent content. Thus, on this future industrial development project, too, one must question the Bank's adherence to its own stated goals as well as those of the Central Bank and OFIPLAN. The aluminum project does not seem capable of resolving the Costa Rican trade deficit, nor will it initially use Costa Rican bauxite, two of the primary goals set down by IDB. Additionally, employment projections cited earlier in this chapter suggest that, due to the low labor intensity of mining and the mechanization of the bauxite smelting process, unemployment and underemployment will continue at a high rate.

## Economic Infrastructure

An area that has traditionally supported and complimented industrial development programs is that of transportation and communications, or economic infrastructure. Infrastructure investment in Costa Rica since 1961 has been $27.5 million in three transportation projects, accounting for 19.2 percent of the Bank's total assistance to Costa Rica. Prior to the funding of the Arenal energy project in 1975, transportation was IDB's largest investment sector, comprising 30.7 percent of all allocations.[31] The three transportation projects, sponsored in conjunction with the Costa Rican Ministry of Transportation and Public Works, were primarily for the construction of 442 kilometers of access or feeder roads, bridges, and other necessary equipment, and construction costs.[32] Costa Rica's need for secondary roads is without question. Anyone traveling off the Pan American Highway, the only road running the length of the country, is aware of the poor roads or lack of roads through the countryside.

In a recent survey, as shown in Table 6.10, many communities throughout the country applied a high priority to the development of transportation. However, almost equal importance was placed on water supply, electricity, and public health. There seems to be some merit in road construction and the opening up of the countryside. But the question of what type of development is to follow once the countryside becomes accessible is most important. In Guanacaste and Puntarenas provinces the countryside has been opened to livestock development which, as demonstrated earlier, has tended to marginalize the population. The merit of infrastructure development only becomes apparent when assessed in connection with the development projects, both public and private, that are to follow. In some cases, roads and other infrastructure projects are implemented with no relationship to any development strategy.

Another critical problem in discussing the merit of road construction is the question of the cost to the economy. Traditionally, many development agencies have invested heavily in infrastructure because it was an easy investment. Road development does not require a specific level of economic development, monetary stability, or even political stability. Roads do provide a ready avenue for international

TABLE 6.10

Community Concerns
(based on study of 453 communities)

| Problem | Percentage |
|---|---|
| Roads | 50 |
| Water supply | 50 |
| Electricity | 46 |
| Health services | 38 |
| Education | 31 |

Source: Instituto de Fomento y Asesoría Municipal and Acción Internacional, Tecnica Division de Acción Internacional, Estudio de Servicios Básicos en 30 Cantones, part 1: Resumen General (San José, Costa Rica, September 1974), p. 12.

development lending—and also a fairly good return for the investor. Not only is the investment easy, but road construction projects usually mean that much of the machinery and technical assistance for the project will be provided by an IDB member nation. Since few Central or South American nations manufacture highway construction equipment, this usually means the United States receives a percentage of the return of the IDB loan and, additionally, a percentage of the national government's financing for the project. This is one reason, as demonstrated in Chapter 3, that the United States does not have a balance of payment problem with its international lending programs through such multilateral lending institutions as the Inter-American Development Bank.

Another problem with road construction, since it is easy and requires little planning, is that countries like Costa Rica may be eager for the aid without planning for the increased burden to their debt service capacity. This remains a consideration, of course, for all development sectors.

## Energy

Development of energy resources is part and parcel of economic infrastructure. Since 1961 the Bank has contracted to invest some $57 million in electric energy in Costa Rica. With the exception of an early \$2.7 million grant in 1962 to the ICE (Instituto Costarricense de Electricidad) for expansion of the distribution system, and in 1970 a \$3.8 million grant to develop the electric distribution system in Guanacaste and Limón provinces, IDB's major investment in energy in Costa Rica has been the \$50.5 million Arenal hydroelectric project in 1975.

Until recently, IDB investments in energy in Costa Rica were relatively small. The Arenal project provided IDB with a major foothold in Costa Rica's energy development, thus diminishing, as noted by one Costa Rican official, the monopoly that the World Bank had in energy development.[33] The Arenal project, located near the Arenal Volcano between the Atlantic and Pacific watersheds, is being developed not just as a means for hydroelectric energy; additionally, the dam will provide irrigation to a section of the Tempisque Valley in Guanacaste Province.

This two-pronged approach brings a diversity of costs and benefits. While IDB's \$50.5 million investment promises to expand electric power resources, there are a number of costs that are not so readily apparent. As with all infrastructure projects, the IDB loan of \$50.5 million is only part of the total cost. Unlike projects of less technical sophistication, a hydroelectric project commands a high capital goods cost. According to Bank guidelines, capital goods must be purchased from a member nation. It is highly unlikely that any member nation with the exception of the United States will have the technical capacity to produce the capital goods needed. Hence, a large percentage of IDB's investment and the total cost is likely to return to the United States, tending to increase Costa Rican debt service as well as augmenting the trade deficit. This, of course, has been the criticism of most infrastructure projects, which do not produce an exportable item with which to improve the balance of trade.

The Arenal project also promises to provide irrigation to a drought-plagued area of Guanacaste. But this seeming benefit was undercut by numerous reports in San José newspapers in 1975, to the effect that the land in the watershed of the Arenal project is owned by only six families, including the family of the current president of the country, Daniel Oduber. Monsignor Roman Arrietas, the bishop of Tilaran, has declared that the Arenal irrigation will only serve the rich while little is being done to aid poor farmers or campesinos displaced by the project.[34] The conflict surrounding the Arenal project has incited tension between small farmers and campesinos and large landowners, forcing the government to reconsider its land reform position. A resolution to these problems does not seem likely in the near future.

It is sufficient to note, however, that energy and infrastructure projects in a macroeconomic analysis continue to erode the Costa

Rican balance of trade and to increase debt service. While energy development is certainly needed and electric power is welcome throughout the countryside, these benefits must be weighed in terms of Costa Rica's increased deficit due to Arenal and its impact on unemployment, underemployment, and general economic development. The statistics presented in this chapter suggest that, in spite of the Arenal project and other Bank projects, Costa Rica's deficit will continue to increase and unemployment will remain high throughout the 1980s.[35]

## Social Infrastructure

Social infrastructure accounts for 16 percent of the Bank's total investment in Costa Rica, at a total cost of $22.87 million from 1961 to 1974. IDB projects included two in sanitation, two in urban development, and three in education. IDB's investment in social infrastructure is relatively minor.

Sanitation projects have dealt largely with sewage and water supply at a cost to IDB of $6.3 million. Housing is a social infrastructure project that was particularly popular among IDB officials in the early 1960s. In Costa Rica IDB, working in conjunction with the housing institute, INVU (Instituto Nacional de Vivienda y Urbanismo sponsored two programs at a total cost of $7.1 million. The Bank's housing program has been phased out due to the difficulty of monitoring cost overruns.

Several programs of educational development also have been sponsored by the Bank. Initial programs such as those to the Universidad de Costa Rica helped to augment the quality of university facilities and equipment. More recently, the Bank sponsored a program to develop technical schools throughout the country to provide opportunities in vocational education. Social infrastructure's cost for education, therefore, runs about $9 million for the period 1961-75.[36] The cost of social infrastructure is thus a relatively small percentage of IDB's total assistance to Costa Rica. Health programs, although certainly an important part of assistance in a developing country, have been excluded from consideration.

One factor that has influenced the pattern of funding is that the Bank's preinvestment strategy has not been oriented to consider human needs in education, health, or sanitation. One disadvantage of social projects, which helps explain the lack of enthusiasm for them, is that they don't generate trade opportunities for foreign exporters. The Bank's largest and most recent preinvestment grant of $2.3 million in 1972 was to OFIPLAN, the national planning office. Of the 21 preinvestment studies currently under way, only two are not

TABLE 6.11

IDB Lending for Export Financing, 1961-74
(in dollars)

| Country | Loans | Amount |
|---|---|---|
| Argentina | 1 | 10,511,000 |
| Bolivia | 1 | 195,000 |
| Brazil | 4 | 60,808,000 |
| Mexico | 6 | 32,410,000 |
| Peru | 6 | 2,964,000 |
| Venezuela | 1 | 1,404,000 |

Source: IDB, Fifteen Years of Progress, 1960-1974 (Washington, D.C., 1975), p. 32.

productionist or economic infrastructure-oriented.[37] Through its direct linkages with OFIPLAN, the Bank is able to influence the direction of current and future development projects, thereby perhaps usurping some of the impetus for self-determination away from national development agencies such as OFIPLAN and the semi-autonomous government ministries.

Throughout our discussion of the Bank's development strategy, we have noted that IDB justifies economic infrastructure and productionist projects because in the long-run they will lessen the trade deficit. In many instances, as the statistics presented in this chapter have demonstrated, this IDB assertion is unfounded. IDB projects, in both the long and short run, encourage imports and further erode the national terms of trade and trade deficit position. Indeed, while IDB has a sector of funding for export financing for all of Latin America, it is interesting to note that since 1961 no funds have been available in this category to Costa Rica. Table 6.11 indicates IDB loans to the export financing sector throughout Latin America since 1961.

Costa Rica and most other Central American nations with weak economies and high trade deficits are not included in the Bank's program of export financing. With the exception of Bolivia, most IDB loans in export financing have gone to the more developed Latin American countries. The statistics show that IDB's development objectives are misconstrued when production-oriented projects are not part of a program of national exportation to offset the growing trade deficit and debt service, a part of which is the inherent cost of IDB programs.

The fact that much of IDB financing is tied directly or indirectly to procurement from donor (creditor) countries, particularly the United States with its near-monopoly of the capital goods market in Latin America, means that IDB aid is likely to worsen the terms of trade in projects with a high infrastructure or productionist component. The sheer monopoly of some donor nations in capital goods allows them to sell at uncompetitively higher prices, estimated at an increase as high as 20 to 25 percent. This also weakens the Costa Rican trade position.[38]

The repayment of loans or debt service weakened Costa Rica's terms of trade. One must therefore conclude that, given the above evidence, IDB development programs are contributing to Costa Rica's underdevelopment and economic stagnation, in at least the short run. The role of Costa Rica's state machinery in providing specific constraints on Bank development objectives is discussed in the following chapter.

## NOTES

1. The Tico Times (San José, Costa Rica), March 21, 1975, p. 16; Universidad (San José, Costa Rica), December 9, 1974, p. 13.

2. IDB, Economic and Social Progress in Latin America (Washington, D.C.: annual report, 1974), p. 44.

3. American Embassy, Annual Economic Report (San José, Costa Rica: January 17, 1975), pp. 2-7.

4. Economic and Social Progress in Latin America, pp. 251-52.

5. Annual Economic Report (American Embassy), p. 6.

6. Economic and Social Progress in Latin America, pp. 248-54.

7. United Nations Development Program, Costa Rica, La Situación Socio-Economíca Actual En Función del Plan Nacional de Desarrollo (San José, Costa Rica: February 1975), p. 15.

8. University of Costa Rica, Income Distribution Survey (San José, Costa Rica: 1971).

9. International Bank for Reconstruction and Development, Economic Report of Costa Rica, vol. 1 (Washington, D.C.: Latin America and Caribbean Regional Office, March 15, 1974), p. 12.

10. Ibid., pp. 22-24.

11. IDB, Costa Rica, Estrategía 1975-1977 (Washington, D.C.: Department of Economic and Social Development, October 25, 1974), p. 23.

12. IDB, "News Release—Inter-American Development Bank Lends 13.6 Million to Foster Development of Fisheries in Costa Rica" (Washington, D.C.: May 1, 1975), pp. 1-3.

13. IDB, "Loan Document, Costa Rica, Loan to Banco Nacional de Costa Rica, Livestock Development Program," PR 507 (Washington, D.C.: December 14, 1971), pp. 30-60.

14. Annual Economic Report (American Embassy), p. 5.

15. Instituto de Fomento y Asesoría Municipal, "Regional Overview of Acción Internacional Canton Reports and Studies," unpublished papers (San José, Costa Rica: 1975), p. 11.

16. Instituto Interamericano de Ciencias Agrícolas, "Algunos Aspectos de la Producción Agropecuaria de Costa Rica," unpublished (San José, Costa Rica: 1975), p. 7.

17. Regional Overview, p. 7.

18. Ibid., p. 4.

19. Ibid., pp. 16-20.

20. Ibid., pp. 23-40.

21. Fifteen Years of Activities, p. 17; see the list of loans, Table 6.6.

22. IDB, "Loan Document, Loan to the Banco de Costa Rica," Industrial Development Loan (Washington, D.C.: February 31, 1970), p. 30.

23. Ibid., p. 31.

24. IDB, Economic and Social Progress in Latin America (Washington, D.C.: December 1973), p. 177.

25. Ibid., p. 251.

26. Annual Economic Report (American Embassy), pp. 1-6.

27. "Industrial Development Loan," Appendix B, p. 3.

28. Economic Report of Costa Rica, vol. 1, p. 9.

29. Dirección General de Estadística y Censos, Ministerio de Economíca, Industria y Comercio, Comercio Exterior, Costa Rica, 1973 (San José, Costa Rica: 1975), pp. xviii-ix.

30. Interview, San José, Costa Rica, April 1975.

31. IDB, Fifteen Years of Activities, p. 44.

32. IDB, Costa Rica, Estrategía 1975-1977, pp. 2, 12, 19.

33. Interview, San José, Costa Rica, April 25, 1975.

34. Articles in San José newspapers such as Excelsior, April 9, 1975, p. 1; La Nación, March 31, 1975, p. 2A; and the Tico Times, April 11, 1975, p. 7, describe the impact of the Arenal project and Monsignor Arrietas's protest.

35. Economic Report of Costa Rica, vol. 1, pp. 9, 77.

36. IDB, "Detalle de los Préstamos Ortorgodos a Costa Rica" (San José, Costa Rica: 1975).

37. Oficina de Planificación Nacional y Política Economíca, Estudios Completados y Proyectos Resultantes (San José, Costa Rica: December 31, 1974), p. 1.

38. See Paul Streeten, The Frontiers of Development Studies (New York: John Wiley, 1972), pp. 181-83.

CHAPTER

# 7

# THE ROLE OF THE STATE IN COSTA RICAN DEVELOPMENT

The Costa Rican government is the central internal arbiter of the country's bid for industrialization and modernization. Knowledge of the government's role in directing domestic development is, therefore, paramount to an understanding of the impact of the Inter-American Development Bank in Costa Rican development. Historically, the part played by the Costa Rican government has been weak, with the interests of the cafetaleros (coffee barons) and foreign investors, such as the giant United Fruit Company on the Atlantic Coast, dictating the development goals of the country.

The modern period for Costa Rica begins in the 1940s with the period leading up to the Revolution of 1948. The politics of contemporary Costa Rica were defined and modern parties and leaders were born during this transitional period. During the period in the wake of the Great Depression a medical doctor, Rafael Calderón Guardia, an extremely popular leader, was elected to the presidency. Calderón Guardia and his followers, known as Calderonistas, acted progressively in reestablishing the defunct National University and with the assistance of the president's personal National Republican Party (PRN) put forth Costa Rica's first labor code. The alliance of Calderón Guardia with leftist elements in labor and the progressive legislation that his administration supported drew the line with the more moderate and conservative elements in Costa Rica and led to the Revolution of 1948, headed by José Figueres and his National Liberation Movement. The defeat of the Calderón Guardia government set the stage for the future dominance in Costa Rican politics of the Liberaciónistas. By 1951 Figueres had founded the Partido Liberación Nacional (Party of National Liberation), which remains Costa Rica's dominant party. The events surrounding the Revolution of 1948 set the stage for expanded state intervention in the modern Costa Rican society and economy.[1]

During the 1920s and 1930s the role of government remained minimal, its place in development largely limited to providing tax exemptions. The public sector depended primarily on import duties as its chief source of revenues, which were restricted by the slow growth of imports. With scarce revenues, government could provide only limited public employment opportunities for expanding the public sector. During the 1930s, under the strain of the Great Depression, public protests demanded state interventions to improve conditions, especially the high rate of unemployment. The government's response was circumscribed by the economic conditions of the time, and also by the tremendous political power of the coffee industry.[2]

During the 1930s economic conditions lessened the strength of foreign and coffee interests in Costa Rica and public outcry increased for improved economic and social conditions. In the period 1930-50, a Costa Rican Communist movement became vocal in organizing public opinion in the Meseta Central and among agricultural workers on the coasts. In 1934 the Communists were effective in organizing the banana workers to strike on the Atlantic Coast plantations. The traditional elite was particularly disturbed by these demands for reform, and in their anxiety to quench the public thirst for reform and diminish the influence of the Communists, Presidents Ricardo Jiménez Oreamuno (1932-36) and Léon Cortes Castro (1936-40) widened suffrage. Representation, however, was severely limited for such Communist parties as the Bloque de Obreros y Compesinos. In spite of this fact, under the competent and respected leadership of Manuel Mora, the Communists had obtained considerable strength by the 1930s and were eventually able to elect Mora to the Congress.

By 1940 popular outcry for reform was more widespread with the Centro para el Estudio de los Problemas Nacional (Centro), a segment of the National Republican Party, joining the Communists in the demand for economic and social reform. By 1940 Calderón Guardia, the candidate of the National Republican Party, assumed the presidency and faced the difficult task of appeasing popular demand and maintaining social equilibrium. Under severe criticism from the Communist groups, Calderón Guardia stressed social and economic improvement to win popular support. While the Calderón Guardia program provided a viable alternative to that of the Communists, it made him, to members of the elite, indistinguishable from the Communists. He established the Social Security system in 1941, the first in Central America; provided labor legislation to regulate working conditions, collective bargaining, and a minimum wage; established a labor ministry and labor courts; and formed an amendment to the Constitution making explicit certain social rights previously considered implicit. These reforms on the part of the new president were anathema to his class and the oligarchy or elite clearly pictured the Calderonistas in the same camp with the Communists. José Figueres Ferrer and his followers were able to capitalize upon the latent fear of the elite, which eventually resulted in the Revolution of 1948.

Calderón Guardia's acceptance of direct support from Manuel Mora's leftist Vanguardia Popular in 1943 paved the way for the president's downfall. During the period 1945-48, new international factors provided additional support to Figueres as the West and particularly the United States became acutely aware of communism and embroiled in the Cold War. Seizing upon the disputed outcome of the 1948 elections, José Figueres launched an armed rebellion to save Costa Rica from the Communist threat. This resulted in the formation of the Second Republic in May 1948.[3]

The Revolution of 1948 allowed for a radical departure from the role that the state had played in Costa Rica, although the conditions of the 1930-50 period and the administration of Calderón Guardia had paved the way for increased state intervention. The state was moved to center stage as the main provider of economic incentive for development. In the wake of Calderón Guardia's program of social reform in social security and labor legislation, Figueres increased the state's direct involvement in capitalist development. Perhaps the most significant increase in the economic sector was the expansion of the state's involvement in economic infrastructure. Figueres quickly nationalized the banks, taking the control of Costa Rica's financial institutions out of the hands of the traditional interests such as the coffee industry and foreign investors, and established the state as the central arbiter of domestic development priorities. Figueres also expanded the state's role in social welfare programs, an area in which Calderón Guardia had been accused of having Communist leanings, for expanding such programs in order to gain and maintain popular support.

The role of the government since the Revolution of 1948 has continued to grow in Costa Rica. Between 1950 and 1966 the government doubled the percentage of the national work force that it employs.[4] The rapid rate of public sector expansion continues, as is evident from the fact that public sector operations increased from 330.9 million colones in 1960 to 1,195.8 million colones in 1972.[5] The initial impact of the revolution was the expansion of the central government into the financial arena. Today public financial institutions include the Central Bank, all but two of the commercial banks (the private ones being foreign-owned), the National Insurance Institute, the National Housing and Urban Institute, the Community Development Bank, the Municipal Development Bank, the Land Colonization Institute (ITCO), the recently created Development Corporation (CODESA), and the Institute of Cooperatives established in 1973. All the above are state-owned.

Several other state institutions are also extremely important, as seen in the state's rapid growth since 1948. Certainly the Caja Costarricense de Seguro Social, the Social Security Agency, for which Calderón Guardia's legislation paved the way in 1943 (well before the revolution), has expanded its operations so that today it is Costa Rica's second largest public employer. The largest state enterprise is the Costa Rican Electricity Institute (ICE), which was established in 1949 and is headed by Alex Murray McNair, who was second in importance to José Figueres during the revolution. Other government-sponsored agencies are the Medical Assistance Institute (IAMS), 1950; Social Assistance Institute (IMAS), 1971; National Apprenticeship Institute (INA), 1968; Costa Rican Technological Institute (ITRC), 1971; Costa Rican Tourist Institute (ICT), 1955; Center for the Promotion of Investments and Exports (CEMPO), 1971; National Water and Sewage Service (SNAA), 1961; and the Atlantic Development and Port Authority (JAPDEVA), 1963.[6] These institutes plus the government ministries are evidence of the very sizable increase in the role of the state since the Revolution of 1948.

Several areas of state control are particularly important for our understanding of the impact of IDB on Costa Rica's development. The following areas comprise the state's development role: social welfare; development financing and the control of credit; tax incentives and development priorities; and planning and project elaboration.

Therefore, the role of the state as an instrument of development is important for our consideration of the Bank's impact on Costa Rica's development because the state is a prime vehicle or intermediary for national development. The Costa Rican state provides the primary access point for the linkage between external assistance and internal national development. Internally the state provides primary access for development through the following resources:

1. The state controls the financial apparatus of the society—the central banks, all domestic banks except two that are foreign-owned—and exercises total control of tax and credit policies.

2. The state embodies and represents the dominant class interests of the society and tends to represent and perpetuate those interests.

3. The state controls the primary vehicles of social demobilization and control through its extensive welfare programs and national police force (social demobilization by undercutting popular unrest through coercive police methods and the distributive benefits of the national welfare system).

4. The state has primary control of the planning instrument of the society through the National Planning Office (OFIPLAN) and the planning departments of the various government ministries.

5. The state is a major project elaborator and developer by providing public sector investment funds (a large percentage of which are externally financed), particularly in the area of economic infrastructure.

As a result of the Revolution of 1948 under José Figueres came the expansion of the state's role in the above areas as well as increased sophistication in expediting the state-defined functions. Although state control of the financial apparatus has been discussed briefly from a structural point of view (the nationalization of the banking system after 1948), the issue needs further elaboration.

## STATE CONTROL OF CREDIT AND TAXATION

A consideration of the state's control of banking, particularly credit and taxation after 1948, is important to understanding development. It is important to note that the government, through the Central Bank, has total control of the flow of credit, a vital factor determining the direction of development. On a trimester basis the Central Bank allocates the specific amount of credit to be provided by all banks in Costa Rica. This allows the state, through the Central Bank, to establish the direction of development financing. For instance, in March and December 1975 credit was allocated in the manner shown in Table 7.1.

The patterning of credit reflects not only the economic orientation of the nation but also to some degree mirrors its social structure. Costa Rica is still an agriculturally oriented export economy and most of the elite sector is composed of large landowners whose livelihood is in coffee, sugar, or another primary agricultural export product. It is within this sort of credit environment that the IDB operates. The Costa Rican credit economy, as we can see from Table 7.1, emphasizes agricultural production over all other sectors and provides less than half as much for industrial development. It is interesting to note that in the period from January 1961 to June 1974, only the Inter-American Development Bank contributed almost as much to industrial development and mining (17.5 percent) as to agricultural development (19.8 percent), while the two other major lending agencies, USAID and the World Bank, lent 52 percent and 8.2 percent, respectively, for agriculture and only 12.5 percent and 2.0 percent for industrial development and mining.[7] This pattern for funding on the part of

TABLE 7.1

Credit Allocated by the Central Bank
(millions of colones)

| Sectors | 1975 March | 1975 December |
|---|---|---|
| 1. Agriculture | 1327.4 | 1215.1 |
| Financing coffee harvest 1975-76 | 89.4 | 270.0 |
| Financing coffee harvest 1974-75 | 232.6 | 6.2 |
| Sugar | 150.0 | 13.3 |
| Cotton | | |
| Cacao | | |
| Rice | | |
| Tobacco | | |
| Plan for canal renovation | 10.0 | 40.0 |
| Basic grains | | |
| Others | | |
| Cattle | | |
| National Production Council | | |
| 2. Industrial | 702.7 | 733.6 |
| 3. Small agricultural production | 210.7 | 219.3 |
| Agriculture | | |
| Cattle | | |
| 4. Other activities | 197.8 | 197.8 |
| Interdepartmental loans | | |
| Tourism | | |
| Other | | |
| 5. Emergencies | 86.1 | 65.1 |
| 6. Financing section | 712.5 | 900.0 |
| 7. Capitalization of economy | 29.0 | 29.0 |
| 8. Securities investment | 216.3 | 216.3 |
| Subtotal | 3482.5 | 3576.2 |
| 9. Special lines: agriculture and cattle, industry, SBN/AID (small agriculture), importation of buses from Hungary, other | 427.0 | 700.0 |
| 10. National Production Council | | |
| Total | 3909.5 | 4276.2 |

Source: Letter from the Banco Central de Costa Rica, San José, February 6, 1975, outlining the limits of national credit from the first trimester 1975.

USAID and the World Bank in Costa Rica has tended to capitalize on the traditional pattern in the economy, which emphasizes agricultural over industrial interests. In the case of credit, therefore, the traditional political and social interests seem to be controlling the direction of development through the national banking system's limitations on credit, and this pattern is being adhered to and supported by the international lending agencies.

The role of the Costa Rican state in tax policy also has significant impact on national development plans. Taxation and forms of taxation such as the imposition of import duties can provide needed investment revenue for development. Costa Rica has a graduated income tax ranging from 5 to 40 percent; property taxes, sales and excise taxes, and tax revenues constitute about 14 percent of gross national product. One reason for the relatively low revenue from taxes is the high incidence of fraud and tax evasion.[8] Historically, import duties always have been the most important source of revenue, and at one time furnished as much as 60 percent of total tax income. This percentage has dropped dramatically, however, in direct proportion to the growth of duty-free imports from the Central American Common Market (CACM), which Costa Rica joined in 1963, and with the Industrial Development and Protection Law of 1959. The Industrial Development and Protection Law is a program of tax incentives for the development of the CACM and involves a number of tax concessions, primarily import duty, tax exemptions, and an income tax on profits of only 1 percent for the initial years of development. This law, along with the CACM agreements such as the Central American Agreement on the Equalization of Import Charges and the General Treaty on Central American Economic Integration in 1963, and the protocols to those documents, resulted in a significant loss of potential investment revenue and were the major contributing factors behind the balance of payment deficit that Costa Rica had accrued with Central American neighbors (see Table 7.2).[9]

The state incentives to foster economic integration through CACM, therefore, have had a devastating effect on Costa Rica's direction of trade, weakening the economy, contributing to domestic inflation, and thereby slowing economic development. It also should be pointed out that, as a result of the state's total industrial tax incentive program, revenues have been declining continuously since 1970.[10] With the continuing trade deficit, which was approximately $270 million in 1974, the government has had to increase domestic taxes and restrict credit in order to offset this deficit. Most Costa Ricans were adversely affected by the government's efforts to institute an "austerity program" with large tax increases in 1975. The consumption tax on durable goods hurt those individuals who could not postpone purchase of such items until the balance of payments crisis

TABLE 7.2

Costa Rican Trade Balance with CACM Countries, 1965-71
(in millions of U.S. dollars)

| | Trade Balance | | | | | | |
|---|---|---|---|---|---|---|---|
| Country | 1965 | 1966 | 1967 | 1968 | 1969 | 1970 | 1971 |
| Guatemala | -1.0 | -4.4 | -5.7 | -7.8 | -8.8 | -10.5 | -11.7 |
| El Salvador | -0.1 | -1.6 | -6.2 | -7.4 | -5.6 | -9.6 | -10.0 |
| Honduras | 1.6 | 2.4 | 1.2 | 0.9 | 2.0 | 4.5 | 3.2 |
| Nicaragua | 3.1 | 5.6 | 3.5 | 1.6 | -1.1 | -7.1 | -10.9 |
| Total | 3.6 | 2.0 | -7.3 | -12.6 | -13.5 | -22.6 | -29.4 |

Source: International Bank for Reconstruction and Development, Economic Report of Costa Rica, vol. 1 (Washington, D.C.: Latin America and Caribbean Regional Office, March 15, 1974), Table 3:9.

had improved (a possibility that does not seem likely in the near future). The general sales tax was increased from 5 to 8 percent and a 2 percent tax that will rise to 5 percent by 1978 was imposed on payrolls. In addition, the government has been forced to enact strict credit restrictions on imported luxury items in order to stem the sizable dollar outflow.[11]

State policy and control of the financial apparatus in Costa Rica thus has had a significant impact on the shape and direction of development. In areas of taxation and credit, state policies have fostered a particular pattern of development that emphasized traditional agricultural export interests and promoted industrialization within the parameter of economic infrastructure and the Central American Common Market. Both avenues of state-fostered development have serious economic limitations. Countries exporting primary agricultural products have long been held to be at a comparative disadvantage with their trading partners, while industrial development through economic integration, as Table 7.2 above aptly indicates, has placed an increasing economic burden upon Costa Rican society, particularly the working classes.

The role of the Costa Rican state has a central impact on development through its control of the financial apparatus. It is also a key access and control point for the traditional agricultural interests that want to continue an export-oriented economy and for the external groups, particularly multinational corporations, that want to take advantage of the increased market potential, tax incentives, and cheap labor to be found by fostering economic integration through CACM. The interests of these latter groups are served by international organizations such as IDB and the Central American Bank for Economic Integration (CABEI), which sponsor loans of direct financing for economic integration. The media of the Organization of American States (OAS), where dominant international actors such as the United States have lobbied for plans of economic integration with CACM and the Latin America Free Trade Association (LAFTA), also has been successful in shaping the development scheme of the Costa Rican state. The external impact of the imperial states, such as the United States, will be dealt with in Chapter 8. However, the access points that the state provides for the manipulation of national development by dominant class interests provide another framework for the discussion of the state and its relationship to IDB priorities and programs.

## THE LINKAGE BETWEEN CLASS INTERESTS AND THE STATE

In the recent book, La Dinastía de los Conquistadores, Samuel Stone, a prominent Costa Rican political scientist, outlines the limited nature of the Costa Rican elite. According to Stone's lengthy study, the majority in the Costa Rican ruling elite, or upper classes, have been related to one of Costa Rica's founding conquistadores, Juan Vásquez de Coronado. In total, 31 out of the 40 presidents and some 285 deputies have been descendants of Vásquez de Coronado.[12] According to Stone, power and wealth have always been concentrated in the hands of a few families. However, some new groups have been allowed to enter through a bargaining process to relieve social and political pressures.

Stone's work demonstrates a coherent class interest, beyond the mere desire to rule, and provides insight on the limited nature of elite circulation and mobility. The elite class is cohesive not only in regard to its heritage and ethnic background, which naturally influence its outlook and its willingness to accept new groups, but also, seemingly, in terms of its class social and economic interests. Stone provides evidence of the linkage between a cohesive class heritage and common economic as well as social goals in several case studies, the first of which is that of the role of the cafetaleros or coffee grower elite. A study of the coffee elite from 1820-80 concludes that approximately one-third of the families were descendants of Juan Vásquez de Coronado and another third were related to Antonio de Acosta Arévalo, a prominent founder of Costa Rica. Of the total group, approximately three-fourths of the cafetaleros occupied important political posts in Costa Rica. Stone has established a linkage between family background, economic interest, and a ruling and governing elite.[13] The cohesion of the cafetaleros as an economic class and their control of at least part of the state mechanism provided them with significant potential leverage for shaping Costa Rica's development. Carlos Joaquin Saenz in a recent study has commented on the impact of the coffee growers on Costa Rican development:

> Scarcity of labor coupled with state policies perhaps explain the failure to establish an industrial sector which could have provided economic opportunities when the coffee industry lagged. This and a financial structure directed toward coffee production as well as the lack of state interest in protecting and stimulating industrial activity effectively killed an effort to industrialize . . . . At the beginning of the twentieth century, then, the capitalist sector was no longer able to absorb the natural increases in population and a subsistence sector began to be recreated. The problem was not yet very serious, for coffee prices did rise again and the population, not too large, was located almost exclusively in the Meseta Central.
>
> The institutional framework developed around coffee production continued to serve interests of coffee growers, who were to become proportionally fewer in number. However, these institutions were unable to meet the needs of the rest of the population. Economic opportunities in the coffee industry grew scarce, and real wages continually deteriorated as money wages declined with the demand for labor. Meanwhile, the prices of basic foods increased as local production failed to provide for local needs.[14]

Saenz's account provides a succinct explanation of the effect of the cafetalero on Costa Rican development in the early part of the twentieth century.

The conjunction of development priorities under the cafetaleros, coupled with the economic conditions of the Great Depression, produced a watershed of social unrest, labor activity, and strikes in the 1920-40 period, which culminated in the Revolution of 1948.

Until the 1940s, coffee was king in Costa Rica and those who controlled coffee also controlled the economy and the state mechanism. Table 7.3 demonstrates the importance of coffee in Costa Rica's primary product exporting economy in the 1930s.

The cafetaleros, however, experienced a gradual erosion of their power as the Great Depression took its toll on the world price of coffee. From a high of $0.60 per kilo in 1927-28, the price of

TABLE 7.3

Importance of Coffee in Relation to
All Exports, 1930-39

| Year | Percentage |
|---|---|
| 1930 | 59 |
| 1931 | 66 |
| 1932 | 58 |
| 1933 | 70 |
| 1934 | 69 |
| 1935 | 65 |
| 1936 | 55 |
| 1937 | 53 |
| 1938 | 49 |
| 1939 | 51 |

Source: Samuel Stone, La Dinastía de los Conquistadores (San José, Costa Rica: Editorial Universitaria Centro Americana or EDUCA, 1975), p. 298.

coffee declined to a low point of $0.22 per kilo in 1939-40 and averaged about $0.30 per kilo during the 1930-40 period, or about one-half the pre-depression price.[15]

Costa Rica's singular dependence on coffee rapidly moved the economy from a boom to a bust position, with increasing unemployment. The position of the cafetaleros was further eroded as various leftwing groups were able to capitalize on popular unrest, undermining the normally secure positions of the cafetalero elite. It was onto such a stage that José Figueres Ferrer came in 1948, allowing new groups to enter the political arena and strengthening the role of the state. José Figueres, in the Revolution of 1948, in effect defused the potential threat of the left to the traditional cafetalero elite by coopting popular unrest through the expansion of social services, outlawing the Communist Party, disbanding the army, and consolidating the machinery of the state by nationalizing all domestic banks and creating a number of autonomous institutions such as ICE, the national electric company, and the national insurance company.

The Revolution of 1948 under Figueres was not, therefore, a true revolution in the sense that dramatic adjustment took place in the social and political structure. Rather, it served largely to protect the interests of the traditional elite group while incorporating some new and rising economic groups in agriculture and industry, thus allowing the state mechanism to be expanded so that it became the major instrument of social and political control and of capitalist development, as we shall see.

Once the state mechanism was expanded it tended to perpetuate itself by developing a class of middle-level bureaucrats who identified their interests with those of the state. In 1950, just two years after the revolution, public sector employment represented 6 percent of the active work force. By 1958 this sector expanded to 10 percent of the work force, providing sizable support for state policies.[16] Popular support for the state also increased through the expansion of social services under the Caja Costarricense de Seguro Social and the instruments of the aguinaldo, or Christmas bonus, provided by national legislation to a large percentage in both public and private sectors. The state, then, for many Costa Ricans, has become the ultimate benefactor or patrón, maintaining loyalty and providing the political stability so necessary for the economic development schemes advocated by the dominant agricultural elites in coffee, cattle, sugar cane, as well as foreign investors, particularly in bananas and other agricultural products on the Atlantic and Pacific coasts.

The state, therefore, through its expansion after 1948, was able to reassert the traditional economic interests and to coopt popular unrest. The data in Table 7.4 show that the traditional agricultural economic interests have been maintained, while the only dramatic shift in the value of the principal exports took place in manufactured goods after the formation of the Central American Common Market, which Costa Rica joined in 1963.

Traditional agricultural interests, in spite of the proclaimed Revolution of 1948, have maintained themselves although they have become more diversified as a result of the fluctuating price of coffee and the increased demand for other commodities, particularly sugar and cattle. The state's control of credit through the Central Bank, as outlined in Table 7.1 above, clearly demonstrates that domestic credit has been limited for industrialization, suggesting that the Revolution of 1948 did maintain the basic structure of the traditional society, with agricultural interests favored over industrial interests. The expansion of the traditional economic sector to include industry and manufacturing took place after the development of CACM, through a program of economic integration that was largely inspired by the external direction of the United States as a dominant member of the OAS, through the international lending instruments and IDB. The intricacies of the role of the Costa Rican state as a vehicle for the expansion of external capitalist investment will be discussed in the subsequent chapter. However, it is important to emphasize that the Costa Rican state, as it developed after the Revolution of 1948,

TABLE 7.4

Value of Principal Costa Rican Exports, 1962 and 1966-72

| | 1962 | 1966 | 1967 | 1968 | 1969 | 1970 | 1971 | 1972 |
|---|---|---|---|---|---|---|---|---|
| In millions of dollars | | | | | | | | |
| Total exports, f.o.b. | 92.7 | 135.7 | 143.3 | 170.0 | 189.6 | 231.0 | 224.6 | 278.3 |
| Agricultural goods | 88.2 | 102.2 | 110.5 | 127.2 | 143.8 | 173.5 | 162.9 | 209.8 |
| Coffee | 48.4 | 52.6 | 54.8 | 55.3 | 55.8 | 73.1 | 59.3 | 77.8 |
| Bananas | 26.9 | 29.2 | 30.9 | 42.8 | 51.5 | 66.8 | 64.0 | 85.3 |
| Beef | 2.7 | 5.5 | 8.6 | 12.0 | 15.1 | 18.0 | 20.5 | 27.9 |
| Sugar | 2.8 | 8.7 | 8.4 | 8.7 | 9.1 | 10.1 | 12.9 | 10.8 |
| Cacao | 4.9 | 3.1 | 3.1 | 3.0 | 7.1 | 1.9 | 1.5 | 3.0 |
| Other | 2.5 | 5.9 | 4.7 | 5.4 | 5.2 | 3.6 | 4.7 | 5.0 |
| Manufactured goods | 2.4 | 27.4 | 29.8 | 40.7 | 42.2 | 53.4 | 58.6 | 65.7 |
| Pharmaceutical goods | — | 0.9 | 1.4 | 1.3 | 1.9 | 4.4 | 5.6 | 6.4 |
| Fertilizers | — | 2.4 | 2.8 | 4.4 | 3.0 | 2.4 | 3.9 | 6.1 |
| Tires | — | 1.3 | 1.5 | 1.4 | 1.8 | 1.9 | 3.3 | 3.2 |
| Clothing, shoes, and synthetic textiles | — | 3.9 | 3.6 | 2.7 | 3.0 | 6.0 | 5.1 | 7.2 |
| Refrigerators and freezers | — | 0.3 | 0.4 | 1.2 | 1.3 | 1.8 | 2.2 | 2.8 |
| Margarines and fats | — | 0.4 | 0.7 | 1.8 | 1.1 | 1.5 | 1.4 | 2.1 |
| Plastic goods | — | 0.4 | 0.4 | 0.6 | 0.9 | 1.0 | 1.9 | 2.0 |
| Dry batteries | — | 0.2 | 0.8 | 1.4 | 1.3 | 1.7 | 1.9 | 2.0 |
| Metal containers | — | — | — | 0.9 | 1.8 | 1.6 | 1.7 | 1.8 |
| Processed woods | — | 1.6 | 1.0 | 1.2 | 1.5 | 1.2 | 1.4 | 1.7 |

| | | | | | | | | |
|---|---|---|---|---|---|---|---|---|
| Beverage concentrates | — | — | 0.5 | 1.3 | 1.8 | 2.3 | 2.0 | 1.6 |
| Insecticides and fungicides | — | 0.3 | 0.3 | 0.4 | 0.4 | 0.6 | 0.8 | 1.4 |
| Pulp and paper products | — | — | — | 0.1 | 0.3 | 1.1 | 1.1 | 1.3 |
| Transmitters and radio receivers | — | 0.6 | 1.0 | 1.1 | 1.0 | 1.4 | 1.4 | 1.2 |
| Furniture and accessories | — | 1.2 | 1.2 | 1.2 | 1.0 | 1.1 | 0.6 | 0.9 |
| Galvanized sheets | — | 1.3 | 1.5 | 1.9 | 1.6 | 1.5 | 1.8 | 1.8 |
| Other | — | 12.6 | 12.7 | 22.9 | 18.5 | 21.9 | 22.5 | 22.2 |
| Other exports | 2.1 | 7.9 | 3.0 | 2.1 | 3.6 | 4.1 | 3.1 | 2.8 |
| In percentages | | | | | | | | |
| Total exports, f.o.b. | 100.0 | 100.0 | 100.0 | 100.0 | 100.0 | 100.0 | 100.0 | 100.0 |
| Coffee | 52.2 | 38.8 | 38.2 | 32.5 | 29.4 | 31.6 | 26.4 | 28.0 |
| Bananas | 29.0 | 21.5 | 21.6 | 25.2 | 27.2 | 28.9 | 28.5 | 30.7 |
| Beef | 2.9 | 4.1 | 6.0 | 7.1 | 8.0 | 7.8 | 9.1 | 10.0 |
| Sugar | 3.0 | 6.4 | 5.9 | 5.1 | 4.8 | 4.4 | 5.7 | 3.9 |
| Manufactured goods | 2.6 | 20.2 | 20.8 | 23.9 | 22.3 | 23.1 | 26.1 | 23.6 |
| Pharmaceuticals | — | 0.7 | 1.0 | 0.8 | 1.0 | 1.9 | 2.5 | 2.2 |
| Fertilizers | — | 1.8 | 2.0 | 2.6 | 1.6 | 1.0 | 1.7 | 2.2 |
| Clothing, shoes, and synthetic textiles | — | 2.9 | 2.5 | 1.6 | 1.6 | 2.6 | 2.3 | 2.6 |
| Tires | — | 1.0 | 1.0 | 0.8 | 0.9 | 0.8 | 1.5 | 1.1 |
| Refrigerators and freezers | — | 0.2 | 0.3 | 0.7 | 0.7 | 0.8 | 1.0 | 1.0 |

Source: International Bank for Reconstruction and Development, Economic Report of Costa Rica, vol. 1 (Washington, D.C.: Latin America and Caribbean Regional Office, March 15, 1974), Table 3:4.

continued to serve the dominant class interests and, in fact, the revolution seems to have strengthened their position and their hold over social and economic policy.

## LABOR AND THE STATE

An aspect of the revolution that defused social unrest was the stifling of the Costa Rican labor movement. The state, as it was reorganized after the revolution, played a dominant role in demobilizing any major efforts at syndicalism. As mentioned earlier, labor reforms under Calderón Guardia were a threat to the traditional ruling classes and provided one impetus for the revolution. The 1930-40 period was the height of the Costa Rican labor movement. Today the labor movement in Costa Rica is relatively small, its top leadership in 1949 being siphoned off by the dominant government party, Liberación Nacional.[17] The outlawing of the Communist Party, Vanguardia Popular, and the increase in social benefits after the revolution also contributed to the undercutting of the labor movement. The 1973 census indicated that with a total population of 1,889,109, of which 607,000 or 32.1 percent constituted the economically active work force, only 57,748 or 9.5 percent belong to unions. The current number of unions is 258, a figure subject to wide fluctuations demonstrating the weak and ephemeral nature of the labor movement in Costa Rica.[18] For example, between 1965 and the end of 1966 the number of unions fell from 360 to 216.

Union activity is also low because collective bargaining agreements between unions and management are unusual. For instance, one of the largest and oldest unions, the National Railroad Union (Union Ferrovaria Nacional) negotiated its first collective bargaining contract at the end of 1968 with the Pacific Electric Railroad (Ferrovarial Electrico al Pacífico). In fact, during the whole of 1967, only one collective bargaining contract was negotiated.[19] Another indication of the weakness of Costa Rica's labor movement is the specialization with which labor organizing has taken place. Generally the pattern is that for each 10 persons employed, only one belongs to a union. However, these figures become even more meaningful when one considers the areas of unionization. For white-collar workers, two out of five are unionized, while for transportation workers the figure is one out of three, and for professional and technical workers one out of six. These three categories of workers comprise the largest percentage of government employees and also the groups with the highest percentage of unionization. On the other hand, unionization is singularly low among industrial workers (one out of 20), while among small agricultural producers one out of 50 workers is unionized.

TABLE 7.5

Wage Comparison of Costa Rican Work Force for Key Sectors
(1973 census)

| | Working Population | | | Urban | | | Rural | | |
|---|---|---|---|---|---|---|---|---|---|
| | Total | Men | Women | Total | Men | Women | Total | Men | Women |
| Costa Rica | | | | | | | | | |
| Total | 410,076 | 309,354 | 100,722 | 200,937 | 129,122 | 71,815 | 209,139 | 180,232 | 28,907 |
| less than 100 colones | 7,549 | 2,714 | 4,835 | 2,988 | 758 | 2,230 | 4,561 | 1,956 | 2,605 |
| 100– 399 | 164,810 | 118,453 | 46,357 | 53,615 | 22,683 | 30,932 | 111,195 | 95,770 | 15,425 |
| 400– 699 | 116,718 | 96,895 | 19,823 | 58,500 | 44,194 | 14,306 | 58,218 | 52,701 | 5,517 |
| 700– 999 | 52,425 | 42,446 | 9,979 | 32,871 | 24,744 | 8,127 | 19,554 | 17,702 | 1,852 |
| 1,000–1,299 | 28,695 | 19,436 | 9,259 | 20,559 | 12,977 | 7,582 | 8,136 | 6,459 | 1,677 |
| 1,300–1,599 | 12,472 | 7,426 | 5,046 | 9,350 | 5,412 | 3,938 | 3,122 | 2,014 | 1,108 |
| 1,600–1,899 | 6,778 | 4,731 | 2,047 | 5,152 | 3,494 | 1,658 | 1,626 | 1,237 | 389 |
| 1,900–2,199 | 5,819 | 4,355 | 1,464 | 4,867 | 3,583 | 1,284 | 952 | 772 | 180 |
| 2,200–2,499 | 1,902 | 1,353 | 549 | 1,676 | 1,157 | 519 | 226 | 196 | 30 |
| 2,500–2,799 | 2,207 | 1,768 | 439 | 1,923 | 1,518 | 405 | 284 | 250 | 34 |
| 2,800 or more | 10,701 | 9,777 | 924 | 9,436 | 8,602 | 834 | 1,265 | 1,175 | 90 |
| Professional and technical workers | | | | | | | | | |
| Total | 43,121 | 22,027 | 21,094 | 33,953 | 17,023 | 16,930 | 9,168 | 5,004 | 4,164 |
| less than 100 colones | 40 | 29 | 11 | 30 | 24 | 6 | 10 | 5 | 5 |
| 100– 399 | 626 | 363 | 263 | 477 | 259 | 218 | 149 | 104 | 45 |
| 400– 699 | 2,467 | 1,365 | 1,102 | 1,845 | 946 | 899 | 622 | 419 | 203 |
| 700– 999 | 6,455 | 2,193 | 4,262 | 4,955 | 1,586 | 3,369 | 1,500 | 607 | 893 |
| 1,000–1,299 | 9,973 | 3,452 | 6,521 | 7,490 | 2,335 | 5,155 | 2,483 | 1,117 | 1,366 |
| 1,300–1,599 | 1,149 | 2,814 | 4,335 | 5,260 | 1,944 | 3,316 | 1,889 | 870 | 1,019 |
| 1,600–1,899 | 4,028 | 2,279 | 1,749 | 2,980 | 1,590 | 1,390 | 1,048 | 689 | 359 |
| 1,900–2,199 | 3,175 | 1,939 | 1,236 | 2,632 | 1,552 | 1,080 | 543 | 387 | 156 |
| 2,200–2,499 | 1,319 | 811 | 508 | 1,173 | 695 | 478 | 146 | 116 | 30 |
| 2,500–2,799 | 1,282 | 913 | 369 | 1,142 | 800 | 342 | 140 | 113 | 27 |
| 2,800 or more | 6,607 | 5,869 | 738 | 5,969 | 5,292 | 677 | 638 | 577 | 61 |

(continued)

(Table 7.5 continued)

| | Working Population | | | Urban | | | Rural | | |
|---|---|---|---|---|---|---|---|---|---|
| | Total | Men | Women | Total | Men | Women | Total | Men | Women |
| Managers and administrators | | | | | | | | | |
| Total | 6,352 | 5,739 | 613 | 5,180 | 4,644 | 536 | 1,172 | 1,095 | 77 |
| less than 100 colones | 1 | 1 | — | 1 | 1 | — | — | — | — |
| 100– 399 | 134 | 82 | 52 | 66 | 26 | 40 | 68 | 56 | 12 |
| 400– 699 | 570 | 437 | 133 | 334 | 229 | 105 | 236 | 208 | 28 |
| 700– 999 | 621 | 544 | 77 | 464 | 392 | 72 | 157 | 152 | 5 |
| 1,000–1,299 | 924 | 816 | 108 | 734 | 637 | 97 | 190 | 179 | 11 |
| 1,300–1,599 | 500 | 452 | 48 | 416 | 371 | 45 | 84 | 81 | 3 |
| 1,600–1,899 | 347 | 313 | 34 | 272 | 243 | 29 | 75 | 70 | 5 |
| 1,900–2,199 | 566 | 525 | 41 | 493 | 456 | 37 | 73 | 69 | 4 |
| 2,200–2,499 | 144 | 138 | 6 | 120 | 114 | 6 | 24 | 24 | — |
| 2,500–2,799 | 307 | 288 | 19 | 265 | 249 | 16 | 42 | 39 | 3 |
| 2,800 or more | 2,238 | 2,143 | 95 | 2,015 | 1,926 | 89 | 223 | 217 | 6 |
| Agricultural workers | | | | | | | | | |
| Total | 117,225 | 114,600 | 2,625 | 8,073 | 7,827 | 246 | 109,152 | 106,773 | 2,379 |
| less than 100 colones | 1,726 | 1,596 | 130 | 139 | 130 | 9 | 1,587 | 1,466 | 121 |
| 100– 399 | 87,081 | 84,931 | 2,150 | 5,337 | 5,144 | 193 | 81,744 | 79,787 | 1,957 |
| 400– 699 | 20,635 | 20,352 | 283 | 1,811 | 1,780 | 31 | 18,824 | 18,572 | 252 |
| 700– 999 | 4,929 | 4,889 | 40 | 326 | 324 | 2 | 4,603 | 4,565 | 38 |
| 1,000–1,299 | 1,745 | 1,738 | 7 | 196 | 194 | 2 | 1,549 | 1,544 | 5 |
| 1,300–1,599 | 413 | 403 | 10 | 78 | 72 | 6 | 335 | 331 | 4 |
| 1,600–1,899 | 188 | 187 | 1 | 43 | 43 | — | 145 | 144 | 1 |
| 1,900–2,199 | 126 | 124 | 2 | 45 | 44 | 1 | 81 | 80 | 1 |
| 2,200–2,499 | 37 | 37 | — | 12 | 12 | — | 25 | 25 | — |
| 2,500–2,799 | 54 | 54 | — | 10 | 10 | — | 44 | 44 | — |
| 2,800 or more | 291 | 289 | 2 | 76 | 74 | 2 | 215 | 215 | — |

| | | | | | | | | | |
|---|---|---|---|---|---|---|---|---|---|
| Transportation workers | | | | | | | | | |
| Total | 13,791 | 13,791 | — | 8,420 | 8,420 | — | 5,371 | 5,371 | — |
| Less than 100 colones | 26 | 26 | — | 11 | 11 | — | 15 | 15 | — |
| 100- 399 | 1,277 | 1,277 | — | 578 | 578 | — | 699 | 699 | — |
| 400- 699 | 5,744 | 5,744 | — | 3,189 | 3,189 | — | 2,555 | 2,555 | — |
| 700- 999 | 4,473 | 4,473 | — | 2,974 | 2,974 | — | 1,499 | 1,499 | — |
| 1,000-1,299 | 1,670 | 1,670 | — | 1,171 | 1,171 | — | 499 | 499 | — |
| 1,300-1,599 | 426 | 426 | — | 337 | 337 | — | 89 | 89 | — |
| 1,600-1,899 | 100 | 100 | — | 89 | 89 | — | 11 | 11 | — |
| 1,900-2,199 | 29 | 29 | — | 26 | 26 | — | 3 | 3 | — |
| 2,200-2,499 | 5 | 5 | — | 5 | 5 | — | — | — | — |
| 2,500-2,799 | 5 | 5 | — | 5 | 5 | — | — | — | — |
| 2,800 or more | 36 | 36 | — | 35 | 35 | — | 1 | 1 | — |
| Blue-collar workers and day laborers | | | | | | | | | |
| Total | 30,688 | 28,097 | 2,591 | 14,884 | 13,672 | 1,212 | 15,804 | 14,425 | 1,379 |
| less than 100 colones | 197 | 182 | 15 | 114 | 106 | 8 | 83 | 76 | 7 |
| 100- 399 | 8,760 | 7,390 | 1,370 | 4,334 | 3,577 | 757 | 4,426 | 3,813 | 613 |
| 400- 699 | 17,285 | 16,242 | 1,043 | 7,979 | 7,567 | 412 | 9,306 | 8,675 | 631 |
| 700- 999 | 3,564 | 3,439 | 125 | 1,819 | 1,799 | 20 | 1,745 | 1,640 | 105 |
| 1,000-1,299 | 646 | 613 | 33 | 456 | 444 | 12 | 190 | 169 | 21 |
| 1,300-1,599 | 128 | 123 | 5 | 100 | 97 | 3 | 28 | 26 | 2 |
| 1,600-1,899 | 61 | 61 | — | 46 | 46 | — | 15 | 15 | — |
| 1,900-2,199 | 30 | 30 | — | 27 | 27 | — | 3 | 3 | — |
| 2,500-2,799 | 2 | 2 | — | — | — | — | 2 | 2 | — |
| 2,800 or more | 15 | 15 | — | 9 | 9 | — | 6 | 6 | — |

Source: Republic of Costa Rica, Censos Nacionales de 1973, vol. 2: Población (San José, Costa Rica, April 1975), pp. 342-43.

The overall pattern of the Costa Rican labor movement is away from blue-collar workers incorporating effectively with white-collar workers. It is the white-collar workers who comprise a small middle economic sector of the Costa Rican social structure, a large percentage of them government bureaucrats and employees who are considered "safe" for unionization because they are unlikely to be radicalized. Unionized blue-collar workers in agriculture and industry comprise only 26.2 percent of the total union population. Within this blue-collar sector certain groups seem to be in a particularly unfavorable position. For instance, small agricultural producers comprise only 2 percent of the total unionized population, and workers in industry and construction number only 8.5 percent of the union members among their ranks.

The obvious conclusion is that the labor movement in Costa Rica is fundamentally of the middle class.[20] The middle classes, as the most unionized, receive the greatest benefits of the labor movement and, in turn, are ardent supporters of the state. For the traditional elite classes, the labor movement's appeal to the middle classes has several advantages. First, it broadens support for the state, the most effective apparatus for the maintenance of elite hegemony. Second, the failure to unionize agricultural and industrial workers on a large scale keeps wages low, protecting the elite's economic position. The low wages among industrial workers also attract foreign investors, particularly after the expansion of the national market through economic integration and CACM. Thus, the state since 1948 has been an effective instrument for protecting the elite's class interests, but it also has effected income distribution in favor of the middle class.

Table 7.5 clearly demonstrates the decided salary advantage of middle-class white-collar workers and the more unionized categories such as transportation workers have over the largely nonunionized agricultural, blue-collar, and service workers.

## GOVERNMENT, POLITICAL PARTIES, AND INTEREST GROUPS IN DEVELOPMENT

In discussing the role of the state in Costa Rican development, we have attempted to disaggregate the state mechanism into components. One component often held to be synonymous with the state is that of government, political parties, and interest groups. Government policy, the influence of political parties, and interest groups provide constraints for a particular development environment for the Inter-American Development Bank in Costa Rica. Government as an aspect of the role of the Costa Rican state mechanism, vis-a-vis IDB, can be examined in the following areas: planning, public policy, project elaboration, and public investment. In a collateral role one finds interest groups and political parties either supporting or opposing the government in the above endeavors.

An analysis of the planning vehicles indicates links between the Inter-American Development Bank's planning process with that of the Costa Rican government. While not all planning between the government and IDB seems to overlap, certain areas of common ground are discernible. The planning function for Costa Rica is established by statute. OFIPLAN, the planning office, was encouraged by a U.S. mission in 1960 and is headed by a cabinet-level minister. OFIPLAN is charged with the coordination of government planning. In fact, however, the planning function is informally diffused, with each ministry conducting its own planning and often submitting its project requests directly to the Office of the Vice President of the Republic. OFIPLAN, however, has compiled a national development plan for 1974-78 along with considerable statistical information, which has an influence on the direction of development. Several members of the IDB staff in fact stated that the national development plan is IDB's planning model. Further investigation reveals that in truth IDB's impact on OFIPLAN may be greater than vice versa. For instance, OFIPLAN's Department of Project Promotions received in 1972 a $2.3 million grant from IDB to plan development projects. This grant has been used by OFIPLAN on a subcontract basis with the various ministries for project development. While the nature of the projects proposed was largely productionist, the important points to note are the Bank's access and direct linkage into OFIPLAN and other government ministries. This provides IDB, at least to some extent, with a two-edged sword, allowing influence in the planning process as well as a voice in the final approval of projects.[21]

Another access point for IDB is through the various IDB missions. Missions provide another planning linkage between the Bank and the government, by assisting various government agencies in project development. The direct assistance to OFIPLAN and the role of the missions, especially the technical mission from IDB's Washington office, provides IDB with direct access to the governmental planning apparatus. However, the more significant impact of IDB is less visible.

IDB's sister agencies, the other international lending agencies, also use lobbying techniques in Costa Rica and employ a similar influence on development strategy. These sister agencies provide clout for IDB's planning suggestions and in some cases have a greater impact, through their large permanent missions, on the planning process. (An elaboration of the impact of external forces on Costa Rica's development is taken up in the following chapter.) Nevertheless, the Costa

Rican government, interest groups, and political parties provide the national environment that to a large degree determines receptiveness for external development.

Political parties and interest groups in Costa Rica, while presenting many different labels, in reality represent groups with a similar outlook. Political parties, as an outgrowth of the social system, largely represent the interests of the traditional agricultural elite groups. The Party of National Liberation (PLN) emerged from the Revolution of 1948 as Costa Rica's dominant political party. Since that time, governing Costa Rica has been an exchange between PLN forces or a coalition of anti-PLN forces, which represent similar interests. Political life definitely centers around PLN, which has a fairly well developed party machine and has been quite successful at getting out the vote. Table 7.6 below illustrates this tradeoff pattern.

In recent elections the PLN has been victorious in electing José Figueres for a third time in 1970 and Daniel Oduber as president

TABLE 7.6

Costa Rican Voting Behavior, 1953-66

| | Presidential Vote | Legislative Vote |
|---|---|---|
| 1953 | | |
| PLN | 123,444 | 114,043 |
| Anti-PLN | 67,324 | 49,391 |
| Total | 190,768 | 163,434 |
| 1958 | | |
| PLN | 97,788 | 86,081 |
| Anti-PLN | 126,761 | 110,610 |
| Total | 224,549 | 196,691 |
| 1962 | | |
| PLN | 192,850 | 184,138 |
| Anti-PLN | 187,273 | 185,526 |
| Total | 380,123 | 369,664 |
| 1966 | | |
| PLN | 218,590 | 202,891 |
| Anti-PLN | 222,810 | 178,905 |
| Total | 441,400 | 381,796 |

*Source*: Charles F. Denton, *Patterns of Costa Rican Politics* (Boston: Allyn and Bacon, 1971), p. 71.

in May 1974. Table 7.7 gives an analysis of the 1974 presidential election by province.

As is evident from Table 7.7, the PLN in 1974 won three times as many votes as any other party and is only to be outdone by the formation of an opposition coalition. However, any coalition to be formed is of the right or center, representing interests similar to those of the Partido Liberación Nacional. Parties of the left such as the Socialist Action Party or Partido Acción Socialista (PAS), seldom can have any real impact without widespread unionization and the development of a national labor movement. Political parties reflect the elite social structure and provide another mechanism for the maintenance of class interests, as well as a mass vehicle for diffusing popular demand through the national party organization, especially PLN. The PLN party machine, through its leftist rhetoric, helps to diffuse opposition by simply addressing pressing social issues such as land reform without concrete action to gain public support. Using reformist legislative or administrative agencies like ITCO, the Agrarian Reform Agency, that will not solve the problem but will address the issue, PLN has been able to gain popular support. Political parties, then, have supported the state machinery and stabilized the national environment for elite-oriented development.

Pressure groups have served a similar function. With the exception of the National Association of Education (ANDE) and its 13,000 members from the public education system, most pressure groups represent traditional economic interests and not interests that would have widespread public impact.[22] The political party system has determined, to some extent, that income will be distributed in favor of the upper classes. Pressure groups also help to determine who will get what. Interest groups, such as the Chamber of Coffee Growers, Chamber of Sugar Growers, Chamber of Transportation, Chamber of Guanacaste Cattlemen, and the Asociación Nacional de Fomento Económico (the Association of National Economic Development) pressure the government for limited economic resources.

The inability of the PLN to adopt some of the basic reforms advocated by the leftist branch of its party in the Patio de Agua document in 1968, such as agrarian reform, public housing, and the nationalization of certain industries, demonstrated again the empty nature of PLN rhetoric.[23] It is in this sort of economic development ideology that the Bank finds itself in Costa Rica. The nature of government domestic development policy, however, is to be found in what the government does rather than what it advocates.

TABLE 7.7

Votes for President and Vice President, 1974 Election, by Province

| Provincia | PD | PRD | PAS | PLN |
|---|---|---|---|---|
| San José | 10,633 | 34,127 | 5,487 | 119,222 |
| Alajuela | 2,014 | 11,657 | 1,352 | 54,385 |
| Cartago | 2,027 | 4,380 | 1,114 | 32,652 |
| Heredia | 1,561 | 4,880 | 1,285 | 22,055 |
| Guanacaste | 450 | 2,877 | 1,168 | 29,390 |
| Puntarenas | 1,394 | 2,822 | 3,443 | 24,737 |
| Limón | 753 | 1,077 | 2,232 | 12,168 |
| Total | 18,832 | 61,820 | 16,081 | 294,609 |

Key: Partido Demócrata (PD)
Partido Renovación Democrática (PRD)
Partido Acción Socialista (PAS)
Partido Liberación Nacional (PLN)

## PUBLIC INVESTMENT

Public investment in Costa Rica provides a clear picture of national development priorities. As shown above, the state plays an overwhelming role in Costa Rica's development and is linked with elite interests. Public investment by the central government provides a glimpse of national development priorities, which seem strikingly similar to those of the IDB and other international development agencie operating in Costa Rica. The central government's public investment program places a heavy emphasis on infrastructure, as do the international lending agencies, which should not be surprising since many of the projects are cosponsored and cofinanced. Table 7.8 provides an overview of the structure of public investment in Costa Rica in 1965-72.

Table 7.8 illustrates the high percentage of investment in infrastructure. Health seems the only aberration from this pattern. However, a closer examination of public health investment reveals that in 1965-70 a large percentage of that cost was committed to water and sewage, an infrastructure component. An estimation of public sector

| PSC | PNI | PUN | PDC | Total Votes |
|---|---|---|---|---|
| 1,467 | 25,122 | 82,132 | 1,264 | 285,558 |
| 596 | 14,953 | 33,847 | 418 | 122,917 |
| 352 | 11,873 | 21,965 | 468 | 77,446 |
| 202 | 5,671 | 15,334 | 371 | 52,561 |
| 322 | 6,826 | 17,777 | 463 | 62,596 |
| 302 | 6,913 | 22,726 | 323 | 65,414 |
| 176 | 2,430 | 12,368 | 154 | 32,848 |
| 3,417 | 73,788 | 206,149 | 3,461 | 699,340 |

Partido Socialista Costarricense (PSC)
Partido Nacional Independiente (PNI)
Partido Unificación Nacional (PUN)
Partido Democráta Cristiano (PDC)

Source: The 1974 presidential material was obtained from the Tribunal Supremo de Elecciónes, San José, Costa Rica, June 1975.

spending by the national planning office reveals the pattern set forth in Table 7.9 for 1975.

The pattern of public investment emphasizes infrastructure or projects of low social impact. In 1966-72 public sector investment almost doubled, from 4.0 percent to 7.6 percent of gross domestic product, and it was projected to continue at a rate in excess of 7 percent through the 1970s.[24] The doubling of public sector investment affords the government considerable leverage, the dominant domestic leverage, in shaping national development priorities and projects. When one considers that total public sector investment is 7 percent of total gross domestic product, the impact on the direction of development is critical.

Not only does public sector investment represent a major area of influence in strategies for development on the part of the government and, therefore, the Costa Rican state mechanism, but it also provides another critical access point for the joining of internal and external development strategies. In 1974 some 94 public sector projects totaled $955 million. Of these projects, 28 were sponsored in part by the Central American Bank of Economic Integration (CABEI),

TABLE 7.8

Structure of Public Direct Investment, 1965-72
(in percentages)

| | 1965-66 | 1967-68 | 1969-70 | 1971-72 |
|---|---|---|---|---|
| Transportation | 19 | 29 | 34 | 32 |
| Power | 28 | 12 | 16 | 21 |
| Telecommunication | 14 | 10 | 3 | 7 |
| Education | 5 | 6 | 7 | 5 |
| Health | 18 | 12 | 23 | 6 |
| Water and sewage | * | * | * | 5 |
| Housing | 6 | 10 | 6 | 6 |
| Municipalities | 4 | 5 | 5 | 5 |
| Other | 6 | 16 | 6 | 3 |

*Included in Health.

Source: International Bank for Reconstruction and Development, Economic Report of Costa Rica, vol. 1 (Washington, D.C.: Latin American and Caribbean Regional Office, March 15, 1974), p. 33.

TABLE 7.9

Public Sector Investment, 1975
(millions of colones)

| | Colones | Percent |
|---|---|---|
| Basic infrastructure | 1,025,145 | 56.0 |
| Infrastructure and social services | 466,113 | 25.5 |
| Public administration | | 6.5 |
| Production | 103,100 | 5.6 |
| Agrarian reform and colonization | 80,082 | 4.4 |
| Protective services | 29,160 | 1.6 |
| Multiple development | 6,696 | 0.4 |

Source: OFIPLAN, Invesiones Publicas, Plan Operativo, 1975 (San José, Costa Rica, 1975), p. 17.

11 were cosponsored by IDB, and two were sponsored by the World Bank. The remainder were cosponsored by USAID or other, primarily U.S., public or private lenders to a local Costa Rican government unit (see Appendix). The points of linkage between internal functions of development and their external counterparts are obvious. The nature of the Costa Rican state has tended to facilitate the strength of that bond.

As was noted, the state's influence and size has multiplied since the Revolution of 1948. The state has become the prime instrument for determining the direction of development, through its control of the national financial apparatus (banking, taxes, and credit), through its connection with political parties and government, as well as through its influence in national planning and public investment. With little or no opposition from labor unions, interest groups, or opposition political parties, and lacking a military organization, the Costa Rican state/system implements the development choice of its dominant social classes. Samuel Stone in La Dinastía de los Conquistadores has pointed out aptly that the dominant class interests remained largely the same in Costa Rica, before and after the Revolution of 1948. These interests favor an agricultural elite whose concern has been to export agricultural products. Stone has clearly demonstrated that the elite also is well represented in the mechanism of the state, thus maintaining its development interests.

Until recently the traditional agricultural elite was not concerned with industrial development. However, particularly since the 1960s with the development of CACM the elite has been receptive to schemes of industrial development financed by private foreign investors and international lending agencies, particularly those sponsored by the United States. It was into this national development environment that the Bank stepped in the early 1960s. The state, because of its cohesive class nature and its domination of the development arena, provided an easy and logical access point for IDB investment proposals, as well as those of other public and private international investment agencies. The following chapter illustrates the impact of the external factors of development on Costa Rica.

## NOTES

1. Charles F. Denton, Patterns of Costa Rican Politics (Boston: Allyn and Bacon, 1971), pp. 29-38.

2. Carlos Joaquin Saenz, Population Growth, Economic Progress, and Opportunities on the Land: The Case of Costa Rica (Madison, Wisconsin: Land Tenure Center, University of Wisconsin-Madison, June 1972), pp. 31-33.

3. John Patrick Bell, Crisis in Costa Rica: The 1948 Revolution (Austin: University of Texas Press, 1971), pp. 131-54.

4. Denton, Patterns of Costa Rican Politics, p. 18.

5. International Bank for Reconstruction and Development, Economic Report of Costa Rica, vol. 2 (March 15, 1974), p. 1.

6. Ibid., p. 4.

7. IDB, office files, San José, Costa Rica, lending data on IDB, World Bank, and USAID for the period January 1961-June 1974.

8. Howard I Blutstein, et al., Area Handbook for Costa Rica (Washington, D.C.: Government Printing Office, October 1970), p. 188.

9. Costa Rican Ministry of Economics, Industry, and Commerce Convenio Centroamericano de Incentivos Fiscales al Desarrollo Industrial, San José, Costa Rica, 31 de julio de 1962, y Protocolo al Convenio Centroamericano de Incentivos Fiscales al Desarrollo Industrial, Protocolo sobre Tratado Preferencial a Honduras, Managua Nicaragua, 23 de septiembre de 1966 (San José, Costa Rica, 1973); Economic Report of Costa Rica, vol. 2, Table 5:17.

10. IDB, Economic and Social Progress in Latin America, annual report (Washington, D.C., 1974), p. 251.

11. American Embassy, Annual Economic Report on Costa Rica (San José, Costa Rica, January 17, 1975), pp. 3-6.

12. Samuel Stone, La Dinastía de los Conquistadores (San José, Costa Rica: Editorial Universitaria Centro Americana, 1975), pp. 148-88.

13. Ibid., pp. 190-94.

14. Saenz, Population Growth, pp. 26, 28-29.

15. Stone, La Dinastía, p. 298.

16. Ibid., p. 330.

17. Robert O. Tomasek, "Costa Rica," in Political Forces in Latin America, ed. Ben G. Burnett and Kenneth F. Johnson (Belmont, Calif.: Wadsworth, 1970), p. 138.

18. Oscar Santiago and Cuellar Quevedo, "Algúnos Antecedentes Sobre la Organización Sincical in Costa Rica," unpublished manuscript, May 1974.

19. Blutstein, et al., Area Handbook for Costa Rica, pp. 252-56

20. Santiago and Quevedo, "Algúnos Antecedentes," pp. 24-28.

21. Interview, OFIPLAN, San José, Costa Rica, April 1975.

22. Denton, Patterns of Costa Rican Politics, p. 48.

23. La Nación (San José, Costa Rica), July 25, 1968, pp. 66-82.

24. International Bank for Reconstruction and Development, Economic Report of Costa Rica, vol. 1 (March 15, 1974), pp. 32, 35.

# PART III

# INTERNATIONAL LENDING AND LATIN AMERICA

CHAPTER

# 8

# THE HEGEMONIC STATE AND DEVELOPMENT

It is difficult to speak of the role of the Inter-American Development Bank and the United States in Costa Rica without discussing Central America. The role of IDB in Costa Rica, Central America, and throughout Latin America is understood more fully when viewed in conjunction with the other international lending agencies and their relationship to the United States.

The U.S. role in Latin America, particularly in Costa Rica and Central America, is a double-edged sword. U.S. interests in the area involve a twofold strategy of developing economic markets and, at the same time, maintaining a political/military climate favorable to the United States. IDB's role as an instrument of U.S. international economic policy is one segment in a multifaceted approach, with other U.S.-oriented international lending agencies operating to advance the economic interests of the United States. IDB and the other international lending agencies operate within Central America and Latin America in an environment that has been made friendly through the second U.S. strategy of political/military leverage.*

---

*A similar double U.S. strategy of advancing economic interests within a stable political/military environment is prevalent throughout Latin America, as events in Chile and events in Brazil since 1964 have made evident. However, this study discusses only the hegemonic role of the United States and IDB in Central America, to further elaborate on the example of IDB in Costa Rica. Minor imperial roles are played by other Western European and Japanese interests, primarily in the field of foreign investment. However, the overwhelming support (over 60 percent U.S. foreign investment in all Central America) of

Chapter 4 outlined a definite leverage relationship between U.S. foreign policy, economic integration, and the IDB, particularly in Central America. The context of IDB's role in national development is defined and subject to the constraints of external forces as well as internal forces, such as the Costa Rican state. In Central America the role of the United States as an external actor is paramount. National development and development policies are shaped not only by the Costa Rican government but also by external forces, such as the United States. The U.S. role in Central America provides further insight into IDB within the context of internal and external state building. These internal and external state forces define IDB activities, but additionally, IDB is one aspect of the total external state building mechanism operating in Central and South America.

The dual U.S. strategy in Central America involved the establishment of CACM and military/political stability.

## MILITARY STRATEGY

The Central American Defense Council (CONDECA) was established in 1964 as a defensive instrument of the Central American State Organization (ODECA). For the United States, the formation of CONDECA was essential for maintaining U.S. hegemony in the whole Caribbean area. Events in Cuba since the Revolution of 1959 had given further impetus to stabilizing the region against national liberation movements, to maintain stable national governments in Central America. Military exercises such as Operation Falconview, an exercise to defend the isthmus against subversive elements from the Caribbean, became commonplace.[1] The role of CONDECA as an instrument of U.S. foreign policy was distinctly enunciated by U.S. Assistant Secretary for Inter-American Affairs Jack Hood Vaughn in 1965:

> The United States hopes to develop close relations with the Central American Defense Council Organization, which will strengthen the defenses against the forces of international Communism which threaten our society.[2]

---

the United States, both economically and militarily, and its dominant interest and control in the IDB and other international lending agencies, makes the imperial role of the United States the focus of discussion.

FIGURE 8.1

CONDECA and the American Military Establishment: An Organizational Model

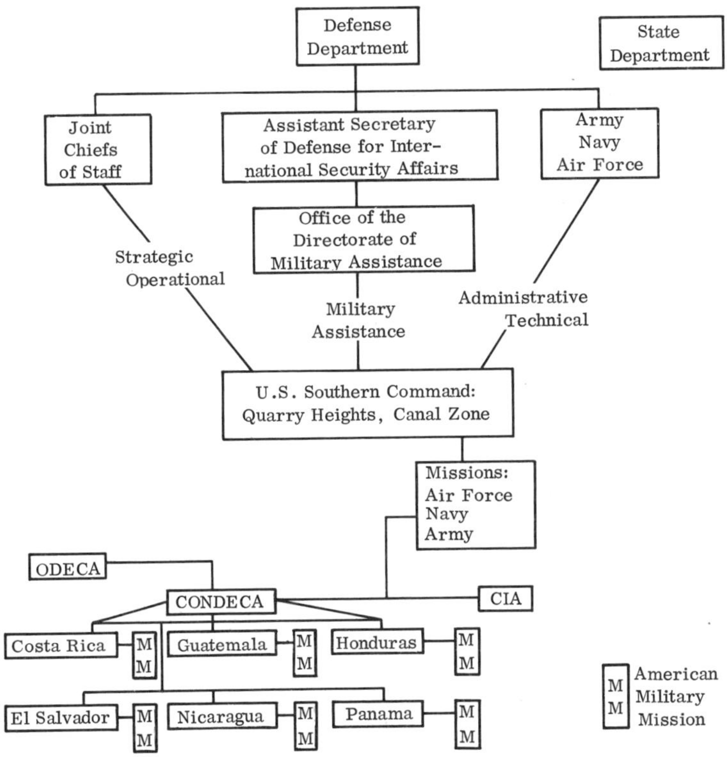


Source: "Integration of the Big Guns: The Central American Defense Council," North American Congress on Latin America (NACLA) 7 (May-June 1973): 23.

CONDECA serves U.S. interests in a number of ways. First, it provides the U.S. military with substantial control and influence in Central America. Second, CONDECA illustrates the use of military aid to strengthen Central American national forces, thus stabilizing the region against subversive elements and providing the political and social equilibrium necessary for economic development and foreign investment. CONDECA, as such, is a model for the proposed U.S. Inter-American Defense Force in Latin America.[3]

A large part of CONDECA's effort has been to integrate Latin American national military defense system under its wing. A study by Phillipe Schmitter has commented, "The external—i.e., U.S. impact on integration in [the military sector] has been great, if not determinate."[4] The military integration of Central America has been complete since 1966 when CONDECA's charter was amended to include security officers, thus allowing Costa Rica to participate and, thereby, avoiding Costa Rica's prohibition of a national army.[5]

The organizational chart in Figure 8.1 illustrates U.S. military integration of Central America. This integration provides access for U.S. influence, and through various training programs encourages support for U.S. development ideas. Counterinsurgency and civic action training have been important in stabilizing the region and have been given special attention by the U.S. Defense Department. The School of the Americas in the Canal Zone had trained over 16,000 Latin American students in counterinsurgency and civil action by 1964, almost half of them Central Americans. By country, the distribution is outlined in Table 8.1. Thus even before the arrival of a fully

TABLE 8.1

Military Training in Latin America

| Country | Number |
|---|---|
| Costa Rica | 1,639 |
| El Salvador | 358 |
| Guatemala | 958 |
| Honduras | 2,969 |
| Nicaragua | 1,420 |
| Total for Central America | 8,154 |
| Total for Latin America | 16,343 |

Source: Willard F. Barber and C. Neale Ronning, Internal Security and Military Power (Columbus: Ohio State University Press, 1966), p. 149.

integrated U.S.-oriented military unit through CONDECA, the socialization and recruitment of the Central American political and military leadership was well under way. CONDECA institutionalized the military integration of the region and provided formal access points for U.S. military influence through the hierarchical organization structure and through the advice of U.S. military missions in each country. U.S. defense policy in Central America complements the strategy of economic integration and the formation of CACM. Within this stabilized military and political environment, the IDB and other international lending agencies are able to advance U.S. economic and political interests.

## POLITICAL/ECONOMIC STRATEGY

The Bank and the other international lending agencies provide development aid to Latin America in support of integration. Development through integration—as shown in the analysis of IDB's funding pattern in Latin America, Central America, and particularly Costa Rica—has emphasized infrastructure projects. Such infrastructure projects as bridges, highways, communications and transportation systems, and hydroelectric facilities further integration and favor the penetration of foreign investors. These investors are attracted to a politically stabilized region with abundant economic infrastructure necessary for the expansion of markets and integrated industrialization.

A second advantage of infrastructure projects is their impact on U.S.-Latin American trade. The building of infrastructure projects initially creates new markets for U.S. manufacturers to sell capital goods, and infrastructure projects also establish a pattern of development that most assuredly will mean an expanded future market for U.S. manufactured goods, as will be demonstrated later in this chapter. Before analyzing the importance of infrastructure projects to U.S. economic interests, this study offers an overview of the roles of other international lending agencies in infrastructure building. It shows IDB is just one component in an intricate process involving a multiplicity of actors as instruments of U.S. foreign economic policy, which favors infrastructure projects.

## ALIGNMENT OF INTERNATIONAL LENDERS, THE UNITED STATES, AND IDB

Among the international lending agencies that operate in Latin America, along with IDB, in advancing U.S. economic interests by promoting trade and export opportunities are: the U.S. Export-Import

TABLE 8.2

U.S. and Multilateral Assistance, by Sector: Summary for 1961-70
(in millions of dollars)

| Sector | IDB | SPTF | IBRD | IFC | UNDP | Eximbank | USAID | | Total |
|---|---|---|---|---|---|---|---|---|---|
| | | | | | | | Loans | Grants | |
| Food and agriculture | 973.2 | 58.1 | 390.9 | — | 80.8 | 62.8 | 467.7 | 138.9 | 2,172.4 |
| Education | 114.8 | 27.8 | 67.5 | — | 25.7 | — | 220.7 | 122.9 | 579.4 |
| Industry and mining | 619.6 | — | 172.3 | 157.9 | 56.2 | 1,218.7 | 107.5 | 33.6 | 2,365.8 |
| Transportation and communications | 661.1 | — | 937.5 | — | — | 854.2 | 367.6 | 25.1 | 2,845.5 |
| Health and sanitation | 321.2 | 167.1 | 61.8 | — | 14.2 | — | 147.9 | 48.3 | 760.5 |
| Public administration and planning | 68.2 | — | 2.0 | — | 15.0 | — | 26.2 | 63.3 | 174.7 |
| Community development and social welfare | — | — | — | — | 5.3 | — | 15.0 | 28.1 | 48.4 |
| Housing | 135.6 | 241.5 | — | — | 2.2 | — | 180.0 | — | 559.3 |
| Power | 550.5 | — | 1,780.3 | — | 27.4 | 242.7 | 277.0 | — | 2,877.4 |
| Private enterprise promotion | — | — | — | — | — | — | 283.9 | 12.1 | 296.0 |
| Population | — | — | — | — | — | — | 29.2 | — | 29.2 |
| Relending | — | — | — | — | — | 107.5 | — | — | 107.5 |
| Export financing | 52.9 | — | — | — | — | — | — | — | 52.9 |
| Regional, general and miscellaneous | — | 22.2 | — | — | 0.5 | — | 117.3 | 291.1 | 431.1 |
| Program loans | — | — | — | — | — | 456.5 | 1,308.1 | — | 1,764.6 |
| Rescheduling of debt and refinancing/refunding | — | — | — | — | — | 856.8 | — | — | 856.8 |
| Total | 3,496.6 | 516.7 | 3,412.3 | 157.9 | 227.3 | 3,799.2 | 3,548.1 | 763.4 | 15,921.5 |

Key: Inter-American Development Bank (IDB)
Social Progress Trust Fund (SPTF)
World Bank and International Development Association (IBRD)
International Finance Corporation (IFC)
United Nations Development Program (UNDP)
Export-Import Bank (Eximbank)
Agency for International Development (AID)

Source: U.S. House of Representatives, Committee on Foreign Affairs, Development Assistance to Latin America, 1961-1971: Selected Tables (Washington, D.C.: Government Printing Office, April 14, 1971), p. 11.

Bank (Eximbank); the U.S. Agency for International Development (USAID); the World Bank group; and ADELA, the Atlantic Community Group for the Development of Latin America. (The United Nations Development Program, or UNDP, is relatively small and its impact less significant.) In Central America these organizations have operated successfully within the framework of CONDECA's military security system, advancing development via integration and contributing to a more favorable U.S. trade position. Table 8.2 illustrates the pattern of U.S. bilateral and multilateral assistance for Latin America (including Central America) by sector.

The U.S. government and the international lending agencies outlined in Table 8.2 all place heavy emphasis on infrastructure projects, which are expressed by sectors under the categories of power, transportation, and communications. In conjunction with infrastructure building, public sectoral spending in food, agriculture, industry, and mining also contribute to the establishment of the necessary infrastructure for industrial and production-oriented sectors of later foreign investment.

The Atlantic Community Group for the Development of Latin America (ADELA) is an important agency that operates largely as a private international investment company, with almost half its capitalization from the United States. ADELA tends to stress industrial and manufacturing projects leaving the infrastructure building to the United States and its aligned international lenders.[6] Table 8.3 demonstrates the financing sectors that ADELA tended to emphasize in Latin America in April 1970.

The alignment of economic interests favoring the United States in the international lending agencies reflects several factors. The U.S. Export-Import Bank and USAID are both arms of the U.S. government and, therefore, the alignment with U.S. economic interests is readily expected. In the case of the World Bank group, U.S. orientation is for similar reasons as those behind the IDB's alignment with the United States. Central to the World Bank's position is the 23 percent share of voting power that the United States controls, far overshadowing the next two most important voting members, the United Kingdom with 9.29 percent and West Germany with 4.92 percent.[7] Latin America's voting power in the World Bank is only 7.54 percent for all nations and the combined voting power of the CACM countries of Costa Rica, El Salvador, Nicaragua, Honduras, and Guatemala equals only 0.63 percent of the total World Bank votes.[8] Latin America's role in decisions affecting itself in the World Bank is quite limited, while the United States exercises considerable influence.

The role of the international lending organizations in providing infrastructure for foreign investors like ADELA, and particularly those from the United States, is illustrated dramatically in Central

TABLE 8.3

Sector Distribution of ADELA Projects,
April 30, 1970

| Sector | Number of Projects | Amount (thousands of U.S. dollars) | Percent |
|---|---|---|---|
| Agriculture, fishing, and food processing | 18 | 16,570 | 20.2 |
| General manufacturing | 16 | 13,855 | 16.9 |
| Pulp and paper | 3 | 10,200 | 12.4 |
| Financial institutions | 21 | 9,185 | 11.2 |
| Textiles | 4 | 6,520 | 7.9 |
| Wood products | 5 | 6,160 | 7.5 |
| Chemical and allied products | 8 | 5,425 | 6.6 |
| Capital goods machinery and metal working | 9 | 4,910 | 5.9 |
| Service industries | 8 | 4,195 | 5.1 |
| Iron and steel | 6 | 4,160 | 5.1 |
| Mining and mineral processing | 1 | 1,000 | 1.2 |
| Total | 99 | 82,180 | 100.1 |

Source: Hector Milo and Israel Yost, "Funding the Empire: Part 2, The Multinational Strategy," North American Congress on Latin America (NACLA) 4, no. 3 (May-June 1970): 12.

America. IDB and the international lending organizations clearly have established in Central America the basis for future foreign investment. Tables 8.4 and 8.5 show the types of infrastructure projects developed in Central America by two of the most important international lenders, the World Bank and the U.S. Export-Import Bank.

The impact of the various international lenders in promoting development through infrastructure and productionist projects with a high capital goods component, has rapidly expanded markets and investment opportunities for U.S. foreign investors and exporters. By 1969 the U.S. percentage of direct foreign investment in the CACM countries was 60 percent or better, as illustrated in Table 8.6 (time sequence data).

The creation of CACM in 1960 made possible this expansion of U.S. markets, through the lowering of tariff barriers between Common Market nations. Imports from outside CACM were subject to an external tariff, thus encouraging many U.S. producers to locate within the CACM region. However, in spite of the gradual creation of external tariffs, in the initial years U.S. exports continued to grow, for example, from $210 million in 1961 to $360 million in 1966. The continuation of heavy exports to CACM is due largely to the market's relatively low external tariff, which averages about 36 percent ad valorem in comparison to 186 percent for Brazil, 78 percent for Chile, and 13 percent for the European Economic Community.[9]

A U.S. document in 1969 emphasized the advantage of CACM to U.S. producers, especially in infrastructure projects: "Opportunities for U.S. suppliers of capital equipment should remain good for the entire area because of infrastructure projects, but higher taxes and increased local production can be expected to cause a decline in import of consumer goods."[10] U.S. firms locating within the region could take advantage of the broader market with little competition from domestic producers. CACM created a market size with potential for economies of scale that demanded expertise and resources in financing, management, technology, production, and distribution that could not be met by most local producers.[11] Investment competition from other industrialized nations remained minimal, allowing heavy U.S. investment without substantial competition, as is evident from Figure 8.2.

U.S. dominance as Central America's major trading partner has been maintained since the inception of CACM. Inflation and the high cost of petroleum and petroleum products have slowed the growth of U.S. trade with Central America. However, the dollar value of that trade for 1975 was expected to increase. Loans by Venezuela, particularly through the Venezuelan Trust Fund of the Inter-American Development Bank, also helped to offset the increased cost of petroleum to nonproducers.[12] The United States anticipates a sagging import demand by the non-oil producers in Latin America such as the CACM nations, except for infrastructure and productionist projects of the international lenders, as noted in a recent report by the U.S. Department of Commerce:

> The countries in the third petroleum needy group are likely to have sagging import demand except for equipment directly related to export agriculture and/or mining and those large development projects financed by international lending institutions like the World Bank.[13]

The international lenders play an important role in stimulating trade even in the face of declining economic growth in Central America. In Latin America as a whole, the process of development through integration continues to open up markets to U.S. investors. During 1975

TABLE 8.4

Investment in Central America by the World Bank Group
(round figures, in millions of U.S. dollars)

| | Bank Loans | | IDA[a] Credits | | IFC[b] Commitments | | Bank/IDA/IFC Total | |
|---|---|---|---|---|---|---|---|---|
| Country/Purpose | Number | Original Amount | Number | Original Amount | Number | Original Amount | Number of Operations | Original Amount |
| Costa Rica | | | | | | | | |
| Agriculture | 4 | 18.50 | — | — | — | — | 4 | 18.50 |
| Education | 1 | 6.20 | — | — | — | — | 1 | 6.20 |
| Electric power and telecommunications | 6 | 73.30 | — | — | — | — | 6 | 73.30 |
| Industry | 2 | 5.00 | — | — | 2 | 0.59 | 4 | 5.59 |
| Transportation | 3 | 22.60 | 1 | 5.50 | — | — | 4 | 28.10 |
| Total | 16 | 125.60 | 1 | 5.50 | 2 | 0.59 | 19 | 131.69 |
| El Salvador | | | | | | | | |
| Education | 1 | 4.90 | — | — | — | — | 1 | 4.90 |
| Electric power | 5 | 52.69 | 1 | 5.60 | — | — | 5 | 58.29 |
| Industry | — | — | — | — | 1 | 0.14 | 1 | 0.14 |
| Telecommunications | 2 | 19.00 | — | — | — | — | 2 | 19.00 |
| Tourism | — | — | — | — | 1 | 0.93 | 1 | 0.93 |
| Transportation | 3 | 18.90 | 1 | 8.00 | — | — | 4 | 26.90 |
| Total | 11 | 95.49 | 2 | 13.60 | 2 | 1.07 | 15 | 110.16 |

| | | | | | | | | |
|---|---|---|---|---|---|---|---|---|
| Guatemala | | | | | | | | |
| Agriculture | 1 | 4.00 | — | — | — | — | 1 | 4.00 |
| Education | 1 | 6.30 | — | — | — | — | 1 | 6.30 |
| Electric power | 2 | 22.00 | — | — | — | — | 2 | 22.00 |
| Telecommunications | 1 | 16.00 | — | — | — | — | 1 | 16.00 |
| Transportation | 1 | 18.20 | — | — | — | — | 1 | 18.20 |
| Total | 6 | 66.50 | — | — | 2 | 15.20 | 8 | 81.70 |
| Honduras | | | | | | | | |
| Agriculture | — | — | 2 | 9.20 | — | — | 2 | 9.20 |
| Education | 1 | 3.00 | 1 | 3.00 | — | — | 2 | 6.00 |
| Electric power | 5 | 35.55 | 2 | 9.50 | — | — | 7 | 45.05 |
| Industry | — | — | — | — | 4 | 0.45 | 4 | 0.45 |
| Transportation | 7 | 53.90 | 2 | 12.50 | — | — | 9 | 66.40 |
| Total | 13 | 92.45 | 7 | 34.20 | 4 | 0.45 | 24 | 127.10 |
| Nicaragua | | | | | | | | |
| Agriculture | 5 | 14.35 | — | — | — | — | 5 | 14.35 |
| Earthquake reconstruction | — | — | 1 | 20.00 | — | — | 1 | 20.00 |
| Education | 1 | 4.00 | — | — | — | — | 1 | 4.00 |
| Electric power | 8 | 66.30 | — | — | — | — | 8 | 66.30 |
| Industry | — | — | — | — | 1 | 2.07 | 1 | 2.07 |
| Transportation | 4 | 21.20 | — | — | — | — | 4 | 21.20 |
| Water supply | 1 | 6.90 | 1 | 3.00 | — | — | 2 | 9.90 |
| Total | 19 | 112.75 | 2 | 23.00 | 1 | 2.07 | 22 | 137.82 |

[a]International Development Association.

[b]International Finance Corporation.

Source: International Bank for Reconstruction and Development, The World Bank Group in the Americas (Washington, D.C., May 1974), pp. 37, 48, 51, 57, 75.

TABLE 8.5

Investment in Central America by the U.S. Export-Import Bank

| Country (guarantor shown in parentheses) | Purpose | Amount |
|---|---|---|
| Central America totals (1972-73) | | |
| Costa Rica | | 998,867 |
| El Salvador | | 88,070 |
| Guatemala | | 13,500,000 |
| Honduras | | 7,540,847 |
| Nicaragua | | 0 |
| Costa Rica | | |
| Instituto Autonomo del Ferocarril (Banco Nacional de Costa Rica) | dredging equipment | 264,150 |
| Total off and relending loans (13) | | 734,717 |
| Total for Costa Rica | | 998,867 |
| El Salvador | | |
| Total off and relending loans (4) | | 88,070 |
| Guatemala | | |
| Exmibal (Explorer Metal Co.) | nickel producing facility | 13,500,000 |
| Total for Guatemala | | 13,500,000 |
| Honduras | | |
| Republic of Honduras | agricultural and road maintenance equipment | 900,000 |
| Cementos de Honduras SA | expansion of cement plant | 684,454 |
| Servicio Aereo de Honduras SA (Republic of Honduras) | aircraft, commercial jet (1) | 3,272,750 |
| Total off and relending loans (65) | | 2,682,643 |
| Total for Honduras | | 7,540,847 |

Source: U.S. Export-Import Bank, Statement of Condition, Fiscal Year 1973 (Washington, D.C.), pp. 28-38.

TABLE 8.6

U.S. Percentage of Direct Foreign Investment in Central America in 1969

| U.S. Direct Foreign Investment | Percent of Total |
|---|---|
| Costa Rica | 75 |
| El Salvador | 60 |
| Guatemala | 86 |
| Honduras | 95 |
| Nicaragua | 80 |

Note: U.S. private investment in Central America (in millions) was as follows:

| 1961 | 1962 | 1963 | 1964 | 1965 | 1966 | 1967 | 1968 | 1969 |
|---|---|---|---|---|---|---|---|---|
| 1 | 7 | 28 | 34 | 26 | 47 | 62 | 24 | 36 |

Source: Gert Rosenthal, "The Role of Private Foreign Investment in the Development of the Central American Common Market," Guatemala draft, 1971, based on figures from the central bank of each of the Central American countries; U.S. Congress, House Committee on Foreign Affairs, Development Assistance to Latin America, 1961-1970, 92nd Congress, 1st Session (Washington, D.C.: Government Printing Office, April 14, 1971), p. 18.

U.S. exports to Latin America were estimated to have risen to over $20 billion, on the heels of the 61 percent increase in U.S. exports to Latin America estimated for 1974.[14] Major infrastructure projects and a number of hydroelectric projects with the Andean Common Market, LAFTA, and the Caribbean Common Market also contributed to the growth of U.S. exports in the 1970s. In Central America the combined efforts of CACM, the international lending agencies, and IDB reflect the larger image of U.S. economic policy, which aims to provide the United States with a favorable trade balance.

In the case study of Costa Rica in Chapter 7, the linkage between the IDB and the state structure was established. The preceding section showed links among the IDB, other international lenders, and the United States and their substantial impact on Costa Rican development. The United States as the major imperial power in Central America, partly as a result of the efforts of IDB and other international lending

FIGURE 8.2

U.S. Trade in CACM and Panama
(percent of market)

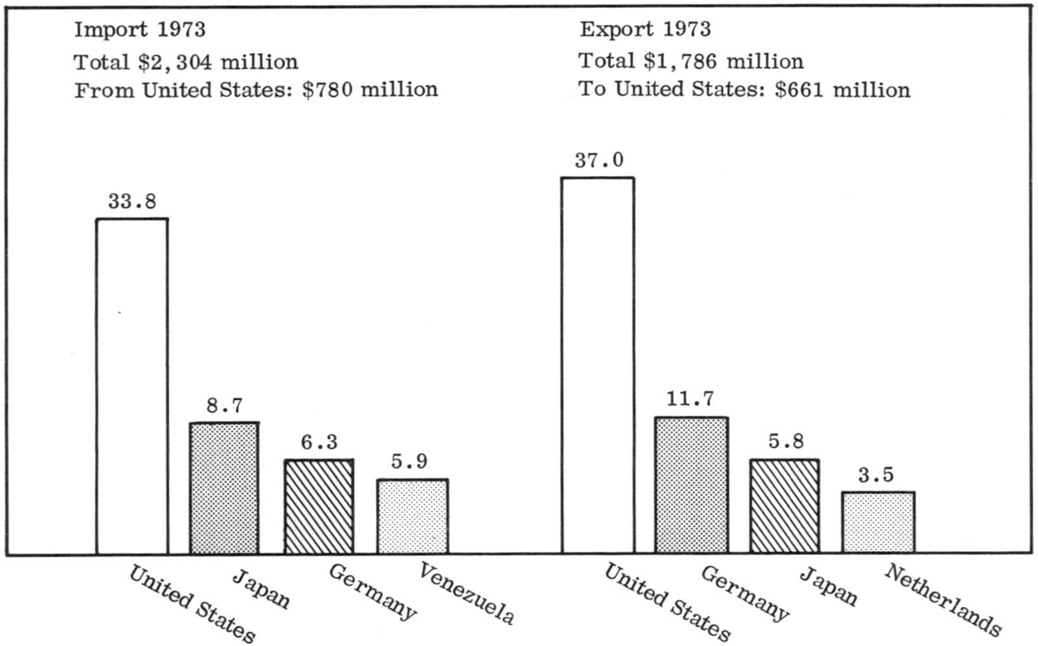


*Source*: U.S. Department of Commerce, *Overseas Business Report*, OBR 75-14 (March 1975), p. 6.

agencies, has been able to shape the direction of political, economic, and even social development to its advantage. The U.S. role in economic integration through the formation of CACM has been exploited to the primary economic advantage of the United States. The IDB and other multilateral and bilateral lenders played an important role in the institutionalization of economic integration in Central America and in shaping national priorities and development projects that have served U.S. economic interests.

This pattern in Costa Rica and Central America is seemingly being replicated in the newer common market areas. U.S. exports to the six Andean Common Market countries of Bolivia, Chile, Colombia, Ecuador, Peru, and Venezuela were estimated to grow in 1975 to nearly $5 billion. This is due largely to the increased demand for U.S. exports reflecting oil revenues in Venezuela and Ecuador. However, industrial and infrastructure projects in Peru and Bolivia also were expected to increase U.S. exports.[15] Figure 8.3 illustrates the U.S. trade advantage in the Andean Common Market (ANCOM) area.

The pattern in the newer Caribbean Common Market (CARICOM) is similar. U.S. exports to the six major Caribbean countries exceeded $1.7 billion in 1974, an increase of 40 percent over 1973.[16]

This study established the links of IDB with U.S. national interests and Costa Rican development. Likewise, the direction of development in other Central and South American countries is also within the constraints of U.S. policy via IDB and the other international lenders. The linkage, however, between IDB and the United States externally, and IDB and U.S. policy internally (in Costa Rica and the other Latin American countries) is consummated through a local national elite that maintains an economic and political outlook similar to that of its U.S. counterpart.

Samuel Stone describes this linkage in Costa Rica. In La Dinastía de los Conquistadores, he traces the history of the Costa Rican agricultural elite before and after the Revolution of 1948.[17] This elite, which traditionally has held both economic and political power, incorporated more modern and industrially oriented elements during the revolution. This change in turn contributed to opening Costa Rican development through integration, and to connecting U.S. interests and the Inter-American Development Bank with Costa Rican national development strategy. Stone suggests that in Costa Rica the traditionally powerful cafetaleros (coffee growers) and other powerful agricultural interests were opposed to the integration of Central America, fearing the competition from their neighbors. This initial fear, however, was offset by the declining price of coffee and other agricultural products in international markets and the influence of newer industrially oriented elite groups represented by José Figueres and the Partido Liberación Nacional, Costa Rica's dominant political

FIGURE 8.3

ANCOM and U.S. Trade
(percent of market)

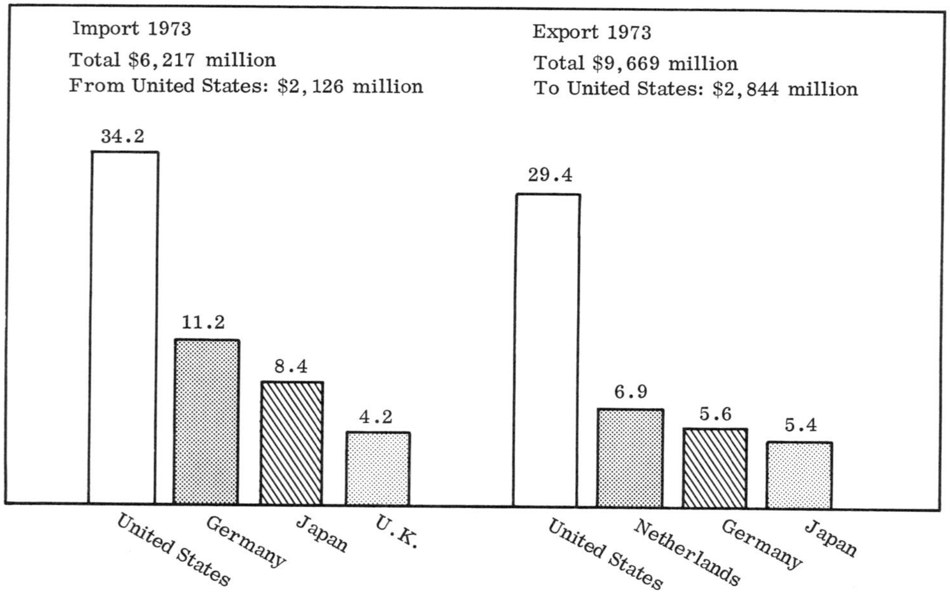


Source: U.S. Department of Commerce, Overseas Business Reports, 75-14 (Washington, D.C., 1975), p. 3.

TABLE 8.7

Industrial Investment by the Costa Rican Ruling Classes, 1960-70

| Year | Amount (in colones) |
|---|---|
| 1960 | 365.000 |
| 1961 | 20.500.000 |
| 1962 | 4.616.000 |
| 1963 | 4.866.000 |
| 1964 | 16.572.000 |
| 1965 | 14.100.000 |
| 1966 | 15.600.000 |
| 1967 | 3.000.000 |
| 1968 | 1.620.000 |
| 1969 | 983.000 |
| 1970 | 3.500.000 |
| Total | 85.722.000 |

Source: Samuel Stone, La Dinastía de los Conquistadores (San José, Costa Rica: Editorial Universitaria Centro Americana, 1975), p. 352.

party. The position of the traditional agricultural interests was weakened by the declining world price of agricultural commodities and they came to support economic integration as a modernizing strategy.[18] After initial debate among the various elite segments on joining CACM, Costa Rica entered the market in 1963. Support for integration came from the internal Costa Rican ruling classes, the dominant political party (Partido Liberación Nacional or PLN), and the machinery of the state. External U.S. support for integrationist development thus was linked to the Costa Rican ruling classes' interests. This linkage is crucial for the success of U.S. economic strategy via IDB in Costa Rica and throughout Latin America. Stone described the bond between the ruling classes in Costa Rica and U.S. investors and provided evidence of their similar economic interests.[19] He supports his allegation of a bond between U.S. foreign investors and the Costa Rican elite with data suggesting a similar pattern of investment by the two groups in 1960-70. Table 8.7 shows the actual investment by the ruling classes in industrial projects for integration, while Table 8.8 compares between the investment pattern of Costa

TABLE 8.8

Number and Value of Industrial Investments, by Group and Sector in Costa Rica, 1975 (value in percent)

| | Group | | | | | |
|---|---|---|---|---|---|---|
| | Costa Rica | | United States | | Others | |
| Sector | Number | Value | Number | Value | Number | Value |
| Footwear and clothing | 53 | 39 | 7 | 8 | 40 | 53 |
| Food and drink | 67 | 37 | 21 | 28 | 13 | 36 |
| Construction material | 72 | 54 | 17 | 23 | 11 | 23 |
| Shipping material | 75 | 34 | 13 | 60 | 12 | 6 |
| Furniture | 67 | 23 | 15 | 52 | 18 | 25 |
| Cosmetics | 86 | 89 | 6 | 6 | 8 | 5 |
| Pharmaceutical goods | 76 | 40 | 24 | 60 | 0 | 0 |
| Electronic equipment | 48 | 8 | 24 | 14 | 28 | 78 |
| Fertilizer | 74 | 6 | 13 | 91 | 13 | 3 |
| Office equipment | 74 | 27 | 19 | 69 | 7 | 4 |
| Agricultural implements | 92 | 88 | — | — | 8 | 12 |
| Other | 73 | 37 | 15 | 62 | 12 | 1 |

Source: Samuel Stone, La Dinastía de los Conquistadores (San José, Costa Rica: Editorial Universitaria Centro Americana, 1975), p. 350.

Rica's elite classes and that of North American investors. Finally, Figure 8.4 illustrates the peak investment periods for the Costa Rican ruling class and U.S. foreign investors.

The quantity of Costa Rican private investment averages 42 percent of all investment for the 1960-70 period. The similarity in types of investments by U.S. foreign investors and Costa Rican elites, and the similarity in peak investment periods, seems to support Stone's contention of a linkage between U.S. foreign capital penetration and the role of the Costa Rican ruling classes. Further empirical evidence is probably necessary to concretize this assertion. Nevertheless, this bond, if clearly established, would provide the linking element between the role of IDB and the other international lending agencies externally and their penetration of the economic and social structure of Costa

FIGURE 8.4

Industrial Investments, 1960-70 (Costa Rica)

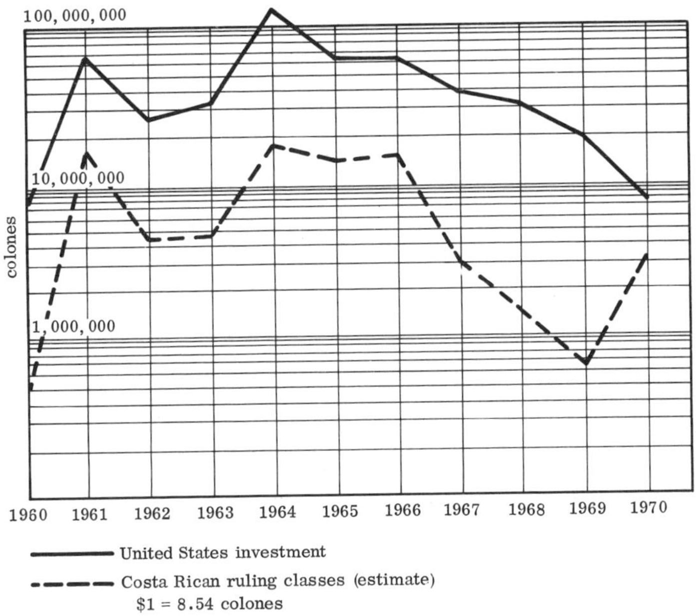


Source: Samuel Stone, La Dinastía de los Conquistadores (San José, Costa Rica: Editorial Universitaria Centro Americana, 1975), p. 346.

Rica and other Central and South American countries in shaping national development to U.S. economic interests.

The IDB, therefore, as one component of the U.S. international economic strategy, is helping to shape the national economies of Central and South America. It is allowed to penetrate those economies on behalf of developed nations, particularly the United States, through the support of the state mechanism and the ruling classes. The United States through the Bank and, it seems, other international lending agencies, has been able to export a model of development that stresses infrastructure and production projects providing favorable markets for North American investors. The concluding chapter discusses the impact and alternatives to this approach in international lending.

## NOTES

1. John Saxe-Fernandez, "The Central America Defense Council and Pax Americana," in Latin American Radicalism, ed. I. L. Horowitz (New York: Random House, 1969), pp. 76-78.

2. Ibid., p. 79.

3. Philippe Schmitter, Autonomy or Dependence as Regional Integration Outcomes: Central America (Berkeley: University of California, Institute for International Studies, 1972), p. 30.

4. Ibid., p. 28.

5. "Integrating the Big Guns: The Central American Defense Council," North American Congress on Latin America (NACLA) 7, no. 5 (May-June 1973): 23.

6. Hector Milo and Israel Yost, "Funding the Empire: Part 2, The Multinational Strategy," North American Congress on Latin America (NACLA) 4, no. 3 (May-June 1970): 13.

7. International Bank for Reconstruction and Development, World Bank/IDA, Annual Report 1973 (Washington, D.C.: 1974), Appendix A, pp. 106-7.

8. Ibid.

9. U.S. Commerce Department, Overseas Business Report, OBR 69-7, "Latin American Economic Integration: Implications for U.S. Business" (April 1969), p. 9.

10. Ibid., p. 12.

11. David Tobias, "The U.S. Investment Bubble in Central America," North American Congress on Latin America (NACLA) 8, no. 5 (May-June 1973): 34.

12. U.S. Commerce Department, Overseas Business Report, OBR 70-43 (Washington, D.C.: September 1970), p. 49.

13. U.S. Commerce Department, Overseas Business Report, OBR 75-14 (Washington, D.C.: 1975).

14. Ibid., p. 2.

15. Ibid., p. 3.

16. Ibid., pp. 5-6.

17. Samuel Stone, La Dinastía de los Conquistadores (San José, Costa Rica: Editorial Universitaria Centro Americana, 1975).

18. Ibid., pp. 339-40.

19. Ibid., p. 335.

# CHAPTER 9
# PROSPECTS FOR LATIN AMERICAN NATIONAL DEVELOPMENT

In this case study of the Inter-American Development Bank and its role in Costa Rican development, several factors affecting national development have been evident. The most important criticism of IDB development strategy is its heavy reliance on economic infrastructure and productionist projects, and the impact of such projects on Costa Rica and other Latin American countries in their terms of trade, balance of payments deficits, and the increasing cost of debt service. The case of Costa Rica demonstrates that IDB's pattern of development assistance has, at least to some extent, been responsible for increasing trade deficits by stressing infrastructure and production projects that demand a high capital goods import component.

IDB's failure to implement national export development projects also has tended to leave Costa Rica dependent on a limited number of primary agricultural exports. IDB's role in encouraging the development of economic integration and the Central American Common Market has further eroded Costa Rica's economic development through the loss of national revenues by tax incentives and tariff reduction schemes. Also, the loss of national profits to foreign and multinational investors with superior capitalization, technical advantages, and industrial and manufacturing economies of scale has allowed a high percentage of the profits accrued in CACM to be repatriated to the foreign investors' home offices. The loss of these two sources of national revenue further eroded Costa Rica's economic development position by increasing dependence on external funding for public investment.

IDB development strategies seem to have undermined development potential by worsening Costa Rica's terms of trade and balance of payments, increasing debt service, and fostering the repatriation of corporate profits. But IDB's strategy has tended to increase middle and traditional elite support for its pattern of development by distributing income to the advantage of these groups.

The social cost of IDB's pattern of development assistance has been high, tending to further marginalize specific population groups; for instance, agricultural workers in Guanacaste were hurt when IDB gave labor-extensive livestock development a high priority. However, the failure of IDB projects to offset Costa Rica's growing trade deficit, which increased in 1973-74 by 124 percent to $270 million (only $30 million of which was due to increased petroleum costs), contributed to giving Costa Rica the highest inflation in Central America (28.1 percent) in March 1975. This fact subjected the working class to severe economic pressures for such basic staples as rice, beans, oil, and meats, as well as numerous other nonluxury items.[1] Foreign exchange reserves grew so low that the national government was forced to impose stringent credit restrictions, curbing the outflow of dollars and discouraging the purchase of imported luxury items.

IDB's assistance strategy for Costa Rica, therefore, has fostered a form of dependent development. It has increased the country's reliance on external market conditions and forced Costa Rica to increasingly look to external funding sources for the public investment needed to meet the national development demands of middle-class and upper-class pressure groups.

It is not surprising, therefore, to find that the political leadership in Costa Rica is somewhat schizophrenic in its advocacy of national development. For instance, in September 1975 at the American Chamber of Commerce, Costa Rican First Vice President Carlos Manuel Castillo reportedly encouraged foreign investment. "From foreign investors," Castillo said prior to the speech, "we want external capital savings to supplement the national savings, and technology, marketing skills and full participation by the foreign investors in the problems of the community." But

> Castillo admitted that [President of Costa Rica] Oduber's visit to the U.S. in search of foreign investment, coupled with his speech on the nationalization of gasoline distribution, seemed contradictory on the surface but, he asserted, Oduber has long thought gasoline distribution was a public service and its private distribution was a concession granted by the government with the understanding that the concession could be withdrawn.[2]

The schizophrenic position in which Costa Rican political leaders find themselves is not uncommon in Latin America, where revolutionary rhetoric often is used to mesmerize the populace while schemes

TABLE 9.1

External Public Debt Outstanding for Latin America, December 31, 1971
(in millions of U.S. dollars)

| Area | Disbursed | Including Undisbursed | | | | | |
|---|---|---|---|---|---|---|---|
| | | | Bilateral | Multi- | Private | | |
| Country | Only | Total | Official | lateral | Suppliers | Banks | Other |
| Argentina | 2,247.0 | 2,908.8 | 464.3 | 693.2 | 849.1 | 308.9 | 593.3 |
| Bolivia | 534.6 | 616.3 | 309.8 | 79.1 | 48.1 | 8.1 | 171.0 |
| Brazil | 3,653.6 | 5,236.2 | 1,846.0 | 1,295.6 | 1,776.9 | — | 317.9 |
| Chile | 2,171.2 | 2,637.1 | 1,190.4 | 232.4 | 561.1 | 376.6 | 276.7 |
| Colombia | 1,354.4 | 2,017.5 | 854.8 | 890.9 | 179.6 | 55.4 | 36.8 |
| Costa Rica | 155.8 | 233.8 | 74.9 | 104.9 | 15.1 | 27.5 | 11.4 |
| Dominican Republic | 231.7 | 275.9 | 217.4 | 37.0 | 14.6 | 6.8 | — |
| Ecuador | 215.6 | 389.9 | 124.7 | 88.2 | 128.8 | 13.7 | 34.5 |
| El Salvador | 91.9 | 134.2 | 51.4 | 65.1 | — | 15.7 | 2.0 |
| Guatemala | 112.8 | 185.4 | 70.0 | 60.7 | 8.4 | 37.0 | 9.3 |
| Guyana | 138.4 | 188.4 | 109.2 | 18.4 | — | — | 60.8 |
| Honduras | 104.8 | 150.2 | 39.5 | 108.2 | 2.5 | — | — |
| Jamaica | 151.8 | 256.2 | 77.3 | 60.2 | 18.2 | 47.0 | 53.6 |
| Mexico | 3,565.1 | 4,243.7 | 460.9 | 1,256.2 | 388.7 | 1,203.7 | 934.2 |
| Nicaragua | 177.5 | 225.3 | 82.8 | 77.0 | 7.9 | 53.7 | 3.8 |
| Panama | 190.1 | 309.1 | 105.5 | 74.4 | 27.4 | 43.3 | 58.6 |
| Paraguay | 106.2 | 161.0 | 84.9 | 44.3 | 28.5 | 1.5 | 1.8 |
| Peru | 923.0 | 1,239.1 | 298.8 | 204.7 | 407.9 | 127.8 | 199.8 |
| Trinidad and Tobago | 90.1 | 106.9 | 22.4 | 43.4 | 4.0 | 23.8 | 13.3 |
| Uruguay | 314.0 | 393.1 | 113.6 | 111.0 | 61.5 | 83.2 | 24.9 |
| Venezuela | 859.4 | 1,143.4 | 119.6 | 450.1 | 145.4 | 385.9 | 42.5 |
| Total | 17, 338.8 | 23,052.5 | 6,718.0 | 5,994.9 | 4,673.9 | 2,819.6 | 2,846.1 |

Source: International Bank for Reconstruction and Development, World Bank/IDA, Annual Report, 1973 (Washington, D.C.), pp. 88-89.

TABLE 9.2

Debt Service on External Public Debt as a Percentage of Latin American Exports, 1965-71

| Country | 1965 | 1966 | 1967 | 1968 | 1969 | 1970 | 1971 |
|---|---|---|---|---|---|---|---|
| Argentina | 20.2 | 25.5 | 27.0 | 27.6 | 23.9 | 21.1 | 21.1 |
| Bolivia | 4.8 | 4.9 | 6.0 | 5.9 | 5.9 | 11.3 | 12.9 |
| Brazil | 20.9 | 21.9 | 22.3 | 19.9 | 18.4 | 16.8 | 17.1 |
| Chile | 12.2 | 10.6 | 12.4 | 19.9 | 18.1 | 17.9 | 19.6 |
| Colombia | 14.4 | 16.5 | 14.1 | 13.4 | 11.8 | 11.9 | 13.8 |
| Costa Rica | 10.3 | 12.0 | 11.9 | 11.9 | 11.5 | 9.7 | 9.9 |
| Dominican Republic | 19.2 | 12.6 | 7.3 | 7.7 | 8.6 | 5.1 | 6.6 |
| Ecuador | 6.3 | 6.4 | 6.3 | 8.3 | 9.3 | 8.8 | 11.9 |
| El Salvador | 3.6 | 3.7 | 2.6 | 2.6 | 2.8 | 3.8 | 6.2 |
| Guatemala | 5.2 | 5.7 | 7.4 | 7.8 | 8.0 | 7.7 | 8.1 |
| Guyana | 4.4 | 4.4 | 4.2 | 5.4 | 4.0 | 3.5 | 2.9 |
| Honduras | 2.4 | 2.2 | 2.1 | 1.7 | 2.3 | 2.8 | 3.3 |
| Jamaica | 1.9 | 1.8 | 2.2 | 3.2 | 3.5 | 3.2 | 4.0 |
| Mexico | 24.8 | 21.9 | 22.1 | 26.3 | 23.4 | 25.5 | 24.7 |
| Nicaragua | 4.2 | 5.6 | 6.3 | 7.5 | 10.0 | 10.7 | 13.6 |
| Panama | 2.5 | 3.0 | 2.9 | 3.2 | 3.2 | 8.8 | 10.5 |
| Paraguay | 6.2 | 5.7 | 7.4 | 10.3 | 9.3 | 9.5 | 11.1 |
| Peru | 7.0 | 9.9 | 11.1 | 14.6 | 13.1 | 13.8 | 19.4 |
| Trinidad and Tobago | 2.0 | 2.0 | 1.7 | 1.3 | 1.7 | 1.7 | 1.6 |
| Uruguay | 6.9 | 12.5 | 19.4 | 20.2 | 19.0 | 18.6 | 22.2 |
| Venezuela | 1.8 | 2.7 | 2.0 | 2.1 | 2.0 | 2.8 | 3.5 |

Note: Debt service ratios are based on debt service actually paid as reported by the countries and not on contractual debt service due. If a country did not pay the entire debt service due during a year, this may be reflected in a lower debt service ratio than would have been the case if contractual debt service had been used in computing the ratio. The debt service ratio is, by itself, an inadequate and incomplete indicator of a country's debt situation. Many other factors also must be considered, such as stability and diversification of the export structure, prospects for future growth, the extent to which imports can be reduced without adversely affecting current production, the time-profile of the country's debt outstanding, the size of foreign exchange reserves and available compensatory financing facilities, and the debt service record of the country.

Source: International Bank for Reconstruction and Development, World Bank/IDA Annual Report, 1973 (Washington, D.C.), pp. 88-89.

of external capitalist development are increasing the country's economic and political dependence. This discussion of the role of the Inter-American Development Bank in one Latin American country, and the dominant role of the United States in the IDB, suggests the part that international lending agencies can play in increasing the economic and political dependence of countries in Latin America, and indeed throughout the Third World.

Besides the problems associated with IDB's development assistance, debt service also is becoming an increasing factor of economic dependence for Costa Rica. Debt service ran about $122.2 million through 1974, equaling approximately 23 percent of the current account receipts of the balance of payments.[3] The impact of debt service in Costa Rica is substantial. As Table 9.1 indicates, it is a significant economic consideration for most Latin American nations. These countries have their largest outstanding obligations to the bilateral and multilateral lending agencies, like IDB. Debt service also brings a need to continually request external financial assistance, in part to meet current debt obligations. At the very least, the sizable debt service obligation of many Latin American countries, such as Costa Rica, puts a damper on economic growth.

Debt service also can serve as a means of political dependency as illustrated in Chile under Allende when lack of creditworthiness and a high rate of debt service were used as justifications by the United States to apply economic sanctions blocking significant sources of international financial assistance available from the IDB and other lending agencies. As illustrated in Table 9.2, debt service also can use up a significant percentage of a country's capital surplus, which is needed for public investment. The high percentage of foreign exchange that must be earmarked for debt service forces many Latin American nations to continue relying on external sources to finance public investment projects, thus perpetuating dependent development.

The argument that aid is offered as a compensation for the less developed nation's comparative disadvantage is sometimes offered to counter the assertion that development assistance through agencies like the IDB tends to undermine rather than improve the terms of trade. Aid is offered on a concessionary basis to offset factors like the near monopoly of the United States in capital goods, which are sometimes sold at uncompetitively high prices with price hikes as much as 20 to 25 percent for loan recipient nations.[4] This compensation may be smaller than appears on the surface. For example, the outflow of interest and amortization expressed as a percentage of new loan disbursements—including suppliers' credits, private and official loans, and loans of international agencies (but excluding private investment)—was 87 percent in 1965-67 in Latin America.[5]

Aid compensation through agencies like the Bank is much smaller than appears from a consideration of loan disbursements that ignores the debt service factor. Additionally, the positive impact of the bilateral and multilateral lending agencies on the U.S. balance of payments, and the favorable overall U.S. balance of payments vis-a-vis Latin America, tends to invalidate any assertion that aid compensates for deteriorating terms of trade for developing nations.

The cost of financial assistance from IDB and any international lending agency, as the case of Costa Rica indicates, is quite high. These costs affect national development in two significant areas: the pattern of development assistance and service on development loans. The analysis of the IDB in Costa Rica, and empirical data from other Latin American nations, strongly suggests that the types of projects, especially the considerable emphasis on economic infrastructure and productionist projects, seem to offer Latin American nations a comparative disadvantage for national development and continuing unfavorable terms of trade. This creates economic dependence, which is heightened by the high cost of aid through IDB and other international lending agencies—and then multiplied with the increasing yearly cost of debt service. The shortcomings of IDB's development assistance program to Costa Rica, and seemingly to Latin America, are substantial. Quite simply, in cost-benefit analysis, the Bank's aid to Costa Rica is more costly to the recipient than to the major IDB donor, the United States.

The impact of U.S. national interest through Bank projects in Costa Rica has brought dependent development and seems to have severely eroded Costa Rica's potential for economic development. IDB projects have weakened Costa Rica's economy and lessened the possibility for successful economic development. In many ways, IDB projects have led not to further development in Costa Rica but to furthering underdevelopment. This pattern is being replicated throughout Latin America.

Implied in this study is an alternative development approach. An obvious solution to the problem of dependent development is to break the dependence by severing ties with the United States and other developed countries that have penetrated the Costa Rican economy and are extracting significant profits from the economy while marginalizing large segments of the population. Some may respond that it is impossible to break economic ties with the developed world because of increased economic and political interdependence, as well as the fact that for Costa Rica the breaking of economic ties with the United States would result in economic chaos and bankruptcy. However, I believe that an alternative development model is available for lessening the influence of the United States and other developed nations in the economies of Latin America without totally severing economic ties.

What is called for is a national economic policy by Costa Rica and the other Latin American nations that is committed to lessening dependence through the following available avenues: diversifying primary product exports; developing and controlling natural resources; industrializing with national ownership; developing nationally owned export industries; bargaining with developed nations for trade preferences for Third World manufactured goods and higher prices for primary product exports; and increasing the priority of social investment projects such as clean water, health, housing, and education to increase the productivity of the Costa Rican population. These suggestions suggest a feasible alternative model of development with which to lessen dependence.

There is no practical reason why the Bank could not sponsor projects that would reflect this alternative development model to lessen dependence. Aid could be provided to assist Costa Rica and other Latin American countries in diversifying their primary product exports, in developing natural resources, in developing export industries owned by nationals, as well as providing increased priority for projects with a high social development content. Practically speaking, the Bank could offer this alternative type of assistance in place of its current development aid, which emphasizes infrastructure projects that benefit the developed nations, particularly the United States, more than Costa Rica.

However, U.S. national economic interests, as articulated and routinized in the IDB development process, have prevented the realization of this alternative development model. Indeed, the ruling classes within Costa Rica and other Latin American nations benefit from the U.S.-oriented development and have encouraged it. In Costa Rica and Latin America the structure of politics must change in order to allow a significant national economic development alternative to take root. At the international level the promise for a change in the policies of the international lending agencies remains weak as long as the national economic interests of the developed nations dominate humanitarian interests in the decision-making process.

## NOTES

1. Tico Times (San José, Costa Rica), March 21, 1975, p. 16; American Embassy, Economic Report for Costa Rica (San José, Costa Rica), January 17, 1975, p. 2.

2. Tico Times (San José, Costa Rica), September 12, 1975, p. 1.

3. Inter-American Development Bank, Economic and Social Progress in Latin America, Annual Report, 1974 (Washington, D.C.), pp. 251-52.

4. Paul Streeten, The Frontiers of Development Studies (New York: John Wiley, 1972), p. 186.

5. Ibid., p. 196.

# APPENDIX

## LOANS TO THE PUBLIC SECTOR IN COSTA RICA

| Lending Agency | Borrower | Project | Amount (in dollars) |
|---|---|---|---|
| USAID | Gobierno[a] | Desarrollo Agropecuario | 79,000,000 |
| CABEI | Gobierno | Plan Maestro Aerop. Santamaria | 475,000 |
| CABEI no. 63 | Gobierno | Carreterra Terron Colorado-Los Chiles | 5,000,000 |
| CABEI no. 72 | Gobierno | Carreterra Circunvalacion | 600,000 |
| CABEI | Gobierno | Aeropverto Liberia | 125,000 |
| CABEI no. 69 | Gobierno | Carreterra Colon-Caldera | 200,000 |
| CABEI | Gobierno | Carreterra Escazu-Santa Ana | 5,500,000 |
| CABEI | Gobierno | Carreterra Santa Ana-Ciudad Colon | 1,698,000 |
| CABEI | Gobierno | Radial Santa Ana-San Antonio Belen | 2,605,000 |
| CABEI | Gobierno | Desarrollo Turistico Bahia Culebra | 41,367,000 |
| CABEI | Gobierno | Carreterra a Escazu | 5,000,000 |
| CABEI | Gobierno | Desjarasit. Ganado Bovino | 222,000 |
| CABEI | Gobierno | Central Aduanera, Terminal Furgones | 117,000 |
| CABEI | Gobierno | Proyecto Central Aduanera Terminal Furgones | 8,400,000 |
| CABEI no. 65 | Gobierno | Factoría Valle Central-Litor. Pacifico | 200,000 |
| CABEI | Gobierno | Parques Nales.-Volcan Poas | 800,000 |
| IDB | Gobierno | FONAPE | 6,000,000 |
| IDB | Gobierno | Ensenanza Técnica | 8,750,000 |
| IDB | Gobierno | Reforma Penitenciaria | 1,000,000 |
| IBRD[b] | Gobierno | Carreterra San José-Siquirres | 28,000,000 |
| First National Bank of Chicago (Pan) | Gobierno | Instrumentos Musicales | 1,000,000 |
| USSR | Gobierno | Maquinaria y Equipo (Trolebuses) | 15,000,000 |
| Varios Bancos | Gobierno | Préstamo "duros" e Inversion + | 50,000,000 |
| Government of Venezuela | Gobierno | Sustentar Precios Café | 11,000,000 |
| Banco Arabe (?) (nd) | Gobierno | Modernizacíon Ferrocarril e Ingenios + | 50,000,000 |
| IDB | Banco Central | Actividad Turistica | 20,000,000 |
| IBRD | Banco Central | Desarrollo Agropecuario | 18,500,000 |
| First National Bank of Chicago (Pan) | Banco Central | Industria Turistica | 10,000,000 |
| Commonwealth Development Corp. | Banco Central | Construccion Viviendas (INS) | 7,500,000 |
| Banco Central Argentino | Banco Central | Linea Crédito | 30,000,000 |
| Wells Fargo Bank | Banco Central | Financiacíon Inversion Privadas | 15,000,000 |
| Manufacturers Hanover Trust | Banco Central | (Decision del Préstatario) | 30,000,000 |

(continued)

(Appendix continued)

| Lending Agency | Borrower | Project | Amount (in dollars) |
|---|---|---|---|
| Kuhn, Loeb & Co.—New York | Banco Central | (Decision del Préstatario) | 30,000,000 |
| Brandts Ltd. (England) | Banco Central | Linea Credito | 2,500,000 |
| Banco do Brasil | Banco Central | Linea Credito | 1,000,000 |
| Marine Midland Bank | Banco Central | Importacíon Maquinaria Agricola | 4,000,000 |
| Banco Nacional Hungria | Banco Central | Importacíon Autobuses | 650,000 |
| IDB | Banco de Costa Rica | Desarrollo Mediana Industria | 15,000,000 |
| Eximbank and others | Banco Nacional | Linea Credito | 4,500,000 |
| Banco Nacional Hungria | Banco Costa Rica | Importacíon Autobuses | 1,350,000 |
| IDB | Banco Anglo | Desarrollo Pesquero | 11,500,000 |
| Marine Midland Bank | Banco Anglo | Desarrollo Ganadero | 1,000,000 |
| CABEI | Banco Credito Agricola | Construcción Viviendas (DECAP) | 7,485,000 |
| CABEI | Banco Credito Agricola | Vivienda Media | 300,000 |
| CABEI | Banco Credito Agricola | Vivienda Bajo Costo | 2,000,000 |
| Banco Nacion Argentina | Banco Credito Agricola | Importación Materias Primas | 2,000,000 |
| (N.D.) | Banco Popular | (Decision del Préstatario) | 5,000,000 |
| IDB | | Construción y Mejoram. Hospitales | 34,000,000 |
| CABEI | C.C.S.S. | Est. para Instalar Fabrica Aluminio | 100,000 |
| (N.D.) | CODESA | Instalación Fabrica de Cemento | 60,000,000 |
| CABEI | CODESA | Programa Hortifruticola | 3,000,000 |
| CABEI | CNP | Almacenamiento de Granos | 6,000,000 |
| First American National Bank | CNP | Construción Bodegas Frijol y Sal | 930,000 |
| CABEI no. 53 | CNP | Est. Barranca-Tipitapa (Cred. Conting.) | 50,000 |
| IDB | ICE | Proyecto Hidroelectrico Arenal + | 50,500,000 |
| IBRD | ICE | Programa Desarrollo Electrico 74-78 + | 50,000,000 |
| Dillon Read | ICE | Refinanciamiento Deudas | 12,000,000 |
| L.M. Ericsson 14186 | ICE | Materiales para Telefónos | 519,000 |
| L.M. Ericsson 14188 | ICE | Ampl. Central Telef. San José Oeste | 486,000 |
| L.M. Ericsson 14357 | ICE | Materiales para Telefónos | 3,000,000 |
| United California Bank | ICE | Pago Cuota Unidades Diesel | 65,000 |
| Citibank | ICE | (N.D.) | 5,000,000 |
| CABEI | ICE | II Et. Red Regional Telecommunicación | 2,000,000 |
| CABEI | ICE | Mercadeo Mayoreo S.J. | 60,000 |

| | | | |
|---|---|---|---|
| CABEI | IFAM (PIMA) | Mercado Mayoreo (Construcción) | 2,300,000 |
| CABEI | IFAM (PIMA) | Est. para Instalación Centro Textil. | 100,000 |
| CABEI | INA | Est. Plan Bahia Culebra | 370,000 |
| Baber Green American | ICT | Banda Transportadora | 922,000 |
| Eximbank and others | INCOP | Cancelar Deuda de Dixie Dredge | 528,000 |
| M.L. Roberts AID | INCOP | Construcción Hatillo y Curridabat | 12,000,000 |
| First Caribbean no. 1 | INVU | Construcción Hatillo y Curridabat | 10,000,000 |
| First Caribbean no. 2 | INVU | Construcción Viviendas Interes Social | 10,000,000 |
| Wells Fargo Bank | INVU | Construcción Hatillo y Curridabat | 10,000,000 |
| Hornblower, Weeks and others | INVU | Construcción Viviendas | 30,000,000 |
| IDB | INVU | Construcción Hatillo y Limón | 9,900,000 |
| Adm., Ing. y Des. S.A. | INVU | Construcción Viviendas | 50,000,000 |
| (Banco Europeo) | INVU | Construcción Viviendas | 15,000,000 |
| MECANOEXPORTIMPORT | INVU | Locomotoras | 2,179,000 |
| (Bco. Ingles) | JAPDEVA | Desarrollo Zona Atlantica | 50,000,000 |
| CABEI | JAPDEVA | Ampliacion Credito Anterior | 60,000 |
| CABEI | JASEMA | Desarrollo Portuario Punta Morales | 1,450,000 |
| Chase Manhattan Bank | LIGA AGR. IND. CANA | Cubrir Dif. Precio Azucar | 15,000,000 |
| (N.D.) | LIGA AGR. IND. CANA | Garantizar Marg. Venta Azucar | 1,000,000 |
| Gobierno Israeli | LIGA AGR. IND. CANA | Municipio Servicio Remun. de Personas | 3,000,000 |
| (N.D.) | Municip. San José | Construcción Mercado Central | 20,000,000 |
| Citibank | Municip. San José | Capital de Trabajo | 3,800,000 |
| IDB | RECOPE | II Etapa Alcant. de San José | 8,000,000 |
| Gobierno Britanico | SNAA | Ampliacion Préstamo Anterior | 3,000,000 |
| CABEI | SNAA | Ampliacion Préstamo Anterior | 3,300,000 |
| | SNAA | II Etapa Acueductos Rurales | 4,500,000 |
| | SNAA | Construcciones Varias | 2,000,000 |
| IDB | Universidad de C.R. | Edificio Facultad de Derecho | 582,000 |
| Total | | | 955,000,000 |
| | | | (¢8,213,000,000) |

[a]Government.
[b]World Bank.
Source: La Nación (San José, Costa Rica), December 22, 1974, p. 1A.

# SELECTED BIBLIOGRAPHY

## BOOKS

Ady, Peter, ed. Private Foreign Investment and the Developing World. New York: Praeger, 1971.

Arias Sanchéz, Oscar. Grupos de Presión en Costa Rica. San José, Costa Rica: Editorial Costa Rica, 1974.

Asher, Robert E. Development Assistance in the Seventies. Washington, D.C.: Brookings Institution, 1970.

Backer, James. La Iglesia y el Sindicalismo en Costa Rica. San José, Costa Rica: Editorial Costa Rica, 1974.

Basch, Antonin, and Milic Kybal. Capital Markets in Latin America. New York: Praeger, 1970.

Bell, John Patrick. Crisis in Costa Rica, The 1948 Revolution. Austin: University of Texas Press, 1971.

Blutstein, Howard I., et al. Area Handbook for Costa Rica. Washington, D.C.: Government Printing Office, October 1970.

Broide, Julio. Banco Interamericano de Desarrollo. Washington, D.C. Banco Interamericano de Desarrollo, 1968.

Castillo, Carlos M. Growth and Integration in Central America. New York: Praeger, 1966.

Cline, William R. Potential Effects of Income Redistribution on Economic Growth: Latin American Cases. New York: Praeger, 1974.

Cochrane, James D. The Politics of Regional Integration: The Central American Case. Vol. 12, Tulane Studies in Political Science. New Orleans: Tulane University, 1969.

Cohen Orantes, Isaac. Regional Integration in Central America. Lexington, Mass.: D. C. Heath, 1972.

Connell-Smith, Gordon. The United States and Latin America. New York: John Wiley, 1974.

Dell, Sidney. The Inter-American Development Bank. New York: Praeger, 1972.

Denton, Charles F. Patterns of Costa Rican Politics. Boston: Allyn and Bacon, 1971.

Editorial Universitaria Centroamericana (EDUCA). Tenencia de la Tierra y Desarrollo Rural en Centroamerica. San José, Costa Rica, 1973.

English, Burt H. Liberación Nacional en Costa Rica. Gainesville: University of Florida Press, 1971.

Facio, Rodrigo. La Moneda y la Banca Central en Costa Rica. San José, Costa Rica: Editorial Costa Rica, 1973.

Fagan, Stuart I. Central American Economic Integration: The Politics of Unequal Benefits. Berkeley: Institute of International Studies, University of California, 1970.

Goldrich, Daniel. Sons of the Establishment: Elite Youth in Panama and Costa Rica. Chicago: Rand McNally, 1966.

Gonzalez Vega, Claudio, et al. The Marketing of Agricultural Products in Costa Rica. AID/ACM Contract no. AID-515-1837. San José, Costa Rica: Associated Colleges of the Midwest and Institute of Economic Investigations, University of Costa Rica, December 1970.

Grunwald, Joseph, et al. Latin American Economic Integration and U.S. Policy. Washington, D.C.: Brookings Institution, 1972.

Hansen, Roger O. Central America: Regional Integration and Economic Development. Washington, D.C.: National Planning Association, 1967.

Hirshman, Albert O. Development Projects Observed. Washington, D.C.: Brookings Institution, 1967.

Jonas (Bodenheimer), Susanne, et al. La Inversión Extranjera en Centro America. San José, Costa Rica: Editorial Universitaria Centro Americana, 1974.

Lizano Fait, Eduardo. Cambio Social en Costa Rica. San José, Costa Rica: Editorial Costa Rica, 1975.

Nelson, Joan M. Aid, Influence and Foreign Policy. New York: Macmillan, 1968.

Nugent, Jeffrey B. Economic Integration in Central America. Baltimore: Johns Hopkins University Press, 1974.

Organization of American States. Official External Financing in Latin American Development Strategy: Implications for the Seventies. Washington, D.C.: Inter-American Economic and Social Council, 1973.

Organization for Economic Cooperation and Development. Flow of Resources to Developing Countries. Paris: the Organization, 1973.

Pearson, Lester B. Partners in Development. New York: Praeger, 1969.

Petras, James, and Morris Morley. The United States and Chile. New York: Monthly Review Press, 1975.

Powelson, John P. Institutions of Economic Growth. Princeton, N.J.: Princeton University Press, 1972.

Prebisch, Raúl. Change and Development: Latin America's Great Task. Washington, D.C.: Inter-American Development Bank, July 1970.

Rockefeller, Nelson A. The Rockefeller Report on the Americas. Chicago: Quadrangle, 1969.

Schmitter, Philippe. Autonomy or Dependence as Regional Integration Outcomes: Central America. Berkeley: University of California, Institute of International Studies, 1972.

Slater, Jerome. The OAS and United States Foreign Policy. Columbus: Ohio State University Press, 1967.

Society for International Development. Political and Social Realities of Development. San José, Costa Rica: Thirteenth World Conference of the Society for International Development, February 22-25, 1973.

Stone, Samuel. La Dinastía de los Conquistadores. San José, Costa Rica: Editorial Universitaria Centro Americana, 1975.

Streeten, Paul. The Frontiers of Development Studies. New York: John Wiley, 1972.

Torres Rivas, Edelberto. Interpretación del Desarrollo Social Centro Americano. San José, Costa Rica: Editorial Universitaria Centro Americana, 1973.

White, John. Regional Development Banks: The Asian, African and Inter-American Development Bank. New York: Praeger, 1972.

Widdicombe, Stacey H., Jr. The Performance of Industrial Development Corporations: The Case of Jamaica. New York: Praeger, 1972.

Wionczek, Miguel S. Latin American Economic Integration. New York: Praeger, 1966.

Yudelman, Montague. Agricultural Development and Economic Integration in Latin America. London: George Allen and Unwin, 1970.

## ARTICLES

Ayres, Robert L. "Development Policy and the Possibility of a Livable Future for Latin America." American Political Science Review, June 1975, pp. 507-25.

Boyer, Mary Helen. "The Eximbank, Export for Empire." North American Congress on Latin America (NACLA) 8 (September 1974): 18-32.

Cooper, Richard W. "Trade Policy in Foreign Policy." Foreign Policy, no. 9 (Winter 1972-73): 18-36.

Denham, Robert Edwin. "The Role of the U.S. as an External Actor in the Integration of Latin America." Journal of Common Market Studies 7 (1968-69): 199-216.

Fallas Monge, Carlos L. "El Movimiento Obrero en Costa Rica-Breve Resumen de su Historia." Unpublished paper. Heredia, Costa Rica: Instituto de Estudios del Trabajo, Universidad Nacional: 1974.

Instituto Interamericano de Ciencias Agrícolas. "Algúnos Aspectos de la Producción Agropecuaria de Costa Rica." Unpublished paper. 1974.

Jonas (Bodenheimer), Susanne. "La Ayuda Externa No Ayuda a la Integración Centro Americana." Estudios Sociales Centroamericanos, no. 7 (January-April 1974): 35-74.

____. "Masterminding the Mini-Market: U.S. Aid to the Central American Common Market." North American Congress on Latin America (NACLA) 7, no. 5 (May-June 1973): 3-21.

Moran, Michael. "Executive Offices Hemispheric Agricultural Marketing Program." Agriculture Price Policies From an Institutional Marketing Perspective. Prepared for Seminar on Agricultural Policy, Inter-American Development Bank, Washington, D.C., March 17-21, 1975.

Saxe-Fernandez, John. "The Militarization of Costa Rica." Monthly Review 24 (May 1972): 61-70.

Sunkel, Osvaldo. "Transnational Capitalism and National Disintegration in Latin America." Social and Economic Studies 22, no. 1 (March 1973): 132-76.

Tobias, David. "The U.S. Investment Bubble in Central America." North American Congress on Latin America (NACLA) 7, no. 5 (May-June 1973): 27-39.

Torres-Rivas, Edelberto. "Poder Nacional y Sociedad Dependiente." Estudios Sociales Centro Americanos (San José, Costa Rica), no. 8 (May-August 1974): 27-63.

Wionczek, Miguel S. "Latin American Integration and United States Economic Policies." In International Organization in the Western Hemisphere, edited by Robert W. Gregg (Syracuse, N.Y.: Syracuse University Press, 1968).

## DOCUMENTS

American Embassy. Annual Economic Report. San José, Costa Rica. January 17, 1975.

Banco Central de Costa Rica. Boletín Estadístico Mensual. San José, Costa Rica, 1974-75.

____. División de Asúntos Económicos. Información Económica Semanal. San José, Costa Rica, 1974-75.

Banco Nacional de Costa Rica. Files on Inter-American Development Bank Agricultural Loans. San José, Costa Rica, 1975.

____. Manual de Instrucciónes Para los Subpréstamos Destinados al Financiamiento Parcial de Proyectos de Desarrollo del Sector Agropecuario, Mediante el Uso de Fondos Obtenidos Por Medio del Préstamos 323 SF/CR del Banco Inter Americano de Desarrollo y de Fondos Propios del Banco Nacional. San José, Costa Rica, 1974.

Dirección General de Estadística y Censos. Ministerio de Economía, Industrial y Comercio. Encuesta Anual de la Industria Manufacturera en el Istmo Centro Americano, República de Costa Rica, 1967-1968. San José, Costa Rica, December 1971.

Instituto de Fomento y Asesoría Municipal. "Regional Overview of Acción Internacional Canton Reports and Studies." Unpublished. San José, Costa Rica, 1975.

____ and Acción Internacional Tecnica. Canton Reports, Producción Agropecuaria, Rama de Actividad, Empleo, Ingresos, Migración Estacional, Immigración. San José, Costa Rica: División de Planificación, 1975.

Instituto Interamericano de Ciencias Agrícolas de la OEA y Banco Inter-Americano de Desarrollo. Ciclo Adiestramiento en Preparación y Evaluación de Proyectos de Desarrollo Agricola. San José, Costa Rica, October 1972-June 1973.

Inter-American Development Bank. Agreement Establishing the Inter-American Development Bank. Washington, D.C., June 30, 1972.

____. "Aide Memoire: Chile and the Inter-American Development Bank during the Administration of Salvador Allende." Washington, D.C., 1973.

____. Annual Reports. Washington, D.C., 1960-74.

____. By-laws. Washington, D.C., December 31, 1973.

____. Canada and the IDB. Washington, D.C., 1973.

____. Contrato de Préstamo entre el Banco InterAmericano de Desarrollo y el Banco de Costa Rica. Préstamo No. 196/OC-CR. Washington, D.C., September 4, 1970.

____. Contrato de Préstamo entre el Banco InterAmericano de Desarrollo y el Banco de Costa Rica. Préstamo No. 255/SF-CR. Washington, D.C., September 4, 1970.

____. Contrato de Préstamo entre el Banco InterAmericano de Desarrollo y el Instituto Costarricense de Electricidad (ICE). Préstamo No. 274/OC-CR. Washington, D.C., January 30, 1975.

____. Contrato de Préstamo entre la República de Costa Rica y el Banco InterAmericano de Desarrollo. Préstamo No. 308/SF-CR. Washington, D.C., December 2, 1971.

____. Contrato de Préstamo entre la República de Costa Rica y el Banco InterAmericano de Desarrollo. Préstamo No. 335/SF-CR. Washington, D.C., November 20, 1972.

____. Costa Rica, Estrategia 1975-1977. Department of Economic and Social Development. Washington, D.C., October 25, 1974.

____. "Detalle de los Préstamos Otorgados a Costa Rica." Internal files. Washington, D.C., 1974.

____. Economic and Social Progress in Latin America, 1973. Washington, D.C., 1974.

____. Economic and Social Progress in Latin America, 1974. Washington, D.C., 1975.

____. El Banco Inter-Americano de Desarrollo y Los Paises no Miembros: Un Decenio de Progreso en Relaciones Mutuas. Washington, D.C., 1969.

____. El BID en Centro America. Washington, D.C., 1969.

____. Fifteen Years of Activities, 1960-1974. Washington, D.C., 1975.

____. Files: Fund for Special Operations Loans by Sector and Country, 1969-73. Washington, D.C., July 11, 1974.

____. General Guideline on the Operating Policy of the Bank. GN 750-1. Washington, D.C., April 28, 1972.

____. Guidelines for Procurement Under IDB Loans. Washington, D.C., March 1975.

____. Loan Document: Costa Rica, Loan to the Banco de Costa Rica, Industrial Development Program. Washington, D.C., March 31, 1970.

____. Loan Document: Costa Rica, Loan to the Banco Nacional de Costa Rica, Livestock Development Program. Washington, D.C., December 14, 1971.

____. Management Improvements. Washington, D.C., 1973.

____. "Memorandum: New Policy Guidelines of the Fund for Special Operations, Preferential Treatment for Economically Less Developed Countries and Countries of Insufficient Market." Washington, D.C., June 4, 1974.

____. "News Release: Inter-American Bank Lends $13.6 Million to Foster Development of Fisheries in Costa Rica." Washington, D.C., May 1, 1975.

____. Presidential Speeches of Felipe Herrera and Antonia Ortiz Mena. Washington, D.C., 1960-75.

____. Proceedings of the Board of Governors. Washington, D.C., 1960-74.

____. Regulations of the Board of Governors. Washington, D.C., December 31, 1973.

____. Statement of Loans, 1973. Washington, D.C., 1974.

____. Structure, Resources and Operations. Washington, D.C., 1972.

____. Trust Fund Agreement Between the Fondo de Inversiónes de Venezuela and the Inter-American Development Bank. Washington, D.C., February 1975.

____. Use of Consulting Firms. Washington, D.C., January 1973.

____, Office of the Deputy Manager for Integration. IDB and Its Relations with the Latin American Integration Process. Washington, D.C., December 1973.

____, Office of the Financial Manager. Funds in Administration. Washington, D.C., April 22, 1974.

International Bank for Reconstruction and Development. Economic Report of Costa Rica, vols. 1 and 2. Washington, D.C.: Latin America and Caribbean Regional Office, March 15, 1974.

____. The World Bank Group in the Americas. Washington, D.C., May 1974.

____. World Bank/IDA, Annual Report, 1973. Washington, D.C., 1973.

Library of Congress, Congressional Research Service. Latin America: Major Policy Issues of the 70's. Washington, D.C., January 25, 1972.

Ministerio de Agricultura y Ganadería, Consejo Agropecuario Nacional Posición de Costa Rica en Relación con una Politica de Integración Agropecuaria a Nivel Centroamericano. San José, Costa Rica, November 6, 1974.

Ministerio de Economía, Industria y Comercio. Convento Centroamericano de Incentivos Fiscales el Desarrollo Industrial, San José, Costa Rica, 31 de julio de 1962 y Protocolo al Convenio Centroamericano de Incentivos Fiscales al Desarrollo Industrial Protocolo Sobre Tratado Preferencial a Honduras, Managua, Nicaragua, 23 de Septiembre de 1966. San José, Costa Rica, 1973.

____. Memoria Anual, 1974. San José, Costa Rica, 1974.

National Advisory Council on International Monetary and Financial Policies. Annual Report. Washington, D.C., July 1, 1972-June 30, 1973.

____. Manual of Procedures and Policy Criteria Employed by the United States in the Appraisal of Financial Commitments of the International Lending Institutions. Washington, D.C., March 1973.

Oficina de Planificación. Plan Nacional de Desarrollo, Sectores Público, Versión Preliminar. San José, Costa Rica, 1974.

Oficina de Planificación, Departamento Promoción de Proyectos y Financiación. "Estudios Completados y Proyectos Resultantes." San José, Costa Rica, 1975.

Oficina de Planificación Nacional y Politica Económica. Plan Operativo 1975, Vols. 1-5. San José, Costa Rica, 1975.

____, División de Inversiónes. Situación de la Deuda Pública Externa Ingreso de Capital y Servicio de la Deuda Pública de Costa Rica Ano 1974 y Estimaciones para 1975. San José, Costa Rica, March 1975.

Organization of American States, Inter-American Economic and Social Council. United States Economic Cooperation in Latin America. Washington, D.C., July 1974.

Presidencia de la Repúblic, Oficina de Planificación y Politica Económica. "Report of Inter-American Development Bank Mission in October and December 1974." San José, Costa Rica, 1975.

Task Force on International Development. U.S. Foreign Assistance in the 1970's: A New Approach. Washington, D.C.: Government Printing Office, March 4, 1970.

United Nations Development Program: Costa Rica. La Situación Socio-Económica Actual En Función del Plan Nacional de Desarrollo. San José, Costa Rica, February, 1975.

U.S. Agency for International Development. Programa de Desarrollo Rural 1975-1976, Documento de Antecedentes para el Préstamo. AID 515 T 025 entre El Gobierno de la República de Costa Rica y el Gobierno de los Estados Unidos de América. San José, Costa Rica, November 1974.

U.S. Commerce Department. The Multinational Corporation: Studies on U.S. Foreign Investment. Vol. 1 and 2. Washington, D.C., March 1972 and April 1973.

____. Overseas Business Reports. Washington, D.C., 1960-75.

U.S. Congress. "Expropriation Policy" (Gonzalez Amendment). Congressional Record. Washington, D.C., January 19, 1972, H105.

U.S. Congress, House Committee on Appropriations. Foreign Assistance and Related Agencies Appropriations for 1975. 93rd Congress, 2nd Session, Part 1. Washington, D.C.: Government Printing Office, 1974.

U.S. Congress, House Committee on Banking and Currency. Inter-American Development Bank Amendment. 89th Congress, 1st Session, February 3-5, 1965. Washington, D.C.: Government Printing Office, 1965.

____. To Authorize the United States to Provide Additional Financial Resources to the Asian Development Bank and the Inter-American Development Bank. 92nd Congress, 1st Session, October 26, 1971. Washington, D.C.: Government Printing Office, 1971.

____. To Provide Additional Funds for the Inter-American Development Bank. 91st Congress, 2nd Session, June 30 and July 1, 1970. Washington, D.C.: Government Printing Office, 1970.

U.S. Congress, House Committee on Foreign Affairs. Development Assistance to Latin America, 1961-1970. 92nd Congress, 1st Session, April 14, 1971. Washington, D.C.: Government Printing Office, 1971.

____. Foreign Assistance Act of 1974. 93rd Congress, 2nd Session. Washington, D.C.: Government Printing Office, 1974.

____. Foreign Assistance Program Authorizations and Appropriations for Fiscal Years 1972, 1973 and 1974. 92nd Congress, 1st Session, September 19, 1973. Washington, D.C.: Government Printing Office, 1973.

____. Inter-American Relations. 93rd Congress, 1st Session, November 1973. Washington, D.C.: Government Printing Office, 1973.

____, Subcommittee on Inter-American Affairs. New Directions for the 1970's, Part 2: Development Assistance Options for Latin America. 92nd Congress, 1st Session, February 18; July 12,

19, 20, and 27; August 4, 1971. Washington, D.C.: Government Printing Office, 1971.

____. Treasury Department Management of U.S. Participation in the Inter-American Development Bank. 92nd Congress, 2nd Session, September 21, 1972. Washington, D.C.: Government Printing Office, 1972.

____. The United States and Multinational Development Banks. 93rd Congress, 2nd Session, March, 1974. Washington, D.C.: Government Printing Office, 1974.

U.S. Congress, House Subcommittee of the Committee on Appropriations. Foreign Assistance and Related Agencies Appropriations for 1975. 93rd Congress, 2nd Session, Part 1. Washington, D.C.: Government Printing Office, 1974.

U.S. Congress, House Subcommittee on International Finance of the Committee on Banking and Currency. Inter-American Development Bank: Role in Agricultural Development. 89th Congress, 2nd Session, August 29, 1966. Washington, D.C.: Government Printing Office, 1966.

____. To Authorize the United States to Provide Additional Financial Resources to the Asian Development Bank and the Inter-American Development Bank. 92nd Congress, 1st Session, October 26, 1971. Washington, D.C.: Government Printing Office, 1971.

U.S. Congress, Senate Committee on Appropriations. Foreign Assistance and Related Program Appropriations, Fiscal Year 1974. 93rd Congress, 1st Session, Part 1 and 2. Washington, D.C.: Government Printing Office, 1974.

U.S. Congress, Senate Committee on Foreign Relations. Inter-American Development Bank Fund for Special Operations. 92nd Congress, 1st Session, June 4, 1971. Washington, D.C.: Government Printing Office, 1971.

U.S. Congress, Senate Subcommittee on Multinational Corporations of the Committee on Foreign Relations. Multinational Corporations and United States Foreign Policy, Part 3. July 18, 19, 20, 30, 31 and August 1, 1973. 93rd Congress, 1st Session. Washington, D.C.: Government Printing Office, 1973.

U.S. General Accounting Office. Report to the Congress by the Comptroller General of the U.S. on the Progress Made Toward

Independent and Comprehensive Audits of IDB. B161470, July 19, 1971. Washington, D.C.: Government Printing Office, 1971.

U.S. President. International Economic Report of the President. Washington, D.C.: Government Printing Office. February 1974.

____, Office of the White House Press Secretary. Policy Statement, Economic Assistance and Investment Security in Developing Nations. Washington, D.C., January 19, 1972.

U.S. State Department, Bureau of Public Affairs. "News Release: Good Partner Policy for Americas Described by Secretary Kissinger." Washington, D.C., April 20, 1974.

____. "News Release: U.S. Participation in Inter-American Development Bank." Washington, D.C., July 29, 1975.

## THESES AND MONOGRAPHS

Saenz, Carlos Joaquin. "Population Growth, Economic Progress, and Opportunities on the Land: The Case of Costa Rica." Madison: Land Tenure Center, University of Wisconsin-Madison, June 1972.

Santiago, Oscar, and Quevado, Cuellar. "Algúnas Antecedentes Sobre la Organización Sindical en Costa Rica." Unpublished paper. May 1974.

# INDEX

## ABOUT THE AUTHOR

R. PETER DEWITT, JR., is an Assistant Professor in the Department of Political Science and the School of Management at the State University of New York, Binghamton.

Dr. DeWitt was formerly an Organization of American States Fellow and a consultant to the Instituto Interamericano de Ciencias Agricolas, San José, Costa Rica. He has a forthcoming article entitled "Current Status of Regional Organizations in Latin America" in the Political Handbook of the World—1977.

Dr. DeWitt holds a B.A. from Pennsylvania State University, an M.A. from San Diego State University, and a Ph.D. in political science from the State University of New York at Binghamton. His current research is a study of the political economy of U.S. foreign direct investment.